Knitting for Babies & Kids

Edited by Jeanne Stauffer
Exclusively using Plymouth yarns

HOUSE of
WHITE
BIRCHES

PUBLISHERS
SINCE 1947

Knitting for Babies & Kids

Copyright © 2003 House of White Birches, Berne, Indiana 46711

Executive Editor: Jeanne Stauffer
Editor: Carol Alexander
Associate Editor: Rachelle Haughn
Pattern Editors: E.J. Slayton, Diane Zangl
Copy Editors: Michelle Beck, Mary Martin

Photography: Tammy Christian, Kelly Heydinger, Christena Green
Photo Stylist: Tammy Nussbaum
Photography Assistant: Linda Quinlan

Art Director: Brad Snow
Publishing Services Manager: Brenda Gallmeyer
Graphic Arts Supervisor: Ronda Bechinski
Book Design: Amy S. Lin
Graphic Artist: Amy S. Lin
Production Assistants: Janet Bowers, Marj Morgan
Traffic Coordinator: Sandra Beres
Technical Artists: Liz Morgan, Mitch Moss, Chad Summers

Chief Executive Officer: John Robinson
Publishing Director: David McKee
Book Marketing Director: Craig Scott
Editorial Director: Vivian Rothe
Publishing Services Director: Brenda R. Wendling

Printed in the United States of America
First Printing: 2003
Library of Congress Number: 2002108788
ISBN: 1-59217-007-2

Welcome

If you love babies and children, you will love this collection of adorable sweaters, breezy summer tops, jazzy jumpers, delightful shorts, cozy hats, fun coats, baby toys, child's bathrobe and slippers, jackets, animal backpack, comfy mittens, kids' afghans, colorful rompers, interesting vests, baby blankets and cuddly animals. You'll find 99 wonderful designs to knit for all your favorite babies and children.

Instructions are given in sizes 6 months, 12 months, 18 months and 24 months for babies and sizes 2, 4, 6 and 8 for children. Most of the designs are great for both boys and girls. All of them are perfect for today's precious babies and active children.

You'll find that each design is part of a set or ensemble. There are baby sets that include matching baby blankets, sweaters, hats and booties. Our Romper Room set includes a Striped Henley Romper Set, Stars & Stripes Romper and Color-Block Romper. Our Ocean Creatures set includes an Octopus Sweater, Goldfish Sweater, Starfish Pillow and Sea Creatures Blanket. The Sunday School Sweaters include David & His Sheep, Jonah & His Whale, and 40 Days & 40 Nights. You'll find a set of Team Colors sweaters, Winter Cuddlers coats, Denim Hearts & Stars outfits for brother and sister, a set of Happy Critters soft toys, an Animal Sweater Collection featuring a cat, dog and bear design and much, much more!

As you can tell, we are really excited about the knitting fun you can have when you knit these delightful baby and kid designs. Believe me, you will have a wonderful, but difficult, time deciding which project to knit first. The designs are knit in all the latest colors and yarns from Plymouth Yarn Company, so we know they will delight kids around the world.

Have a wonderful time knitting!

Warm regards,

Jeanne Stauffer

Contents

Diamond Lace Baby Set

Designs by E. J. Slayton

A lacy pattern of openwork diamonds creates the delicate beauty in this soft baby ensemble. The precious blanket is knit in the round, beginning with double pointed needles.

Blanket

Skill Level
Intermediate***

Finished Size
Approximately 40 inches square (lightly blocked)

Materials
- Plymouth Dreambaby D.K. 50 percent acrylic microfiber/50 percent nylon DK weight yarn (183 yds/50g per ball): 7 balls yellow #104
- Size 4 (3.5mm) double-pointed (set of 5) and circular needles or size needed to obtain gauge
- Stitch markers
- Tapestry needle

Gauge
20 sts = 4 inches/10cm in pat worked in rnds

To save time, take time to check gauge.

Pattern Notes
Change from dpn to circular needles as amount of sts warrant.

When working on circular needle, pm at beg of each section.

Blanket
With dpn, cast on 4 sts. Join without twisting, dividing sts on 4 needles and working with 5th needle.

Rnd 1: *K1, yo, rep from * around. (8 sts)

Rnd 2 and all even rnds: Knit.

Rnd 3: *K1, yo, rep from * around. (16 sts—4 on each needle)

Rnd 5: [K1, yo, k3, yo] 4 times. (24 sts)

Rnd 7: [K1, yo, k5, yo] 4 times. (32 sts)

Rnd 9: [K1, yo, k7, yo] 4 times. (40 sts)

Rnd 11: [K1, yo, k3, ssk, yo, k4, yo] 4 times. (48 sts)

Rnd 13: [K1, yo, k3, ssk, yo, k1, yo, k2tog, k3, yo] 4 times. (56 sts)

Rnd 15: [{K1, yo} twice, ssk, k3, yo, ssk, k2, k2tog, yo, k1, yo] 4 times. (64 sts)

Rnd 17: [K1, yo, k3, yo, ssk, k5, k2tog, yo, k3, yo] 4 times. (72 sts)

Rnd 19: [K1, yo, k5, yo, ssk, k3, k2tog, yo, k5, yo] 4 times. (80 sts)

Rnd 21: [K1, yo, k7, yo, ssk, k1, k2tog, yo, k7, yo] 4 times. (88 sts)

Rnd 23: [K1, *yo, k3, ssk, yo, k4, yo, sl 1, k2tog, psso, yo, k3, ssk, yo, k4, yo] 4 times. (96 sts)

Rnd 25: [K1, yo, k3, ssk, yo, k1, yo, k2tog, k3, yo, ssk, k2, ssk, yo, k1, yo, k2tog, k3, yo] 4 times. (104 sts)

Rnd 27: [{K1, yo} twice, *ssk, k3, yo, ssk, k2, k2tog, yo, k1, yo, rep from * to end of section] 4 times. (112 sts)

Rnd 29: [K1, yo, k3, yo, *ssk, k5, k2tog, yo, k3, yo, rep from * to end of section] 4 times. (120 sts)

Rnd 31: [K1, yo, k5, yo, *ssk, k3, k2tog, yo, k5, yo, rep from * to end of section] 4 times. (128 sts)

Rnd 33: [K1, yo, k7, yo, *ssk, k1, k2tog, yo, k7, yo, rep from * to end of section] 4 times. (136 sts)

Rnd 35: [K1, yo, k3, ssk, yo, k4, yo, *sl 1, k2tog, psso, yo, k3, ssk, yo, k4, yo, rep from * to end of section] 4 times. (144 sts)

Rnd 37: [K1, yo, k3, ssk, yo, k1, yo, k2tog, k3, yo, *ssk, k2, ssk, yo, k1, yo, k2tog, k3, yo, rep from * to end of section] 4 times. (152 sts)

Rnds 39–156: [Rep Rnds 27–38] 9 times, rep Rnds 27–36 omitting center yo's in last set of half-diamonds. (632 sts—158 sts in each section)

Do not bind off.

Edging
Purl 1 rnd, k first st of next rnd.

On LH needle, using backward loop method, cast on 7 sts, turn, k4, yo, k2tog, k last st tog with 1 st of blanket.

Note: *When working yo's at outer edge in Rows 2, 6 and 10, work 2 sts (k1, p1) in each.*

Row 1: K5, yo, k2. (8 sts)

Row 2: K2, [k1, p1] in yo, k2, yo, k2tog, k last edging st tog with 1 st of blanket. (9 sts)

Row 3: K9.

Row 4: K6, yo, k2tog, k last edging st tog with 1 st of blanket.

Row 5: K5, yo, k2tog, yo, k2. (10 sts)

Row 6: K3, [p1, k2] twice, yo, k2tog, k last edging st tog with 1 st of blanket. (12 sts)

Row 7: K12.

Row 8: Bind off 5 sts, k2, yo, k2tog, k last edging st tog with 1 st of blanket. (7 sts)

Rows 9–11: Rep Rows 1–3.

Row 12: Bind off 2 sts, k3, yo, k2tog, k last edging st tog with 1 st of blanket. (7 sts)

*Rep Rows 1–12 to 1st before corner, ending with an odd-numbered row.

Short-Row Corner
[Maintaining pat, work to 4th st from end, sl next st purlwise, bring yarn to front, return st to LH needle, turn and work back to edge; turn and work complete row, joining to next blanket st] 3 times.

Rep from * to final corner, working a

few extra short rows before corner as needed to end corner with Row 11. Turn, bind off 2 sts. Cut yarn, leaving a 10-inch end. Sew or weave beg and end of edging tog.

Block lightly.

Cardigan

Size

To fit 6 (12, 18, 24) months Instructions are given for smallest size, with larger sizes in parentheses. When only 1 number is given, it applies to all sizes.

Finished Measurements

Chest: 21 (23, 25, 27) inches

Length: 11 (11¾, 12½, 13½) inches

Materials

- Plymouth Dreambaby D.K. 50 percent acrylic microfiber/50 percent nylon DK weight yarn (183 yds/50g per ball): 2 (3, 4, 4) balls yellow #104
- Size 3 (3.25mm) 24-inch circular needle
- Size 4 (3.5mm) needles or size needed to obtain gauge
- Stitch markers
- Stitch holders
- Tapestry needle
- 3 (⁷⁄₁₆-inch) shank buttons
- Sewing needle and all-purpose thread

Gauge

20 sts and 32 rows = 4 inches/10cm in pat with larger needles

21 sts and 31 rows = 4 inches/10cm in St st with larger needles

To save time, take time to check gauge.

Pattern Notes

Maintain 2 selvage sts at each edge. These are not shown on chart.

Beg and end pat as indicated on chart, omitting any yo's closer than 2 sts to edge. If there aren't enough sts to work both the yo and its dec, simply k these sts.

Cardigan is shown with 3 button-holes. If preferred, work 5 button-holes evenly spaced between neck edge and lower edge, and purchase 5 buttons.

Special Abbreviations

Cdd (centered double decrease): Sl next 2 sts as if to k2tog, k1, p2sso.

M1 (Make 1): Inc by making a backward loop over RH needle.

Back

With larger needles, cast on 49 (53, 57, 63) sts.

Row 1 (WS): P1, k to last st, p1.

Row 2: Knit.

Rows 3–7: Rep Rows 1 and 2, ending with Row 1.

Row 8: K, inc 4 (6, 6, 6) sts evenly across. (53, 59, 63, 69 sts)

Referring to Chart A, and keeping 2 sts at each edge in St st, beg pat as indicated for desired size. Work even in pat until back measures 7 (7¼, 7½, 8) inches from beg, ending with a WS row.

Shape underarms

Maintaining pat, bind off 4 (5, 6, 7) sts at beg of next 2 rows.

[Dec 1 st each edge every other row] 3 times. (39, 43, 45, 49 sts)

Work even until armhole measures 4¼ (4½, 5, 5½) inches.

Mark center 17 (19, 21, 23) sts for back neck, place all sts on holder.

Left Front

With larger needles, cast on 26 (27, 28, 31) sts and work Rows 1–7 as for back.

Row 8: K, inc 2 (2, 3, 3) sts evenly across. (28, 29, 31, 34 sts)

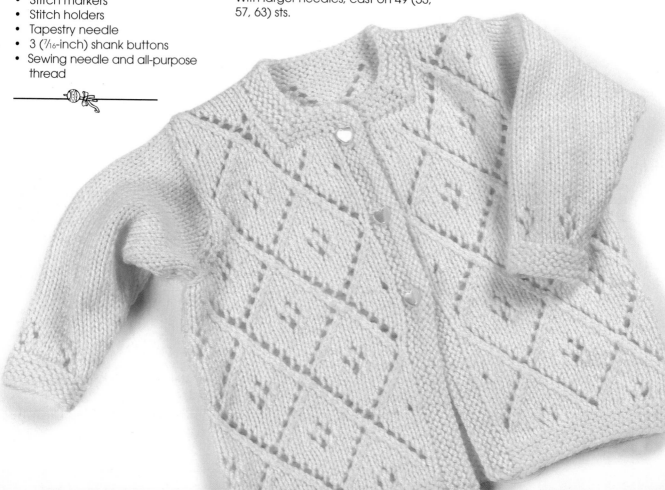

Referring to Chart B, and keeping 2 sts at each edge in St st, beg and end pat as indicated for desired size. Work even in pat until front measures same as back to under-arm, ending with a WS row.

Shape underarm

Bind off 4 (5, 6, 7) sts at beg of next row.

[Dec 1 st at armhole edge every other row] 3 times. (21, 21, 22, 24 sts)

Work even until armhole measures 2¼ (2½, 3, 3½) inches, ending with a RS row.

Shape neck

Bind off 7 (6, 7, 8) sts at beg of next WS row.

[Dec 1 st at neck edge every other row] 3 times. (11, 12, 12, 13 sts)

Work even until front measures same as back at shoulder.

Place remaining sts on holder.

Right Front

Work as for left front, reversing pat placement and shaping.

Sleeve

With larger needles, cast on 29 (33, 35, 37) sts and work Rows 1–7 as for back.

Row 8 (RS): Knit.

Row 9 and all WS rows: Purl.

Row 10: K6 (8, 6, 7), pm, k1, [ssk, yo, k4] 2 (2, 3, 3) times, ssk, yo, k2, pm, k6 (8, 6, 7).

Row 12: K2, M1, k4 (6, 4, 5), [ssk, yo, k1, yo, k2tog, k1] 2 (2, 3, 3) times, ssk, yo, k1, yo, k2tog, k4 (6, 4, 6), M1, k2. (31, 35, 37, 39 sts)

Row 14: K9 (11, 9, 10), [yo, ssk, k4] 2 (2, 3, 3) times, yo, ssk, k8 (10, 8, 9).

Continue to work in St st, inc 1 st at each edge on next and every 4th row until there are 45 (49, 55, 59) sts.

Work even until sleeve measures 6½ (7, 8, 9) inches, ending with a WS row.

Shape cap

Bind off 4 (5, 6, 7) sts at beg of next 2 rows.

[Dec 1 st at each edge every other row] 3 times.

Bind off all sts knitwise on WS.

Bind off front and back shoulder sts tog using 3-needle bind-off method.

Front Border

Beg at bottom right front corner with smaller needles and RS facing, pick up and k 2 sts for every 3 rows to neck edge, pm, 1 st in each bound-off st across front neck, pm, 11 sts along right neck edge, k across back neck sts, 11 sts along left neck edge, and down left front to match right side.

Row 1 (WS): Sl 1, k across.

Row 2: Sl 1, k to first marker, M1, k1, M1, [k to 1 st before next marker, cdd] twice, k to next marker, M1, k1, M1, k to end.

Row 3: Rep Row 1, working 3 evenly spaced buttonholes (k2tog, yo, ssk) approximately 2 inches apart beg at right neck edge, k to end.

Row 4: Rep Row 2, working [k1, p1] in each yo.

Rows 5 and 6: Rep Rows 1 and 2.

Bind off all sts knitwise on WS.

Finishing

Set sleeves into armholes.

Sew sleeve and body seams.

Sew buttons opposite buttonholes.

Bonnet

Size

To fit 6–12 (18–24) months. For larger size, work bonnet with larger needles.

Materials

- Plymouth Dreambaby D.K. 50 percent acrylic microfiber/50 percent nylon DK weight yarn (183 yds/50g per ball): 1 ball yellow #104
- Size 4 (3.5mm) double-pointed (2) and straight needles or size needed to obtain gauge
- Size 5 (3.75mm) needles (for larger size)
- Stitch markers
- Stitch holders
- Tapestry needle

Gauge

20 sts and 32 rows = 4 inches/10cm in pat with smaller needles

To save time, take time to check gauge.

Bonnet

Beg at front edge with smaller (larger), cast on 45 sts.

Row 1 (WS): P1, k to last st, p1.

Row 2: Knit.

Rows 3 and 4: Rep Rows 1 and 2.

Row 5: Rep Row 1.

Row 6: K, inc 8 sts evenly. (53 sts)

Sides

Row 1 and all WS rows: Purl.

Row 2: K2, [yo, ssk, k2, ssk, yo, k1, yo, k2tog, k3] 4 times, yo, ssk, k1.

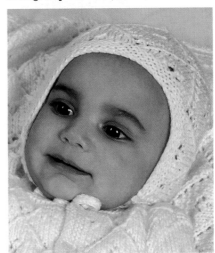

Rep Rows 62 and 63 until all side sts have been worked, remove markers.

With WS facing, pm, pick up and p 2 sts for every 3 rows along left bonnet edge to border, then 3 sts across end of border, turn. Sl 1, k to beg of rib, work established rib across center 14 sts, pm, pick up and k along right bonnet edge to match left side.

Row 1: Sl 1, k to marker, work established rib to marker, k to end.

Rows 2–8: Work as Row 1, dec 1 st at each edge on Rows 5 and 7.

Bind off knitwise on WS, dec 1 st at each edge.

Ties

With dpn, RS facing, pick up and k 3 sts at front corner, work I-cord tie as follows: *Slide sts to other end of needle, pull yarn across back, k3, rep from * until tie measures 6 inches. K3tog, fasten off. Rep for other corner. ✦

Row 4: K3, [yo, ssk, k3, yo, ssk, k2, k2tog, yo, k1] 4 times, k2.

Row 6: K4, [yo, ssk, k5, k2tog, yo, k3] 4 times, k1.

Row 8: K5, [yo, ssk, k3, k2tog, yo, k5] 4 times.

Row 10: K6, [yo, ssk, k1, k2tog, yo, k7] 3 times, yo, ssk, k1, k2tog, yo, k6.

Row 12: K1, [ssk, yo, k4, yo, sl 1, k2tog, psso, yo, k3] 4 times, ssk, yo, k2.

Row 14: K3, [yo, k2tog, k3, yo, ssk, k2, ssk, yo, k1] 4 times, k2.

Row 16: K2, [yo, ssk, k2, k2tog, yo, k1, yo, ssk, k3] 4 times, yo, ssk, k1.

Row 18: K5, [k2tog, yo, k3, yo, ssk, k5] 4 times.

Row 20: K4, [k2tog, yo, k5, yo, ssk, k3] 4 times, k1.

Row 22: K3, [k2tog, yo, k7, yo, ssk, k1] 4 times, k2.

Row 24: K2, k2tog, [yo, k3, ssk, yo, k4, yo, sl 1, k2tog, psso] 3 times, yo, k3, ssk, yo, k4, yo, ssk, k2.

Rows 25–37: Rep Rows 1–13.

Shape back

Row 38: K19, pm, work pat Row 14 across center 15 sts, pm, ssk, turn.

Row 39: Sl 1, p to marker, p2tog, turn.

Row 40: Sl 1, work Row 16 between markers, ssk, turn.

Rows 41–60: Continue in pat, working edge sts tog with sides of bonnet, ending with Row 12.

Row 61: Sl 1, p to last st dec 3 sts evenly, p2tog. (12 sts between markers)

Row 62: Sl 1, k1, [p2, k2] twice, end p2, k1, ssk.

Row 63: Sl 1, p1, [k2, p2] twice, end k2, p1, p2tog.

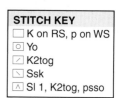

STITCH KEY
- ☐ K on RS, p on WS
- ☉ Yo
- ☑ K2tog
- ◿ Ssk
- △ Sl 1, K2tog, psso

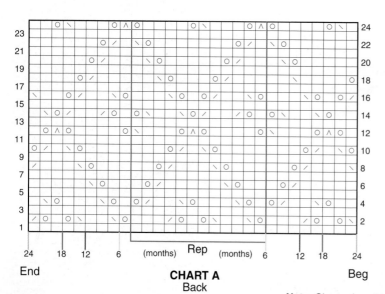

CHART A
Back

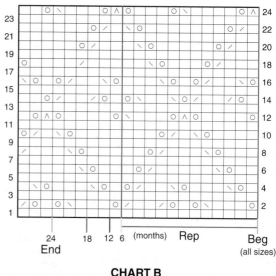

CHART B
Fronts

Note: *Charts do not include selvage sts.*

Bouncing Baby Layette

Designs by Uyvonne Bigham

*Five pieces make up this ensemble to welcome the new baby.
It knits up quickly in worsted weight yarn.*

Skill Level

Easy**

Size

Sweater, Rompers, Hat & Booties:
Newborn (6–9, 12–18) months
Instructions are given for smallest
size, with larger sizes in parentheses. When only 1 number is given, it
applies to all sizes.

Afghan: Approximately 37 x 41 inches

Materials

- Plymouth Encore Worsted 75
  percent acrylic/25 percent wool
  worsted weight yarn (200 yds/
  100g per skein): mint #1201
  Afghan: 5 balls
  Sweater and Rompers: 3 balls
  Booties and Hat: 1 ball will
  make both
- Size 6 (4mm) straight and double-
  pointed needles
- Size 7 (4.5mm) straight and
  double-pointed needles or size
  needed to obtain gauge
- Size 8 (5mm) needles or size
  needed to obtain gauge
- Cable needle
- Stitch holder
- Stitch markers
- Small amount waste yarn
- ⅔ yd (½-inch) elastic
- Yarn needle
- Sewing needle and all-purpose
  thread

Gauge

18 sts and 26 rows = 4 inches/10cm
in Cable & Ribbon Pat with medium
needles

17 sts and 27 rows = 4 inches/10cm
in St st with larger needles

To save time, take time to check
gauge.

Special Abbreviations

C6 (cable 6): Sl next 3 sts to cn and
hold at front of work, k3, k3 from cn.

C4 (cable 4): Sl next 2 sts to cn and
hold at front of work, k2, k2 from cn.

Pattern Stitch

Cable & Ribbon Pattern

Row 1 (RS): Knit.

Row 2 and all WS rows: K5, p to last
5 sts, k5.

Rows 3–8: Rep Rows 1 and 2.

Row 9: K5, p10, *C6, p10, rep from *
to last 5 sts, k5.

Row 11: P10, *k6, p10, rep from * to
end of row.

Row 13: Rep Row 9.

Row 15: Rep Row 11.

Row 17: Knit.

Row 19–24: Rep Rows 3–8.

Row 25: K5, p2, *C6, p10, rep from *
to last 7 sts, p2, k5.

Row 27: K5, p2, *k6, p10, rep from *
to last 7 sts, p2, k5.

Row 29: Rep Row 25.

Row 31: Rep Row 27.

Row 32: Rep Row 2.

Rep Rows 1–32 for pat.

Afghan

With size 7 needles, cast on 164 sts.

Knit 5 rows.

Work in Cable & Ribbon pat until
afghan measures approximately
40 inches, ending with row 8 or 24
of pat.

Purl 5 rows.

Bind off knitwise on WS.

Sweater

Body

With size 6 needles cast on 116 (132,
148) sts.

Knit 5 rows. Change to size 7 needles.

Work even in Cable & Ribbon pat
until body measures 6 (7, 8) inches,
ending with a WS row.

Divide for fronts and back

Next row: Work across 26 (30, 34) sts
and place on holder for right front,
bind off next 6 sts for underarm, work
across 52 (60, 68) sts, place remaining 32 (36, 40) sts on 2nd holder for
left front.

Back

Working on 52 (60, 68) sts of back
only, continue in established pat
until armhole measures 4 inches.

Bind off all sts.

Mark 13 (17, 21) sts at each side
for shoulder.

Right Front

Sl sts from first holder to size 7 needle.

With WS facing join yarn at armhole
edge. Continue in established pat
until armhole measures 3 inches,
ending with a WS row.

Shape neck

At neck edge, k 6 sts and place on
holder, work to end of row.

Work 1 row even.

[Bind off 2 sts at neck edge] twice.

[Dec 1 st at neck edge every other
row] 3 times.

Bind off remaining 13 (17, 21) sts.

Left Front

Sl sts from 2nd holder to size 7 needle.

With RS facing join yarn at armhole
edge.

Next row: Bind off 6 sts, work to end
of row.

Work as for right front, reversing
shaping.

Neck Band

Sew shoulder seams.

With RS facing using size 6 needles, pick up and k 51 (55, 59) sts from neck edge, including sts from st holders.

Knit 1 row.

Eyelet Row: K2, *yo, k2tog, rep from * to last st, k1.

Knit 2 rows.

Bind off all sts.

Sleeves

With size 6 needles cast on 28 (30, 32) sts.

Knit 5 rows. Change to size 7 needles and Cable & Ribbon pat.

[Inc 1 st each side of next and every following 6th (8th, 10th) row] 6 (5, 4) times. (40 sts)

Work even until sleeve measures 7 (7 ½, 8) inches.

Bind off.

Finishing

Sew sleeves into armholes.

Cut a 72-inch length of yarn and fold in half.

Make a twisted cord by inserting a pencil on 1 end and twisting until yarn folds back on itself. Tie ends.

Weave cord through eyelet row at neck.

Rompers

Back

With size 7 needles and waste yarn, cast on 46 (48, 50) sts using a provisional method.

Work in St st for 6 rows. Change to Size 8 needles and work even for 6 more rows.

Next row (RS): Knit, inc 4 sts evenly. (50, 52, 54 sts)

Work even until back measures 6½ (7½, 7½) inches, ending with a WS row.

Bind off 4 sts at beg of next 2 rows.

[Dec 2 sts at each end every other row] 5 times, then [dec 1 st each end every other row] 5 times. (12, 14, 16 sts)

Work even for 2 rows.

Place remaining sts on holder for crotch.

Front

Work as for back.

Finishing

Sew crotch seam, using Kitchener method.

Leg Bands

With size 7 needles and RS facing, pick up and k 30 sts along edge of leg opening.

Knit 1 row.

Bind off all sts.

Sew side seams.

continued on page 188

Embossed Ribs Baby Ensemble

Designs by Janet Rehfeldt

Textured patterns and fish button accents highlight a slightly oversized baby sweater worked in colorful underwater hues.

Skill Level
Easy**

Size
Infant's 6 (12, 18, 24) months
Instructions are given for smallest size, with larger sizes in parentheses. When only 1 number is given, it applies to all sizes.

Finished Measurements
Chest: 20 (22, 24, 26) inches

Total length: 10 (11, 12, 13½) inches

Hat circumference: 14 (15, 16, 17) inches

Booties heel to toe: 3½ (3¾, 4½, 5) inches

Foot circumference (unstretched): 4¾ (4¾, 5¼, 5¼) inches

Materials
- Plymouth Fantasy Naturale 100 percent cotton worsted weight yarn (140 yds/100g per skein): 3 (3, 4, 4) skeins ocean #9936
- Size 7 (4.5mm) 16-inch circular and double-pointed needles
- Size 8 (5mm) 16-inch circular and double-pointed needles or size needed to obtain gauge
- Stitch holders
- Stitch markers
- Tapestry needle
- 4 (¾-inch) Streamline fish buttons from Blumenthal Lansing Co.
- 2 (size 4/0) snaps

Gauge
18 sts and 24 rows = 4 inches/10cm in Reverse St st on larger needles

To save time, take time to check gauge.

Pattern Stitch
Embossed Rib
Rnd 1: *K1-tbl, rep from * around.

Rnds 2–4: *P1, k1-tbl, rep from * around.

Rnd 5: *K1-tbl, rep from * around.

Rnds 6–8: K1-tbl, *p1, k1-tbl, rep from * around.

Rep Rnds 1–8 for pat.

Pattern Notes
Sweater is worked in the round to the underarm, then worked back and forth for the upper bodice.

Hat is worked in the round using circular and dpns.

Booties are worked in the round using dpns. For ease in working, use shorter 5–6-inch size.

Pullover

Body
With smaller needles, cast on 96 (102, 108, 114) sts.

Join without twisting, pm between first and last st.

Work in k1, p1 rib for 4 rnds.

Next rnd: Knit, inc 12 (14, 16, 18) sts evenly. (108, 116, 124, 132 sts)

Change to larger needles and Embossed Rib pat.

(Work rnds 1–8) 2 (3, 3, 4) times, then (work rnds 1–4) 1 (0, 1, 0) times.

Divide for front and back
Purl 1 rnd, dec 4 sts evenly. (104, 112, 120, 128 sts)

Back
Next row (RS): Purl across 52 (56, 60, 64) sts, sl remaining sts to holder.

Work even in rows from this point in Reverse St st until armhole measures 4 (4½, 5, 5½) inches, ending with a RS row.

Shape neck
K 18 (19, 20, 21) sts, sl 16 (18, 20, 22) back neck sts to holder, attach 2nd ball of yarn, k remaining 18 (19, 20, 21) sts.

Next row: Dec 1 st at each neck edge.

Work 4 rows even for button extension.

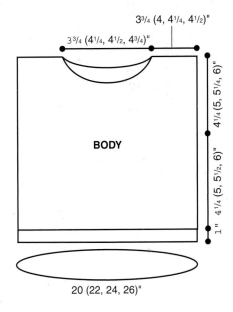

3¾ (4, 4¼, 4½)"

3¾ (4¼, 4½, 4¾)"

4¼ (5, 5¼, 6)"

4¼ (5, 5½, 6)"

1"

BODY

20 (22, 24, 26)"

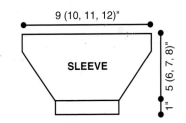

9 (10, 11, 12)"

SLEEVE

1"   5 (6, 7, 8)"

Bind off 17 (18, 19, 20) sts on each shoulder.

Front

Sl 52 (56, 60, 64) sts from holder onto larger needles.

With RS facing, join yarn and purl across.

Work even in Reverse St st until armhole measures 2½ (3, 3, 3½) inches.

Shape neck

Work across 22 (23, 25, 26) sts, sl center 8 (10, 10, 12) sts to holder for front neck, attach 2nd ball of yarn and work across remaining 22 (23, 25, 26) sts.

[Dec 1 st each side of neck every row] 5 (5, 6, 6) times. (17, 18, 19, 20 sts on each side)

Work even until armhole measures 4¼ (4½, 4¾, 5) inches, ending with a WS

Beg buttonhole band

Mark each shoulder for 2 buttonholes, evenly spaced.

Work in k1, p1 rib for 5 rows, making buttonholes on Row 3 by working [yo, k2tog] at each marker.

Bind off all sts.

Back Neck Band

With smaller needles and RS facing, join yarn at right shoulder, pick up and k 5 sts along button placket and right neck edge, 16 (18, 20, 22) sts from back neck holder, and 5 sts along left button placket and neck edge. (26, 28, 30, 32 sts)

Work in k1, p1 rib for 4 rows.

Bind off.

Front Neck Band

With smaller needles and RS facing, join yarn at left shoulder, pick up and k 10 (12, 14, 15) sts along buttonhole band and left neck edge, 8 (10, 10, 12) sts from front neck holder, and 10 (12, 14, 15) sts along right buttonhole band and neck edge. (28, 32, 38, 42 sts)

Work in k1, p1 rib for 4 rows.

Bind off.

Sleeves

With smaller needles, cast on 26 (28, 30, 34) sts.

Work in k1, p1 rib for 4 rows.

Change to larger needles and Reverse St st.

[Inc 1 st each side every 3rd row] 8 (3, 3, 1) times, then [every 4th row] 0 (5, 7, 9) times. (42, 44, 50, 54 sts)

Work even until sleeve measures 6 (7, 8, 9) inches.

Bind off loosely.

Finishing

Lap buttonhole band over button extension. Sew sleeve top to armhole, easing to fit and sewing through all layers at shoulder.

Sew sleeve seams.

Sew buttons to button band.

Sew one snap to each side of neck band near bound-off edge.

Hat

Cuff

With smaller dpn, cast on 64 (68, 72, 76) sts.

Join without twisting, pm between first and last st.

Work in k1, p1 rib for 4 rnds.

Change to larger needles and Embossed Rib pat.

Work Rnds 1–8, then work [Rnds 1–4] 0 (0, 1, 1) time.

Purl 1 rnd, dec 2 sts evenly. (62, 66, 70, 74 sts)

Work even in Reverse St st until hat measures 3 (3½, 4, 4½) inches from beg.

around. (18, 18, 21, 21 sts)

Next rnd: *P1, p2tog, rep from * around. (12, 12, 14, 14 sts)

Cut yarn, leaving a 12-inch end.

Draw end through remaining sts twice and pull tightly.

Weave in end.

Booties

Cuff & Leg

With smaller dpn, cast on 22 (22, 24, 24) sts.

Divide sts onto 3 needles as follows: 5-12-5, (5-12-5, 6-12-6, 6-12-6)

Join without twisting, pm between first and last st.

Work in k1, p1 rib for 3 rnds. Knit 1 rnd.

Work Rnds 1–8.

Heel Flap

Place instep sts of 2nd needle on holder for ease in working heel.

Knit sts of 1st needle onto 3rd needle. Turn.

Work back and forth across 10 (10, 12, 12) heel sts, turning work after each row as follows:

Row 1: Sl 1, p across.

Row 2: *Sl 1, k across.

Rep Rows 1–2 until heel flap measures approximately 1 (1¼, 1½, 1½) inches, ending with a WS row.

Turn heel

Row 1: K5 (5, 7, 7), ssk, k1, turn.

Row 2: Sl 1, p2 (2, 4, 4), p2tog, p1, turn.

Row 3: Sl 1, k3 (3, 4, 4), ssk, k1, turn.

Row 4: Sl 1, p3 (3, 5, 5), p2tog, p1, turn.

Row 5: Sl 1, k3 (3, 5, 5), ssk, turn.

Row 6: Sl 1, p2 (2, 4, 4), p2tog. (4, 4, 6, 6 sts)

Shape gusset

Sl instep sts from holder to 2nd needle.

K 4 (4, 6, 6) heel sts, with same needle pick up and k 7 (8, 10, 10) sts along left side of heel flap, with 2nd needle p across instep sts, with 3rd needle pick up and k 7 (8, 10, 10) sts along right side of heel flap, knit half of heel sts onto last needle.

You should have 9 (10, 13, 13) sts on 1st needle and 3rd needle, and 12 sts on 2nd needle.

Rnd 1: On 1st needle p to last 3 sts, p2tog, p1, p all sts on 2nd needle, on 3rd needle p1, p2tog, purl to end of rnd.

Rnd 2: Purl.

Rep Rnds 1–2 until 22 (22, 24, 24) sts remain.

Foot

Work even in Reverse St st until foot measures 3 (3¼, 4 , 4½) inches from back of heel or ½ inch less than desired length.

Shape toe

Rearrange sts so there are 5-11-6 (5-11-6, 6-12-6, 6-12-6) sts on needles.

Dec rnd: P to within last 3 sts on first needle, p2tog, p1; on second needle p1, p2tog, p to last 3 sts, p2tog, p1, on third needle, p1; p2tog, p to end of rnd.

Rep dec rnd 3 times. (10, 10, 12, 12 sts)

Sizes 18 and 24 month only: P to within last 3 sts on 1st needle, p2tog, p1; on 2nd needle p to within last 3 sts, p2tog, p1; on 3rd needle p all sts without dec. (10 sts)

Cut yarn.

Weave toe sts tog using Kitchener method. ◆

Shape crown

Change to dpn when necessary.

Rnd 1: [P29 (9, 0, 17), p2tog] 2 (6, 0, 4) times. (60, 60, 70, 70 sts)

Rnd 2 and all even-numbered rnds: Purl.

Rnd 3: *P8, p2tog, rep from * around. (54, 54, 63, 63 sts)

Rnd 5: *P7, p2tog, rep from * around. (48, 48, 56, 56 sts)

Rnd 7: *P6, p2tog, rep from * around. (42, 42, 49, 49 sts)

Rnd 9: *P5, p2tog, rep from * around. (36, 36, 42, 42 sts)

Rnd 10: *P4, p2tog, rep from * around. (30, 30, 35, 35 sts)

Rnd 11: *P3, p2tog, rep from * around. (24, 24, 28, 28 sts)

Rnd 13: *P2, p2tog, rep from *

Bubblegum Baby Trio

Designs by Sandi Prosser

Small Fair Isle motifs are used to create the colorful design in this three-piece set for baby.

Skill Level
Intermediate***

Size
Infant's 6 (12, 18, 24) months
Instructions are given for smallest size, with larger sizes in parentheses. When only 1 number is given, it applies to all sizes.

Finished Measurements
Chest: 20 (22, 24, 26) inches
Length: 9½ (10½, 11½, 13) inches
Pants Inseam: 6 (7½, 8, 9) inches

Materials
- Plymouth Wildflower D.K. 51 percent mercerized cotton/49 percent acrylic DK weight yarn (136 yds/50g per ball): Jacket and Hat: 2 (2, 2, 3) balls lilac #50 (MC), 2 balls seafoam #42 (A), 1 (1, 2, 2) balls aqua #15 (B), 1 ball each white #41 (C), bubblegum #54 (D); Pants: 1 (1, 2, 2) balls lilac #50 (MC), 1 ball each seafoam #42 (A), aqua #15 (B), white #41 (C), bubblegum #54 (D)
- Size 3 (3.25mm) needles
- Size 6 (4.25mm) needles or size needed to obtain gauge
- Size E/4 crochet hook
- 1 (⅝-inch) button
- 1 yd (½-inch) elastic
- 3-inch piece of cardboard

Gauge
24 sts and 32 rows = 4 inches/10cm in St st with larger needles

To save time, take time to check gauge.

Stripe Pattern
Work in St st in the following color sequence:
6 rows bubblegum, 4 rows MC, 2 rows white, 6 rows seafoam, 4 rows white, 6 rows aqua, 2 rows MC, 4 rows bubblegum, 2 rows aqua, 4 rows seafoam, 6 rows MC, 4 rows white.

Pattern Note
Carry color not in use loosely across back of work.

Jacket

Back
With MC and smaller needles, cast on 55 (61, 67, 73) sts.

Beg with a WS row, work in garter st for 5 rows, inc 6 sts evenly on last WS row. (61, 67, 73, 79 sts)

Change to larger needles.

Referring to Chart A, beg and end as indicated for chosen size, work even until back measures 5 (5½, 6¼, 7½) inches, ending with a WS row.

Shape armhole
Bind off 3 sts at beg of next 2 rows.

[Dec 1 st each end every other row] 3 times. (49, 55, 61, 67 sts)

Work even until armhole measures 4½ (5, 5¼, 5½) inches, ending with a WS row.

Shape neck
Next row (RS): Bind off 14 (15, 17, 20) sts, work across next 21 (25, 27, 27) sts and sl to holder, bind off rem 14 (15, 17, 20) sts.

Left Front
With MC and smaller needles, cast on 27 (30, 33, 36) sts.

Work in garter st as for back, inc 3 sts evenly across last WS row. (30, 33, 36, 39 sts)

Change to larger needles.

Referring to Chart A, beg and end as indicated for chosen size, work even until front measures same as for back to underarm, ending with a WS row.

Shape armhole
Bind off 3 sts at beg of next row.

[Dec 1 st at arm edge every other row] 3 times. (24, 27, 30, 33 sts)

Work even until armhole measures 2½ (3, 3¼, 3½) inches, ending with a RS row.

Neck shaping
Next row: Bind off 6 sts, work to end of row.

[Dec 1 st at neck edge every row] 3 (3, 5, 5) times, then [every other row] 1 (3, 2, 2) times. (14, 15, 17, 20 sts)

Work even until armhole measures same as for back.

Bind off.

Right Front
Work as for left front, reversing shaping.

Sleeves
With smaller needles and MC, cast on 35 (35, 37, 39) sts.

Work in garter st as for back, inc 6 sts evenly on last WS row. (41, 41, 43 sts)

Change to larger needles.

Referring to Chart B, beg and end as indicated for chosen size, [inc 1 st each end every 4th row] 11 (13, 14, 15) times, working added sts into pat. (57, 61, 65, 69 sts)

Work even in established pat until sleeve measures 5½ (6½, 7½, 8½) inches, ending with a WS row.

Shape cap
Bind off 3 sts at beg of next 2 rows.

[Dec 1 st at each end every other row] 3 times. (45, 49, 53, 57 sts)

Bind off.

Sew shoulder seams.

Neck Band
With RS facing, using MC and

smaller needles, pick up and k 25 (25, 27, 27) sts along right front edge, k 19 (21, 25, 27) sts of back neck, pick up and k 25 (25, 27, 27) sts along left front edge. (69, 71, 79, 81 sts)

Work 4 rows in garter st.

Bind off knitwise on WS.

Front Edgings

With RS facing, using MC and smaller needles, pick up and k 52 (54, 58, 64) sts along front edge.

Knit 2 rows.

Bind off knitwise on WS.

Finishing

Attach MC to top of neck, at right edge for girl or left edge for boy.

With crochet hook, ch 10, sk 2 bound-off sts, sl st in next st. Fasten off.

Sew sleeves into armholes.

Sew sleeve and side seams.

Sew on button.

Pants

Legs

With MC and smaller needles, cast on 35 (39, 43, 45) sts.

Work in k1, p1 ribbing for 1½ inches, inc 34 (38, 42, 44) sts evenly on last WS row. (69, 75, 85, 89 sts)

Change to larger needles.

Working in Stripe pat, [inc 1 st each end of needle every 4th row] 7 (8, 7, 7) times. (83, 91, 99, 103 sts)

Work even until leg measures 6 (7½, 9, 10½) inches ending with a WS row.

Shape crotch

Bind off 3 sts at beg of next 2 rows.

[Dec 1 st each end every other row] twice.

Cut yarn; sl sts to holder.

Work 2nd leg as for first; do not cut yarn.

Next row: With appropriate color, k 73 (81, 89, 93) sts on needle, sl sts from holder to LH needle and k them. (146, 162, 178, 186 sts)

Work even in Stripe pat until pants measures 6½ (7, 7½, 8) inches above bound-off crotch sts, ending with a WS row. Change to MC.

Next row: K1 (2, 1, 2), *k2tog, k1, rep from * across, end last rep k1. (98, 108, 118, 124 sts)

Change to smaller needles.

Work even in k1, p1 ribbing for 1½ inches.

Bind off loosely in ribbing.

Finishing

Sew center front and back seams.

Sew leg seams.

Fold waistband in half to wrong side and sew loosely in position leaving an opening to insert elastic.

Cut elastic to desired waist measurement and insert in casing.

Sew ends of elastic tog securely.

Sew opening of waistband tog.

Hat

With MC and smaller needles, cast on 93 (97, 101, 105) sts.

Beg with a WS row, work in garter st for 7 rows.

Change to larger needles.

Referring to Chart C, work even in pat until hat measures 5½ (6, 6½, 7) inches.

Bind off.

Finishing

Fold hat in half.

Sew top and side seam.

Tassels

Make 2

Wrap MC around cardboard approximately 50 times. Tie one end; cut other end.

Tie another strand tightly around top of tassel, about 1 inch below first tie.

Sew 1 tassel to each corner of hat. ✦

COLOR KEY
- Lilac (MC)
- Seafoam (A)
- Aqua (B)
- White (C)
- Bubblegum (D)

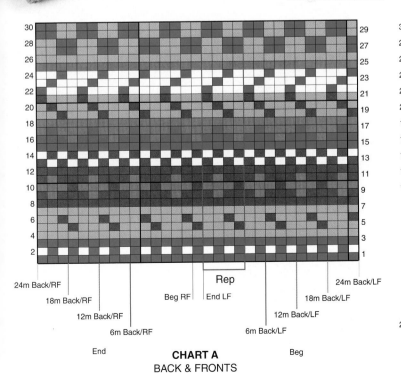

CHART A
BACK & FRONTS

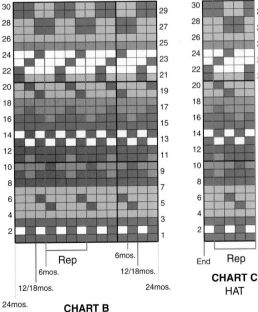

CHART B
SLEEVE

CHART C
HAT

21

Stars & Stripes Romper

Design by Cindy Polfer

Dress your little one in a patriotic romper. This romper would look cute on boys and girls alike.

Skill Level

Intermediate***

Size

Infant's 6 (12, 18, 24) months
Instructions are given for smallest size, with larger sizes in parentheses. When only 1 number is given, it applies to all sizes.

Finished Measurements

Chest: 21 (22, 23, 24) inches

Total length: 15¼ (16¼, 17¼, 18¼) inches

Armhole depth: 4¼ (4½, 4¾, 5) inches

Sleeve length: 2¾ inches

Materials

- Plymouth Wildflower D.K. 51 percent mercerized cotton/49 percent acrylic DK weight yarn (136 yds/50g per ball): 3 (3, 4, 4) balls blue #57 (MC), 1 ball each red #46 (A), white #41 (B)
- Size 3 (3.25mm) needles
- Size 5 (3.75mm) needles or size needed to obtain gauge
- Stitch holders
- Stitch markers
- Tapestry needle
- 4½-inch piece of snap tape
- Small amount of waste yarn
- 3 star appliqués (optional)
- Sewing needle and matching thread

ROMPER ROOM

Gauge
23 sts and 34 rows = 4 inches/10cm in St st with larger needles

To save time, take time to check gauge.

Pattern Stitches
Wrap worked on a knit row: Wyib, sl next st purlwise, bring yarn between needles to front of work, sl same st back to LH needle.

Wrap worked on a purl row: Wyif, sl next st purlwise, bring yarn between needles to back of work, sl same st back to LH needle.

Hiding wraps on a knit row: K to 1 st before wrapped st, insert needle under wrap and knitwise into st and k them tog.

Hiding wraps on a purl row: P to 1 st before wrapped st, insert RH needle from behind into back loop of wrap and place it on LH needle. Purl wrap and st tog.

Striped Pattern Sequence: Work in St st and color sequence of 4 rows red, 4 rows white.

1/1 Striped Rib
Row 1 (WS): With A, k1, *p1, k1, rep from * across.

Row 2: P1, *k1, p1, rep from * across.

Row 3: With B, purl.

Row 4: P1, *k1, p1, rep from * across.

Row 5: With A, purl.

Row 6: P1, *k1, p1, rep from * across.

Pattern Notes
Red and white stripes are worked on front yoke only.

The neck band is worked as a folded band whose last row of sts are not bound off, but rather tacked to the base of the neckline. This is done to provide a very stretchy neck band which will slip over a child's head easily.

The waste yarn used for the neck band will be removed after last row of neck band sts are tacked to neckline. The waste yarn acts as a st holder, making it easier to tack last row of ribbing sts to base of neckline.

Purchased star appliqués may be used in place of knit ones.

Back
Crotch Facing

With MC and larger needles, cast on 13 sts.

Work in St st for 8 rows, ending with a WS row.

Turning row (RS): Purl.

Body

Beg with a purl row, continue in St st for 11 rows.

Shape leg openings

Continuing in St st, [inc 1 st each side every other row] 7 times, then [every row] 5 times. (37 sts)

Cast on 2 sts at beg of next 4 (0, 0, 0) rows, then 3 sts at beg of next 6 (10, 8, 4) rows, and finally 4 sts at beg of next 0 (0, 2, 6) rows. (63, 67, 69, 73 sts)

[Dec 1 st each side every 18th (20th, 22th, 24th) row] twice. (59, 63, 65, 69 sts)

Work even until body measures 6½ (7¼, 8, 8¾) inches from top of leg opening, ending with WS row.

Shape armhole

Bind off 4 sts at beg of next 2 rows.

[Dec 1 st each side every other row] 4 (4, 4, 5) times. (43, 47, 49, 51 sts)

Work even until armhole measures 3½ (3¾, 4, 4¼) inches ending with WS row.

Shape back neck

K 11 (13, 14, 15) sts, join 2nd balls of yarn, k 21 sts and place on holder for back neck, k 11 (13, 14, 15) sts.

Working on each side with separate balls of yarn, [dec 1 st at each neck edge every other row] twice. (9, 11, 12, 13 sts for each shoulder)

Purl 1 row.

Place shoulder sts onto st holders.

Front

Work as for back until front measures 5½ (6¼, 7, 7¾) inches from top of leg opening *except* work 9 rows instead of 11 before shaping leg opening.

Change to Striped Pat Sequence and work even for 1 inch, ending with a WS row.

Shape armhole

Bind off 4 sts at beg of next 2 rows.

[Dec 1 st each side every other row] 4 (4, 4, 5) times. (43, 47, 49, 51 sts)

Work even until armhole measures 2¼ (2½, 2¾, 3) inches, ending with a WS row.

Shape front neckline

K 13 (15, 16, 17) sts, join 2nd ball of yarn, k 17 sts and sl to holder for front neck, k remaining 13 (15, 16, 17) sts.

Working on each side with separate balls of yarn, [dec 1 st at each neck edge every other row] 4 times. (9, 11, 12, 13 sts for each shoulder)

Work even until armhole measures same as for back, ending with a WS row.

Place sts on st holders.

Join right shoulder seam by using 3-needle bind-off method.

Neck Band

Beg at left shoulder seam with RS facing, using A and smaller needles, pick up and k 14 sts along left side of neck, k 17 sts of front neck, pick up and k 18 sts along right side of neck, knit 21 sts of back neck, pick up and k 5 sts along remainder of left neck. (75 sts)

Work 6 rows of 1/1 Striped Rib Pat, [rep Rows 1 and 2] 3 times, then Row 1. (13 rows)

Do not bind off. Beg with a k row, work 6 rows of St st using waste yarn.

Cut yarn and remove sts from needle.

Join left shoulder seam same as for right. Sew neck band seam.

Fold neck band in half to inside and tack last row of ribbing sts to base of neck band, folding back waste yarn as you st. Remove waste yarn.

Sleeves

With A and smaller needle, cast on 41 (43, 43, 45) sts.

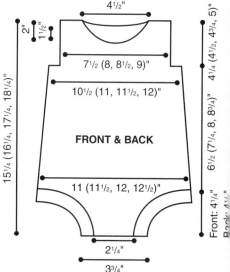

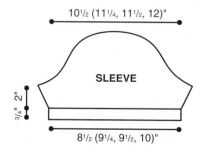

Work 6 rows of 1/1 Striped Rib pat, inc 8 (10, 12, 12) sts evenly on last row. (49, 53, 55, 57 sts)

Change to MC and larger needles.

Purl 1 row.

Working in St st, [inc 1 st each side every other row] 6 times. (61, 65, 67, 69 sts)

Work even until sleeve measures 2¾ inches from beg, ending with a WS row.

Shape cap

Bind off 4 sts at beg of next 2 rows.

[Dec 1 st each side every other row] 4 times. (45, 49, 51, 53 sts)

Purl 1 row.

Next row: K42 (45, 47, 49) sts, wrap next st, turn, p 39 (41, 43, 45) sts, wrap and turn, k 35 (37, 39, 41) sts, wrap and turn, p 31 (33, 35, 37) sts, wrap and turn, k 27 (29, 31, 32) sts, wrap and turn, p 23 (25, 27, 27) sts, wrap and turn, k 19 (20, 22, 22) sts, wrap and turn, p 15 (15, 17, 17) sts, k to end hiding wraps.

Purl 1 row, hiding remaining wraps

Bind off all sts.

Leg Bands

With RS facing, using A and smaller needles, pick up and k 67 (71, 73, 77) sts along edge of leg opening between turning rows.

Work 6 rows 1/1 Striped Band Pat.

Bind off in rib.

Star Appliqué

Make 3

With MC and smaller needles, cast on 45 sts.

Row 1: [Sl 1 wyib, k2, ssk, k2tog, k2] 5 times.

Row 2: [K1, ssk, k2tog, k1, sl 1 wyib] 5 times.

Row 3: [Sl 1 wyib, ssk, k2tog] 5 times.

Row 4: [K2tog, k1] 5 times.

Cut yarn, leaving a 12-inch end.

With tapestry needle, draw end through remaining sts to form circle.

Tack beg of star to end of star.

Sew 3 stars to yoke as shown in photo.

Finishing

Sew in sleeves, joining sleeve to armhole 1 row in from edge.

Sew side and sleeve seams.

Pin snap tape to crotch, centering middle snap. Tuck excess tape under at each end.

Sew tape to crotch, having front overlap back. ✦

Color-Block Romper

Design by Cindy Polfer

Primary colors and a speckled yarn perk up a romper meant for playtime.

Skill Level
Intermediate***

Size
Infant's 6 (12, 18, 24) months
Instructions are given for smallest size, with larger sizes in parentheses. When only 1 number is given, it applies to all sizes.

Finished Measurements
Chest: 21 (22, 23, 24) inches

Total back length: 15¼ (16¼, 17¼, 18¼) inches

Armhole depth: 4¼ (4½, 4¾, 5) inches

Sleeve length: 2¾ inches

Materials
- Plymouth Wildflower Fancy D.K. 53 percent acrylic/43 percent mercerized cotton/4 percent nylon DK weight yarn (116 yds/50g per skein): 3 (3, 4, 4) skeins blue #857 (MC), 1 skein each green #849 (A), yellow #848 (B), red #863 (C)
- Size 3 (3.25mm) needles
- Size 5 (3.75mm) needles or size needed to obtain gauge
- Stitch holders
- Stitch markers
- Tapestry needle
- Small amount of waste yarn
  - 4½-inch piece of snap tape
    - Sewing needle and matching thread

Gauge
21 sts and 29 rows = 4 inches/10cm in St st with larger needles

To save time, take time to check gauge.

Pattern Stitch
Wrap worked on a knit row:
Wyib, sl next st purlwise, bring yarn between needles to front of work, sl same st back to LH needle.

Wrap worked on a purl row: Wyif, sl next st purlwise, bring yarn between needles to back of work, sl same st back to LH needle.

Hiding wraps on a knit row: K to wrapped st, insert needle under wrap and knitwise into st and k them tog.

Hiding wraps on a purl row: P to wrapped st, insert RH needle from behind into back loop of wrap and place it on LH needle. Purl wrap and st tog.

1/1 Striped Rib
Row 1 (WS): With C k1, *p1, k1, rep from * across.

Row 2: P1, *k1, p1, rep from * across.

Rows 3: With MC k1, *p1, k1, rep from * across.

Row 4: With C p1, *k1, p1, rep from * across.

Row 5: With C k1, *p1, k1, rep from * across.

Pattern Notes
Intarsia pat is worked on front only.

Chart begins after leg openings have been worked.

To avoid holes when changing colors, always bring new color up over old.

The neck band is worked as a folded band whose last row of sts are not bound off, but rather tacked to the base of the neckline. This is

done to provide a very stretchy opening which will easily slip over a child's head.

The waste yarn used for the neck band will be removed after last row of neck band sts are tacked to neckline. The waste yarn acts as a st holder, making it easier to tack last row of ribbing sts to base of neckline.

Back
Crotch Facing

With MC and larger size needles, cast on 12 sts.

Work in St st for 6 rows, ending with a WS row.

Turning row (RS): Purl.

Body

Beg with a p row, continue in St st for 9 rows.

Shape leg openings

Continuing in St st, [inc 1 st each side every other row] 5 times, then [every row] 5 times. (32 sts)

Cast on 3 sts at beg of next 6 (4, 0, 0) rows, then 4 sts at beg of next 2 (4, 8, 6) rows, and finally 5 sts at beg of next 0 (0, 0, 2) rows. (58, 60, 64, 66 sts)

Work even until body measures 2½ (2¾, 3¼, 3¾) inches from top of leg opening.

Next row: Dec 1 st each end. (56, 58, 62, 64 sts)

Work even until body measures 6½ (7¼, 8, 8¾) inches from top of leg opening, ending with a WS row.

Shape armhole

Bind off 4 sts at beg of next 2 rows.

[Dec 1 st each end every other row] 4 times. (40, 42, 46, 48 sts)

Work even until armhole measures 3½ (3¾, 4, 4¾) inches, ending with a WS row.

Shape back neck

Next row: K 9 (10, 12, 13) sts, attach 2nd ball of yarn, k 22 sts and place on holder for back neck, k remaining 9 (10, 12, 13) sts.

Working on each side of neck with separate balls of yarn, purl 1 row.

Dec row: Dec 1 st at each neck edge. (8, 9, 11, 12 sts remaining for each shoulder)

Purl 1 row.

Place shoulder sts onto st holders.

Front

Work same as back to top of leg opening except work 7 rows instead of 9 just before shaping leg opening.

Referring to chart for chosen size, work in intarsia pat to armhole, dec 1 st each side on body as indicated.

Shape armhole

Bind off 4 sts at beg of next 2 rows.

[Dec 1 st each side every other row] 4 times. (40, 42, 46, 48) sts.

Work even as charted to front neckline shaping.

Shape front neckline

Continuing in charted pat, work across 11 (12, 14, 15) sts, sl center 18 sts onto holder for front neck, attach 2nd ball of yarn and work across remaining 11 (12, 14, 15) sts.

Working on each side of neck with separate balls of yarn, [dec 1 st at each neck edge every other row] 3 times. (8, 9, 11, 12 sts for each shoulder)

Work even until armhole measures same as for back, ending with a WS row.

Join right shoulder seam by using 3-needle bind-off method.

Neck Band

Beg at left shoulder seam with RS facing, using A and smaller needles, pick up and k 10 sts along left side of neck, k 18 sts of front neck, pick up and k 14 sts along right side of neck, knit 22 sts of back neck, pick up and k 3 sts along remainder of left neck. (67 sts)

Work 5 rows of 1/1 Striped Rib pat, [rep Rows 4–5] 3 times. (11 rows)

Do not bind off.

Beg with a k row and waste yarn, work 6 rows in St st. Cut yarn and remove sts from needle.

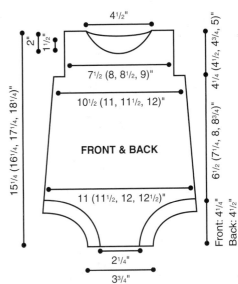

4½"

2" 1½"

7½ (8, 8½, 9)"

10½ (11, 11½, 12)"

15¼ (16¼, 17¼, 18¼)"

4¼ (4½, 4¾, 5)"

6½ (7¼, 8, 8¾)"

FRONT & BACK

Front: 4¼"
Back: 4½"

11 (11½, 12, 12½)"

2¼"

3¾"

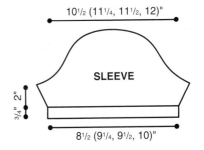

10½ (11¼, 11½, 12)"

SLEEVE

3" 2"

¾"

8½ (9¼, 9½, 10)"

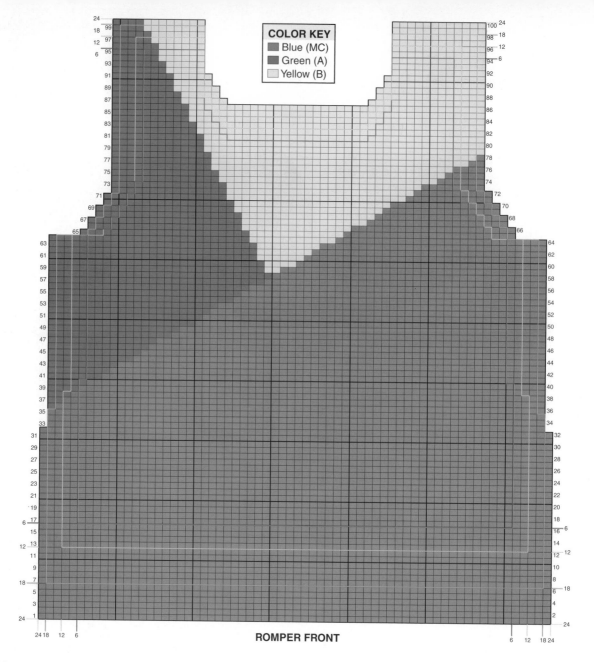

COLOR KEY
- Blue (MC)
- Green (A)
- Yellow (B)

ROMPER FRONT

Join left shoulder seam same as for right. Sew neck band seam.

Fold neck band in half to inside and tack last row of ribbing sts to base of neck band, folding back waste yarn as you st. Remove waste yarn.

Sleeves

With A and smaller needle, cast on 37 (39, 38, 41) sts.

Work 5 rows of 1/1 Striped Rib pat, rep Row 2 inc 7 (9, 12, 11) sts evenly. (44, 48, 50, 52 sts)

Change to blue and larger needles. Purl 1 row.

[Inc 1 st each end of next and every following RS row] 5 times. (54, 58, 60, 62 sts)

Work even until sleeve measures 2¾

inches from beg, ending with p row.

Shape cap

Bind off 4 sts at beg of next 2 rows.

[Dec 1 st each side every other row] 3 times. (40, 44, 46, 48 sts)

Purl 1 row.

Next row (RS): K 37 (41, 43, 48) sts, wrap next st, turn, p 34, 38, 40, 40) sts, turn, k 31 (34, 36, 36) sts, wrap and turn, p 28 (30, 32, 32) sts, wrap and turn, k 25 (26, 28, 28) sts, wrap and turn, p 22 (22, 24, 24) sts, wrap and turn, k 18 (18, 20, 20) sts, wrap and turn, p 14 (14, 16, 16) sts, k to end hiding wraps.

Purl 1 row, hiding remaining wraps. Bind off all sts.

Leg Bands

With RS facing using C and smaller needles, pick up and k 59 (61, 65, 69) sts along edge of leg opening between turning rows.

Work 5 rows of 1/1 Striped Rib pat. Bind off in rib.

Finishing

Sew in sleeves, joining sleeve to armhole 1 row in from edge.

Sew side and sleeve seams.

Tack down crotch facing.

Pin snap tape to crotch, centering middle snap. Tuck excess tape under at each end.

Sew tape to crotch, having front overlap back. ✦

Striped Henley Romper Set

Designs by Kennita Tully

Bright colors in a bold, striped design create the colorful appeal in this captivating set!

Skill Level

Intermediate***

Size

Infant's 6 (12, 18, 24) months
Instructions are given for smallest size, with larger sizes in parentheses. When only 1 number is given, it applies to all sizes.

Finished Measurements

Cuff to cuff measurement: 18¾ (20½, 22, 23¼) inches

Length: 21 (22½, 24, 25½) inches

Hat circumference: 15 (16½, 18½) inches

Materials

- Plymouth Wildflower D.K. 51 percent cotton/49 percent acrylic DK weight yarn (137 yds/50g per ball): 3 (3, 4, 4) balls bright blue #55 (A), 2 (3, 3, 3) balls canary yellow #48 (B)
- Size 4 (3.5mm) straight and 16-inch circular needles
- Size 5 (3.75 mm) double-pointed, 16- and 24-inch circular needles or size needed to obtain gauge
- Stitch holders
- Tapestry needle
- ½ (½, ⅔, ⅔) yd snap tape
- Sewing machine or hand-sewing needle and matching thread

Gauge

22 sts and 32 rows = 4 inches/10cm in St st with larger needles

To save time, take time to check gauge.

Stripe Sequence

Work in St st stripes of 8 rows A, then 8 rows B.

Romper

Back

Beg at left leg with smaller needles and B, cast on 22 (22, 24, 28) sts.

Work in Stripe pat, inc 1 st each end of 7th (5th, 5th, 5th) row.

[Inc 1 st every 8th (6th, 6th, 6th) row] 4 (7, 8, 8) times at inside of leg and *at the same time* [inc 1 st every 8th (6th, 6th, 6th) row] 4 (6, 3, 3) times at outside seam.

Continue to [inc 1 st at outside seam only every 0 (0, 8, 8) rows] 0 (0, 4, 4) times. (32, 37, 41, 45 sts)

Work even until leg measures 6 (6½, 7, 7½) inches, ending with a WS row.

Cut yarn, place sts on holder.

Right Leg

Work as for left leg, reversing shaping. Do not cut yarn.

Join for body

Next row: Keeping to color sequence, k sts of right leg, sl sts of left leg from holder to LH needle, k to end of row. (64, 74, 82, 90 sts)

Body

[Inc 1 st each end every 6th row] twice. (68, 78, 86, 94 sts)

Work even until body measures 9 (9½, 10, 10½) inches above crotch, ending with a WS row.

Shape sleeves

Cast on 3 sts at end of next 8 rows. (92, 102, 110, 118 sts)

Work even for 2½ (3, 3½, 4) inches, ending with a WS row.

Shoulder shaping

Bind off 6 (7, 7, 8) sts at beg of next 10 (4, 10, 4) rows, then 5 (6, 6, 7) sts at beg of following 2 (8, 2, 8) rows.

Bind off remaining 22 (26, 28, 30) sts for back neck.

Front

Work as for back, to beg of sleeve shaping.

Divide for placket

Next row (RS): Work across 31 (36, 40, 44) sts, join 2nd ball of yarn and bind off next 6 sts, work to end of row.

Working on both sides simultaneously with separate balls of yarn, cast on 3 sts at end of next 8 rows for sleeve shaping, *at the same time* work even at placket edge until placket measures 3½ inches.

Shape neck

Bind off at each neck edge 3 sts 1 (1, 1, 2) times, then 2 sts 1 (2, 3, 2) times. [Dec 1 st every other row] 3 (3, 2, 2) times.

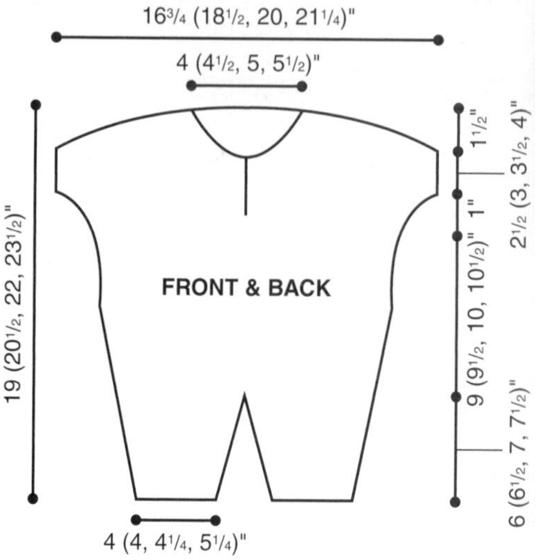

At the same time, when sleeve measures same as for back, shape shoulders as for back.

Front Placket

With smaller needles and A, pick up and k 22 sts along one edge of front opening.

Work even in St st for 20 rows.

Fold placket in half and sew to inside.

Rep for 2nd side.

Sew shoulder seams.

Schematic diagram labels:

16¾ (18½, 20, 21¼)"

4 (4½, 5, 5½)"

FRONT & BACK

19 (20½, 22, 23½)"

1½"

1"

2½ (3, 3½, 4)"

9 (9½, 10, 10½)"

6 (6½, 7, 7½)"

4 (4, 4¼, 5¼)"

Neck Band

With smaller needles and A, pick up and k 17 (17, 19, 19) sts along right side of neck, 22 (26, 28, 30) sts along back neck and 17 (17, 19, 19) sts along left side of neck. (56, 60, 66, 68 sts)

Work even in St st for 12 rows.

Bind off loosely.

Fold neck band to inside and sew in place.

Sleeve Cuff

With smaller needles and A, pick up and k 3 sts for every 4 rows along sleeve edge.

Work even in St st for 18 rows.

Bind off.

Fold cuff in half to inside and sew in place.

Sew sleeve and side seam.

Leg Placket

With smaller needles and A, pick up and k 3 sts for every 4 rows along front of right leg and same amount along left leg.

Work even in St st for 20 rows.

Bind off.

Fold placket in half to inside and sew in place.

Rep for back leg placket.

Cuff

Left Leg

With smaller needles and A, pick up and k 7 sts along front placket, 1 st in each cast-on st of leg. Do not pick up sts in back placket.

Work even in St st for 28 rows.

Bind off.

Rep for right leg, picking up sts along leg first, then along placket.

Finishing

Sew snap tape to leg plackets, beg and ending above cuff. Do not sew tape to cuffs.

Sew leg cuff seam.

Fold cuff in half to inside and sew i n place.

Sew lower end of back leg placket to top of cuff.

Sew snap tape to neck placket.

Overlap lower edges of placket and sew to romper body, joining both plackets.

Hat

With smaller circular needle and A, cast on 84 (90, 102) sts.

Join without twisting, pm between first and last st.

Work in St st for 1½ inches.

Change to larger needles and B, beg stripe sequence.

Work even in Stripe Pat until 5 rnds of 2nd yellow stripe have been completed.

Beg shaping

Dec Rnd: *K12 (13, 15), k2tog, rep from * around.

Work even for 7 rnds.

Dec Rnd 2: *K11 (12, 14), k2tog, rep from * around.

Work even for 7 rnds.

Dec every 8th rnd as before, having 1 less st between each dec until 24 sts remain. Change to dpn when necessary.

Next row: K2tog across row. (12 sts)

Cut yarn, leaving an 8-inch end.

Draw end through all sts twice and fasten off on inside. ✦

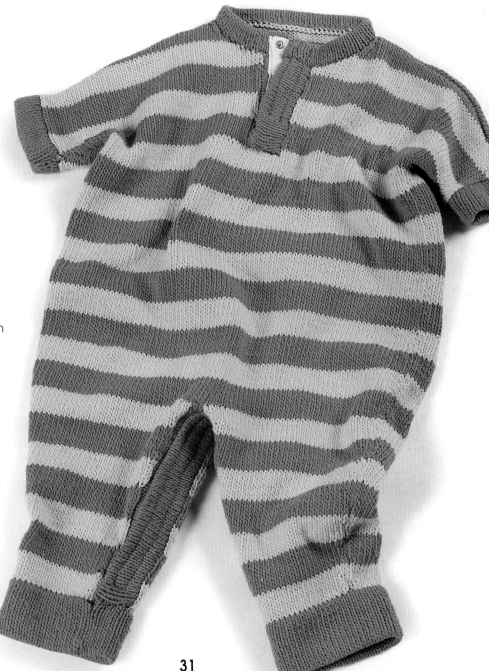

Alphabet Blocks Baby Accessories

Designs by Diane Zangl

Block letters are featured on pastel squares to create an heirloom for that special new baby. This soft afghan and matching wall hanging will be treasured by parents and baby alike. A block for baby completes the collection.

Skill Level
Easy**

Finished Size
Afghan: Approximately 37 x 41 inches

Wall Hanging: 15 x 15 inches

Block: 4 inches square

Materials
- Plymouth Encore Wosted 75 percent acrylic/25 percent wool worsted weight yarn (200 yds/100g per skein): 6 skeins natural #146 (MC), 1 skein each aqua #235 (A), fuchsia #137 (B), lime #3335 (C).
- Size 6 (4mm) needles or size needed to obtain gauge
- ⅝-inch-wide flat wooden stick or dowel
- Polyester fiberfill
- Yarn needle

Gauge
18 sts and 27 rows = 4 inches/10cm in St st

To save time, take time to check gauge.

Pattern Stitch
Seed Pattern
Row 1 (RS): Sl 1 purlwise wyif, *p1, k1, rep from * across, end last rep p1.

Row 2: Sl 1 knitwise wyib, *k1, p1, rep from * across, end last rep k1.

Rep Rows 1 and 2 for pat.

Pattern Notes
Sl first st of every row for afghan and wall hanging.

Wind separate balls of color for each section. To avoid holes when changing colors, always bring new color up over old.

MC is used for Seed pat only; CC blocks are worked in St st. When working a Seed pat block above a CC one, always knit first row to avoid color showing through.

Wall Hanging
With MC, cast on 64 sts. Sl first st of every row, work even in Seed pat for 7 rows.

First Tier of Blocks
Set up pat (RS): With MC, work Seed pat over 5 sts, k18 A, MC Seed pat over 18 sts, k18 B, MC Seed pat over 5 sts.

Keeping MC in Seed pat and color blocks in St st, work even for 25 more rows.

Second Tier of Blocks
Set up pat (RS): Work Seed pat over 5 sts, k18 MC, k18 C, k18 MC, Seed pat over 5 sts.

Keeping MC in Seed pat and color blocks in St st, work even for 25 more rows.

Third Tier of Blocks
Set up pat (RS): Work Seed pat over 5 sts, k18 B, k18 MC, k18 A, Seed pat over 5 sts.

Keeping MC in Seed pat and color blocks in St st, work even for 25 more rows.

Work even in Seed pat only for 8 rows.

Facing
Purl next RS row for turning ridge. Work 7 rows in St st.

Bind off all sts.

Finishing
Turn facing to inside and sew in place.

Referring to charts, duplicate st letters on each color block.

Slide flat wooden stick into casing.

Block

Cast on 18 C, 18 B, 18 A.

Work even in St st for 25 more rows.

Next row (RS): Bind off 18 sts with A, cut B, attach MC, k18 MC, bind off 18 sts with C.

Working with MC on center square only, [work in Seed pat for 25 rows, do not sl first st. Purl next RS row] twice.

Work in Seed pat for 25 rows

Bind off all sts.

Finishing

Referring to charts, duplicate st letters on each color block.

Sew bound-off edge of lime square to side edge of first natural square.

Rep for aqua square.

Lightly stuff block with fiberfill.

Sew 3 sides of remaining natural squares to sides of aqua and lime and tops of all three colored squares.

Afghan

With MC, cast on 156 sts. Work in Seed pat for 7 rows.

First Tier of Blocks

Set up pat (RS): Sl 1, work Seed pat over 5 sts, k18 C, Seed pat over 36 sts, k18 B, Seed pat over 36 sts, k18 A, Seed pat to end of row.

Keeping MC in Seed pat and color blocks in St st, work even for 25 more rows.

Second Tier of Blocks

Set up pat (RS): Sl 1, Seed pat over 41 sts, k18 B, Seed pat over 36 sts, k18 A, Seed pat to end of row

Keeping MC in Seed pat and color blocks in St st, work even for 25 more rows.

Third Tier of Blocks

Set up pat (RS): Sl 1, Seed pat over 23 sts, k18 B, Seed pat over 36 sts, k18 A, Seed pat over 36 sts, k18 C, Seed pat to end of row.

Keeping MC in Seed pat and color blocks in St st, work even for 25 more rows.

Fourth Tier of Blocks

Set up pat (RS): Sl 1, Seed pat over 5 sts, k18 B, Seed pat over 36 sts, k18 A, Seed pat over 36 sts, k18 C, Seed pat to end of row.

Keeping MC in Seed pat and color blocks in St st, work even for 25 more rows.

Fifth Tier of Blocks

Set up pat (RS): Sl 1, Seed pat over 41 sts, k18 A, Seed pat over 36 sts, k18 C, Seed pat to end of row.

Keeping MC in Seed pat and color blocks in St st, work even for 25 more rows.

Sixth Tier of Blocks

Set up pat (RS): Sl 1, Seed pat over 23 sts, k18 A, Seed pat over 36 sts, k18 C, Seed pat over 36 sts, k18 B, Seed pat to end of row.

Keeping MC in Seed pat and color blocks in St st, work even for 25 more rows.

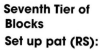

Seventh Tier of Blocks

Set up pat (RS): Sl 1, Seed pat over 5 sts, k18 A, Seed pat over 36 sts, k18 C, Seed pat over 36 sts, k18 B, Seed pat to end of row.

Keeping MC in Seed pat and color blocks in St st, work even for 25 more rows.

Eighth Tier of Blocks

Set up pat (RS): Sl 1, Seed pat over 41 sts, k18 C, Seed pat over 36 sts, k18 B, Seed pat to end of row.

Keeping MC in Seed pat and color blocks in St st, work even for 25 more rows.

Ninth Tier of Blocks

Set up pat (RS): Sl 1, Seed pat over 23 sts, k18 C, Seed pat over 36 sts, k18 B, Seed pat over 36 sts, k18 A, Seed pat to end of row.

Keeping MC in Seed pat and color blocks in St st, work even for 25 more rows.

10th Tier of Blocks

Set up pat (RS): Sl 1, Seed pat over 5 sts, k18 C, Seed pat over 36 sts, k18 B, Seed pat over 36 sts, k18 A, Seed pat to end of row.

Keeping MC in Seed pat and color blocks in St st, work even for 25 more rows.

Top Border

With MC, work in Seed pat for 8 rows.

Bind off all sts.

Referring to charts, duplicate st letters on each color block. ✦

COLOR KEY	
☐	Natural
▨	Aqua
▨	Fuchsia
▨	Lime

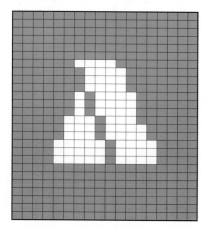

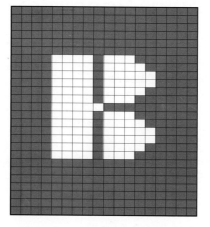

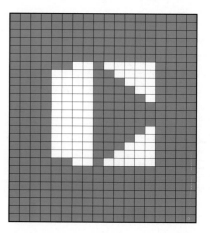

Entrelac Baby Nursery

Designs by Barbara Venishnick

A crib-size afghan and matching window valance will add charm to a baby's room. Make them in the soft pastels shown here, or choose your own bright colors.

Skill Level
Advanced****

Finished Measurements
Afghan: Approximately 36 x 48 inches

Valance: Approximately 36 inches wide x 8 inches tall

Materials
- Plymouth Encore Worsted 75 percent acrylic/25 percent wool worsted weight yarn (200 yds/ 100g per ball)
  Afghan: 2 balls white #208 (MC), 1 ball each peach #597 (A), mint #1201 (B), baby pink #029 (C), baby blue #793 (D)
  Valance: 1 ball of each of the above colors
- Size 8 (5mm) 40-inch circular needles or size needed to obtain gauge
- Size G/6 crochet hook

Gauge
16 sts and 32 rows = 4 inches/10cm in garter st

To save time, take time to check gauge.

Special Abbreviation
M1 (Make 1): With RH needle from back of work, pick up strand between last st knitted and next st. Place st on LH needle and k, twisting the strand by working through the back.

Pattern Notes
Circular needle is used to accommodate large number of sts. Work in rows; do not join.

Valance may be altered in 6-inch increments. For a wider valance, add an additional ball of MC.

Pocket on valance will accommodate a rod of up to 2 inches.

Refer to charts for placement of colors.

Afghan

First Row of Squares
Beg with lower left square and B,

cast on 18 sts.

Purl 36 rows, leaving all sts on needle.

With A cast on 18 sts. Purl 36 rows, leaving all sts on needle.

Continue with colors shown on chart A until 6 squares have been completed.

Bind off all sts of final square.

*Second Row of Squares
Change to MC. With remaining 5 squares on LH needle, pick up and

k 18 sts along left edge of bound-off square, turn.

Row 1 (WS): Knit 18, turn.

Row 2: Knit 17, join last MC st and st of square 5 by working k2tog-tbl, turn.

Rep Rows 1 and 2 until all live sts of square 5 have been joined to new MC square.

Next square: With MC pick up and K 18 sts along the left edge of square 4 of previous row and work as for the first MC square.

Rep this process until 5 MC squares are complete. Leave all squares on RH needle.

Third Row of Squares

With A, cast on 18 sts to RH needle.

Row 1 (WS): P 17 sts, purl last color A st tog with MC st, turn.

Row 2: P18, turn.

Rep Rows 1 and 2 until all MC sts have been joined to square A sts.

With D pick up and p 18 sts along remaining side of first MC square, turn.

Row 3: P18, turn.

Row 4: P17, purl the last color D st tog with MC st, turn.

Complete this square as for previous color A square.

After a total of 5 squares have been completed, work final color D square by picking up and p 18 sts along edge of last MC square.

Purl 36 rows.

Bind off all sts of final square.*

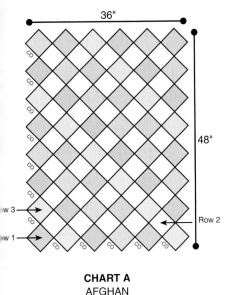

CHART A
AFGHAN

Rep from * to * 6 times more. (14 rows of squares)

Final Row of Squares

Work as for second row of squares, binding off each square as it is completed.

Weave in ends.

Valance

Work first row of squares as for afghan following Chart B for colors, but do not bind off sts of last square.

Left Triangle

With MC k 2 sts of square 6, turn, k2, turn, k1, M1, k2tog-tbl, (one from MC triangle and one from 6th square), turn, k3, turn, k1, M1, k1, k2tog-tbl, turn, k4, turn, k1, M1, k2, k2tog-tbl.

Continue in this manner, inc 1 st at right edge of triangle and working 2 sts tog at opposite edge until all sts of square 6 have been used and there are 18 MC sts in triangle.

Work 5 MC rectangles as for afghan.

Right Triangle

Pick up and k18 sts along edge of last colored square, turn.

K18, turn, k15, k2tog, k1, turn, k17, turn, k14, k2tog, k1, turn, k16.

Continue in this manner, dec 1 st at the end of every RS until 1 st remains, turn.

Top Row of Triangles

All squares are on LH needle.

With MC, p final st of right triangle, pick up and p 17 sts along side of right triangle, turn.

P18, turn, sl 1, p1, psso, p15, p last st of triangle tog with first st of MC square, turn, p17, turn, sl 1, p1, psso, p14, p2tog, turn, p16.

Continue in this manner, dec number of sts on top triangle.

When 2 sts are left on triangle and 2 sts on MC square, p2tog on triangle, p2tog on square and pass first st over 2nd st.

Using this last st as first st, pick up and p 17 sts along edge of the next MC square. Rep as for previous triangle.

When 6 top triangles are complete, bind off last st of final triangle.

Curtain Rod Pocket

With MC, cast on 10 sts.

Row 1 (RS): K1-tbl, k8, sl 1 wyif.

Row 2: K1-tbl, p8, sl 1 wyif.

Rep Rows 1 and 2 until piece measures 36 inches or same length as width of valance.

Bind off all sts.

Join Rod Pocket to Valance

Hold valance with RS facing. Place strip against back of valance with both WS tog. Pin in place.

With crochet hook and MC, *work sc through both layers in first st of top triangle and first edge st of rod pocket, sc through the next st on valance and next edge st of rod pocket, ch 3, rep from * across row allowing ch 3 to form a small loop.

Do not skip any edge sts on rod pocket.

Pin bottom edge of pocket to valance and sew in place.

Bows

Cut 4 strands of yarn, 1 each of A, B, C, and D, each 9 inches long.

Hold all 4 strands tog behind valance between two colored squares.

With crochet hook, pull each end of bundle through to front leaving 1 or 2 sts between ends.

Tie a knot and a bow.

The tail ends of each square may be used to help secure the bows in place.

Rep 4 more times across valance.

Weave in ends. ✦

COLOR KEY
- ☐ White (MC)
- ☐ Peach (A)
- ☐ Mint (B)
- ☐ Baby pink (C)
- ☐ Baby blue (D)

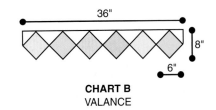

CHART B
VALANCE

Spring Sky Layette

Designs by Laura Polley

The gradual striping effect of this charming baby set will remind you of cottony clouds and soft blue skies.

Skill Level
Afghan and Hat: *Beginner**
Sweater and Socks: *Intermediate****

Size
Sweater: Infant's 6 (12, 18, 24) months
Hat: Infant's 0-6 (6-12, 12-24) months
Socks: Infant's 6-12 (12-18, 18-24) months

Instructions are given for smallest size, with larger sizes in parentheses. When only 1 number is given, it applies to all sizes.

Finished Measurements
Sweater
Chest (buttoned): 23 (25, 27, 29) inches
Length: 11½ (14, 15, 16¾) inches

Hat
Circumference: 16¾ (18½, 20) inches

Socks
Foot length: 3¾ (4¼, 4¾) inches

Afghan
Approximately 31 x 41 inches

Materials
- Plymouth Encore Worsted 75 percent acrylic/25 percent wool worsted weight yarn (200 yds/100g per skein): baby blue #793 (MC)
  Sweater: 2 (2, 2, 3) balls
  Afghan: 3 balls
  Socks and hat: 1 ball will do both
- Plymouth Encore Colorspun 75 percent acrylic/25 percent wool worsted weight yarn (200 yds/100g per skein): blue/yellow variegated #7744 (CC)
  Sweater: 2 (2, 2, 3) balls
  Afghan: 3 balls
  Socks and hat: 1 ball will do both
- Size 6 (4mm) straight and double-pointed needles
- Size 8 (5mm) straight and 29-inch circular needles or size needed to obtain gauge
- Tapestry needle
- 6 (7, 8, 8) ⁵⁄₁₆-inch buttons

Gauge
19 sts and 26 rows = 4 inches/10cm in St st and Stripe pat with larger needles

24 sts and 30 rnds = 4 inches/10cm in St st with dpns
To save time, take time to check gauge.

Special Abbreviation
M1 (Make 1): Insert LH needle from front to back under horizontal bar between st just worked and next st, lift this bar onto LH needle, then knit into back of it.

Pattern Stitches
A. Stripe Sequence (when worked in rows)
Row 1 (RS): With CC, knit.
Row 2: With CC, purl.
Row 3: With MC, knit.
Row 4: With MC, purl.
Rep Rows 1–4 for pat.

B. Stripe Sequence (when worked in rnds)
Rnds 1 and 2: With CC, knit.
Rnds 3 and 4: With MC, knit.
Rep Rnds 1–4 for pat.

Pattern Notes
Body of sweater is worked in 1 piece to armhole. Sleeves are worked flat, then joined to body for raglan yoke.

Circular needle is used to accommodate large number of sts; do not join but turn and work in rows throughout body of sweater. Work afghan in same manner.

Sweater instructions give buttonhole band for boys. If working sweater for girls, place buttonholes on right band.

First and last sts of hat are used as selvage sts.

Sweater

Sleeves
With smaller needles and MC, cast on 32 (32, 34, 36) sts.

Work in garter st for 9 rows, inc 2 (4, 4, 4) sts evenly spaced on last WS row. (34, 36, 38, 40 sts)

Change to larger needles and work Row 1 of Stripe pat across all sts. Continue to work in Stripe pat, [inc one st every 6th row] 5 (6, 6, 7) times. (44, 48, 50, 54 sts)

Work even until sleeve measures 6 (7, 7½, 8½) inches, ending with a WS row.

Place first and last 5 sts on holder for armholes. Place remaining sts on 2nd holder.

Body
With smaller circular needle and MC, cast on 96 (104, 116, 120) sts. Work in garter st for 9 rows, inc 12 (12, 12, 16) sts evenly spaced on last WS row. (108, 116, 128, 136 sts)

Change to larger needles.

Work in Stripe pat until body measures approximately 5 (7, 7, 7½) inches, ending with a WS row and same color stripe as last sleeve row.

Yoke
Next row (RS): Maintaining Stripe pat, k 22 (24, 27, 29) sts for right front, pm, place next 10 sts on holder for right underarm, k 34 (38, 40, 44) sts of first sleeve, pm, k 44 (48, 54, 58) sts for back, pm, place next 10 sts on holder for left underarm, k 34 (38, 40, 44) sts of 2nd sleeve, pm, k 22 (24, 27, 29) sts for left front. (156, 172, 188, 204 sts)

Work even in established Stripe pat for 5 more rows.

Begin raglan shaping

Dec row (RS): [Work to 3 sts before marker, ssk, k1, sl marker, k1, k2tog] 4 times, work to end of row. (8 st dec)

Continue in established pat, [working dec row every 4th row] 4 (4, 3, 4) times, then [every other row] 7 (8, 11, 12) times.

At the same time, when body measures 9½ (11, 12, 13¾) inches from lower edge, begin neck shaping.

Neck shaping

Bind off 8 (8, 8, 7) sts at beg of next 2 rows.

[Dec 1 st at each neck edge every other row] 2 (3, 4, 5) times. (40, 46, 44, 44 sts remain—10 (12, 10, 10) for each sleeve and (20, 22, 24, 24) for back neck)

***Note:** On the last few dec rows, there will be insufficient sts at each edge to maintain the k1 st in between markers. Work these last dec as close as possible to their original position.*

Work 1 row even. Place all sts on holder.

Neck Band

With RS facing using smaller needles and CC, beg at right front neck edge, pick up and k 12 (13, 15, 16) sts along right front neck edge, k 10 (12, 10, 10) sts of first sleeve, k 20 (22, 24, 24) sts from back neck holder dec 2 sts evenly across back neck, k 10 (12, 10, 10) sts of 2nd sleeve, pick up and k 12 (13, 15, 16) sts along left front neck edge. (62, 70, 72, 74 sts)

Work in garter st for 9 rows.

Bind off purlwise on RS.

Button Band

With RS facing using smaller needles and CC, beg at lower edge of right front, pick up and k 50 (56, 64, 70) sts evenly along front of sweater to top of neck band.
Knit 9 rows.

Bind off purlwise on RS.

Buttonhole Band

With RS facing using smaller needles and CC, beg at upper edge of left front neck band, pick up and k 50

(56, 64, 70) sts evenly along front of sweater to lower edge of body.

Knit 3 rows.

Buttonhole row (RS):

6 months size only: K3, (yo, k2tog), [k6, yo, k2tog] 5 times, k3.

12 months size only: K3, (yo, k2tog), [k6, yo, k2tog] 6 times, k3.

18 months size only: K3, (yo, k2tog), [k6, yo, k2tog] 7 times, k3.

24 months size only: K3, (yo, k2tog), [k7, yo, k2tog] 7 times, k3.

Knit 5 more rows.

Bind off purlwise on RS.

Finishing

Join underarm sts of sleeves and body using Kitchener method.

Sew sleeve seams.

With CC and tapestry needle, work half-cross-st embroidery

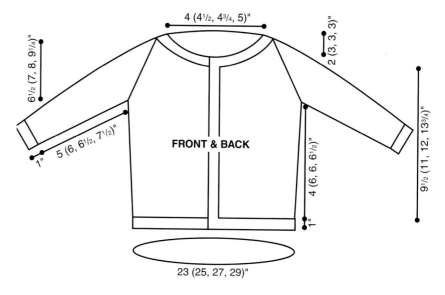

around all garter-st edges of sweater as shown in photo.

Work full cross-sts at corners of neck band and at sleeve seam.

Sew on buttons.

Hat

Sides

With smaller needles and MC, cast on 73 (80, 86) sts.

Work in garter st for 9 rows, inc 9 (10, 12) sts evenly on last WS row. (82, 90, 98 sts)

Change to larger needles and work in Stripe pat until hat measures 4 (4½, 5) inches from beg, end with a WS row.

Shape crown

Row 1 (RS): K1 for selvage st, [k8, k2tog] 10 (11, 12) times, k1 for selvage st. (72, 79, 86 sts)

Row 2: Purl.

Row 3: K1 for selvage, [k7, k2tog] 10 (11, 12) times, k1 for selvage. (62, 68, 74 sts)

Row 4: Purl.

Continue in established pat, working decs every RS row as before, having 1 fewer st between each dec every time until 12 (13, 14) sts remaining, end with a WS row.

Finishing

Cut yarn. Draw end through remaining sts twice and draw tightly to close. Sew back seam.

With CC and tapestry needle, work half cross-st embroidery around garter-st edge of hat as for sweater, working a full cross-sts at hat seam.

Socks

Cuff

With MC and smaller straight needles, cast on 24 sts. Knit 11 rows, inc 4 sts evenly on last row. (28 sts)

With first dpn, [k1, p1] 4 times, k1.

With 2nd dpn, [p1, k1] 5 times.

With 3rd dpn, [p1, k1] 4 times, end p1.

Sts are now divided on 3 dpns as follows: 9 sts on first and 3rd needles and 10 sts on 2nd needle.

Pm and join.

Work 7 rnds more in k1, p1 rib as established.

Work 6 rnds in Stripe pat.

Cut CC.

Heel

With MC, k 7 sts from first needle, turn, purl back across these 7 sts and purl 7 sts from 3rd needle. (14 sts on 1 needle)

Do not remove marker. Divide remaining 14 sts onto 2 needles for instep, to be worked later.

Working back and forth in rows on these 14 heel sts, work in St st for 13 rows, ending with a k row.

Turn heel

Row 1 (WS): P8, p2tog, p1, turn.

Row 2: Sl 1, k3, ssk, k1, turn.

Row 3: Sl 1, p4, p2tog, p1, turn.

Row 4: Sl 1, k5, ssk, k1, turn.

Row 5: Sl 1, p6, p2tog, p1, turn.

Row 6: Sl 1, k6, ssk. Do not turn. (8 sts)

Shape gusset

With same needle used for Row 6 of heel turning, pick up and k 9 sts along left edge of heel. With 2nd needle, k across 14 instep sts. With 3rd needle, pick up and k 9 sts along right edge of heel, then k 4 sts from last needle. 40 sts are now divided on 3 needles as follows: 13 sts on first and 3rd needles, 14 sts on 2nd needle. Marker for beg of rnd is now at center bottom of foot.

Knit 1 rnd.

Rnd 1: With CC, knit to last 3 sts of first needle, k2tog, k1, k across 14 sts of 2nd needle, on 3rd needle k1, ssk, k to end of rnd. (38 sts)

Rnd 2: Knit.

Maintaining Stripe pat, rep Rnds 1 and 2 until 28 sts remain.

Work even in established pat until foot measures approximately 2¾ (3¼, 3¾) inches from back of heel, ending with a full stripe.

Cut CC.

Toe

Rnd 1: With MC, k to last 3 sts of first needle, k2tog, k1. On 2nd needle, k1, ssk, knit to last 3 sts, k2tog, k1. On 3rd needle, k1, ssk, knit to end of rnd.

Rnd 2: Knit.

Rep Rnds 1 and 2 until 12 sts remain, ending with Row 2.

Next row: K9, place 3 unworked sts of 3rd needle onto first needle.

Finishing

Cut MC, leaving an 8-inch end.

Graft tog 6 sts on either side of foot, using Kitchener st.

Sew cuff seam. Turn cuff to RS.

With CC and tapestry needle, work half cross-st embroidery around garter-st cuff as for sweater, working full cross-sts at seam.

Afghan

Main Section

With smaller circular needle and MC, cast on 132 sts.

Knit 12 rows.

Inc row (WS): *K12, M1, rep from * across, end last rep k12. (142 sts)

Change to larger circular needle.

Work even in Stripe pat until main section measures approximately 39 inches from beg, end with a Row 2 of Stripe pat.

Cut CC and change to smaller circular needle.

Dec row (RS): With MC, [k11, k2tog] 10 times, k12. (132 sts)

Knit 13 rows.

Bind off purlwise on RS.

Side Borders

With smaller circular needle and MC, pick up and k 184 sts along 1 side edge of main section, including garter-st sections.

Knit 13 rows.

Bind off purlwise on RS.

Rep for 2nd side.

Finishing

With tapestry needle and CC, working over middle 3 ridges of garter-st borders, work half cross-st embroidery around entire outer edge of afghan as for sweater, working full cross-sts at each corner. ✦

Baby Bumble Bee

Design by Mary Saunders

Knit a delightful toy bee, inspired by the favorite child's song. No need to squash this one, he's very friendly.

Skill Level
Intermediate***

Finished Size
Approximately 9 inches long x 12 inches diameter

Materials
- Plymouth Encore Worsted 75 percent acrylic/25 percent wool worsted weight yarn (200 yds/100g per skein): 1 each black #217, yellow #215, white #208
- Size 7 (4.5mm) double-pointed needles or size needed to obtain gauge
- Polyester fiberfill
- Tapestry needle

Gauge
18 sts and 24 rows = 4 inches/10cm in St st

To save time, take time to check gauge.

Stinger
With black, cast on 3 sts.

[Slide sts to other end of dpn, k3] 4 times.

Body
Rnd 1: Slide sts to other end of needle, k in front and back of each st. (6 sts)

Divide sts onto 3 dpn, pm between first and last st.

Rnd 2: Knit.

Rnd 3: K in front and back of each st. (12 sts)

Rnds 4 and 6: Knit.

Rnds 5 and 7: Rep Rnd 3. (48 sts)

Rnds 8–13: Knit.

Rnds 14–21: Change to yellow and knit.

Rnds 22–29: Change to black and knit.

Rnds 30–37: Change to yellow and knit.

Rnd 38: *K2, k2tog, rep from * to end of rnd. (36 sts)

Rnds 39 and 41: Knit.

Rnd 40: *K1, k2tog, rep from * to end of rnd. (24 sts)

Rnd 42: *K2tog, rep from * to end of rnd. (12 sts)

Head

Rnd 43: Change to black and knit.

Rnd 44: *K1, k in front and back of next st, rep from * to end of rnd. (18 sts)

Rnds 45 and 47: Knit.

Rnds 46 and 48: *K2, k in front and back of next st, rep from * to end of rnd. (32 sts)

Rnds 49–59: Knit.

Rnd 60: *K2, k2tog, rep from * to end of rnd. (24 sts)

Rnds 61 and 63: Knit.

Rnd 62: *K1, k2tog, rep from * to end of rnd. (16 sts)

Rnd 64: *K2tog, rep from * to end of rnd. (8 sts)

Cut yarn leaving an 18-inch end. With tapestry needle, draw end through remaining sts.

Stuff bee with fiberfill. Pull yarn tightly, closing head.

Secure end and pull to inside.

Legs
Make 6

Attach legs to bottom of bee, having 3 along each side at approximately Rnds 17/18, 25/26, and 33/34.

With black, pick up and k 4 sts in a square pat.

[Slide sts to other end of needle, k4] 6 times.

Cut yarn leaving a 9-inch end.

Thread yarn into tapestry needle and draw through all sts twice.

Secure end and hide inside leg.

Face

With white, work duplicate st eyes and mouth on head, referring to photo for placement.

Antennae
Make 2

Attach antennae to top of head approximately 4 sts apart.

With yellow, pick up and k 3 sts.

[Slide sts to other end needle, k3] 10 times.

Cut yarn leaving a 9-inch end.

Thread yarn into tapestry needle and draw through all sts twice.

Secure end and hide inside antennae.

Large Wings
First half

Using 2 dpn and white, cast on 5 sts.

Row 1 (RS): Knit.

Row 2: Purl.

Row 3: Sl 1, yo, k1, p1, k1, yo, k1.

Row 4: Sl 1, *p1, k1, rep from * to last 2 sts, p2.

Row 5: Sl 1, yo, p1, *k1, p1, rep from * to last st, yo, k1.

Row 6: Sl 1, *k1, p1, rep from * to end of row.

Row 7: Sl 1, yo, k1, *p1, k1, rep from * to last st, yo, k1

Rows 8–11: Rep Rows 4–7.

Rows 12, 14, 18 and 22: Rep Row 4.

Row 13: Sl 1, yo, k2tog, p1, *k1, p1, rep from * to last 3 sts, k2tog, yo, k1.

Row 15: K2tog, yo k2tog, k1, p1, k1, rep from * to last 4 sts, k2tog, yo, k2tog.

Rows 16 and 20: Rep Row 6.

Row 17: K2tog, yo, k2tog, p1 ,*k1, p1, rep from * to last 4 sts, k2tog, yo, k2tog.

Row 19: K2tog, yo, k2tog, k1, p1, k1, k2tog, yo, k2tog.

Row 21: K2tog, yo, k2tog, p1, k2tog, yo, k2tog.

Row 23: K2tog, k1, p1, k1, k2tog.

Row 24: P2tog, p1, p2tog.

Row 25: Sl 1, k2tog, psso.

Cut yarn, leaving a 12-inch end. Pull end through final st and secure.

Second half

With RS facing, pick up and k 5 sts along cast-on edge of first wing and knit 1 row.

Rep Rows 2–25.

Small Wings
First half

Using 2 dpn and white, cast on 3 sts.

Row 1: Knit.

Row 2: Purl.

Row 3: Sl 1, yo, p1, yo, k1.

Row 4: Rep Row 6 of large wing.

Rows 5–10: Rep Rows 3–8 of large wing.

Row 11: Rep Row 13 of large wing.

Rows 12–19: Rep Rows 18–25 of large wing.

Second half

With RS facing, pick up and k 3 sts along cast-on edge of first wing and k 1 row.

Rep Rows–19.

Finishing

Stack small wings on top of large wings and sew to center back.

Weave in all yarn ends and conceal inside the bee's body. ✦

Puddle Ducks

Designs by Diane Zangl

Spring showers, puddles, and toddlers go together in a four-piece ensemble for boys and girls. Intarsia colorwork and an interesting raindrop pattern combine in this fun collection.

Skill Level
Intermediate***

Size
Cardigan, pants and romper: Infant's 6 (12, 18, 24) months

Hat: Infant's 6/12 (18/24) months Instructions are given for smallest size, with larger sizes in parentheses. When only 1 number is given, it applies to all sizes.

Finished Measurements
Cardigan
Chest (buttoned): 21½ (22½, 23½, 24½) inches

Armhole depth: 4½ (5, 5½, 5¾) inches

Side length to underarm: 6½ (7, 7½, 8) inches

Sleeve length: 7 (8, 9, 9½) inches

Pants
Waist: 20 (21, 23, 24) inches

Crotch depth: 8½ (9, 9½, 10) inches

Inseam: 7½ (9, 10, 11) inches

Romper
Chest (buttoned): 22 (23, 24, 26) inches

Armhole depth: 5 (5½, 5½, 5¾) inches

Total length: 17¼ (19¾, 22, 24¾) inches

Hat
Head circumference: 17 (18) inches

Materials
- Plymouth Wildflower D.K. 51 percent mercerized cotton/49 percent acrylic DK weight yarn (137 yds/50g per ball): 6 (7, 8, 9) balls white #41 (MC), 5 (5, 6, 6) balls teal #55, 1 ball each yellow #48 and terra cotta #80

Note: *Amounts given are enough to complete all 4 pieces. Specific amount for each garment is given before instructions for that garment.*
- Size 3 (3.25mm) needles
- Size 5 (3.75mm) straight, double-pointed, 16- and 24-inch circular needles or size needed to obtain gauge
- 10 (10, 12, 12) duck buttons, JHB International Skip's Duck #20621
- ⅔ yd (¾-inch wide) elastic
- Snap tape to fit romper crotch (optional)
- Stitch holders
- Stitch markers
- Tapestry needle

Gauge
22 sts and 20 rows = 4 inches/10cm in St st with larger needles

To save time, take time to check gauge.

Special Abbreviations
CS (Cross St): Knit 2nd st, knit first st, sl both sts off needle.

M1 (Make 1): Make a backwards loop and place on RH needle.

Stitch Patterns
Color Stripe

Work 1 row teal, 1 row yellow, remaining rows with white as indicated.

Raindrops (worked in rows)

(multiple of 6 sts + 4)

Rows 1, 3, 7 and 9 (RS): Knit.

All WS rows: Purl.

Row 5: *K4, cs, rep from * across, end last rep k4.

Row 11: *K1, cs, k4, rep from * across, end last rep cross-st, k1.

Row 12: Purl.
Rep Rows 1–12 for pat.

Raindrops (worked in rnds)

(multiple of 6 sts)

Rnds 1–4: Knit.

Rnd 5: *Cs, k4, rep from * around.

Rnds 6–10: Knit.

Rnd 11: K3, *cs, k4, rep from * around end last rep k1.

Rnd 12: Knit.
Rep Rnds 1–12 for pat.

Pattern Notes
Wind separate balls or bobbins of each color for each duck motif.

To avoid holes when changing colors, always bring new color up over old.

Make buttonholes on right band for girls and left band for boys.

Cardigan

Materials
- 2 (3, 3, 4) balls white, small amounts each teal, yellow and orange.

Body
With teal and smaller needles, cast on 113 (119, 123, 129) sts.

Work even in k1, p1 rib in Color Stripe pat for 1 (1, 1¼, 1½) inches, ending with a WS row.

Change to larger needles and work even in St st for 4 rows.

Beg pat (RS): K1 (4, 6, 9), work Row 1 of Chart A over next 111 sts, k1 (4, 6, 9).

Work even in established pat until Row 14 of chart is completed.

Continue in St st with MC only until body measures 6½ (7, 7½, 8) inches from beg, ending with a WS row.

Beg armhole shaping

K 22 (23, 24, 25) sts and sl to holder, bind off 12 (12, 12, 14) sts for right underarm, k 45 (49, 51, 51) sts for back, sl remaining 34 (35, 36, 39) sts to 2nd holder.

Back

Work even on back sts only until armhole measures 4½ (5, 5½, 5¾) inches, ending with a WS row.

Bind off all sts. Mark center 19 (21, 21, 21) sts for back neck.

Left Front

With RS facing, sl sts from 2nd holder to LH needle.

Bind off 12 (12, 12, 14) sts for left underarm, k to end of row.

Work even in St st until armhole measures 2½ (3, 3½, 3¼) inches, ending with a RS row.

Beg neck shaping

Bind off 6 sts at beg of next row.

[Dec 1 st at neck edge [every other row] 3 (3, 3, 4) times.

Work even on remaining 13 (14, 15, 15) sts until armhole measures same as for back.

Right Front

Sl sts from holder to LH needle. With WS facing, join MC at underarm. Work right front as for left, reversing shaping.

Sleeves

With teal and smaller needles, cast on 27 (31, 33, 33) sts. Work in Color Stripe pat as for body until cuff measures 1½ inches, inc 5 (5, 7, 7) sts on last WS row. (32, 36, 40, 40 sts)

Change to larger needles. Work Rows 1–4 of Raindrops pat.

Row 5: K1, M1, k2 (4, 0, 2), *cs, k4, rep from * across, end last rep k2 (4, 0, 2), M1, k1.

Work in established pat, [inc 1 st each end every 4th row] 9 (10, 11, 12) times, working added sts into pat. (50, 56, 62, 64 sts)

Work even until sleeve measures 5½ (6½, 7½, 8) inches from beg.

Mark each end st for underarm.

Continue to work even for 1 (1, 1, 1¼) inches more. Bind off.

Sew shoulder seam.

Neck band

With MC and smaller needles, pick up and k 49 (51, 53, 59) sts around neck.

Work in k1, p1 rib for 3 rows.

Change to yellow and work 1 row. Change to teal and work 1 row.

Bind off loosely.

Button band

With smaller needles and RS facing, working along front edge, pick up and k 2 sts with teal, 1 st with yellow, 3 sts for every 4 rows with white, end 1 st with yellow, and 2 sts with teal. You must have an uneven number of sts.

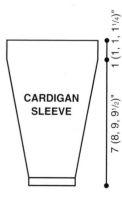

CARDIGAN SLEEVE

1 (1, 1, 1¼)"

7 (8, 9, 9½)"

Keeping to established color pat, work even in k1, p1 rib for 4 rows. Cut white.

Next row: Work 2 sts teal, with yellow work in established rib to last 2 sts, work 2 sts teal. Cut yellow.

Row 2: Work in established rib with teal only.

Bind off loosely in pat.

Buttonhole band

Mark front band for 5 (5, 6, 6) sts evenly spaced.

Work as for button band making buttonholes on Row 3.

Buttonhole row: [Work to marker, yo, k2tog] 5 (5, 6, 6) times, work to end of row.

Finishing

Sew sleeves into armholes, matching underarm markers to center of bound-off sts.

Sew sleeve seams.

Referring to photo, embroider random raindrops with teal between duck motifs.

Sew on buttons.

Pants

Materials

- 3 (3, 4, 4) balls teal

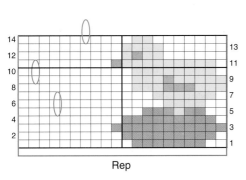

**CHART A
CARDIGAN**

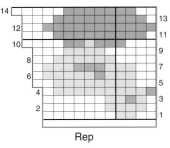

**CHART B
HAT**

COLOR KEY

☐	White (MC)
▨	Teal
▧	Yellow
▩	Orange
⬭	Embroider lazy daisy st with teal

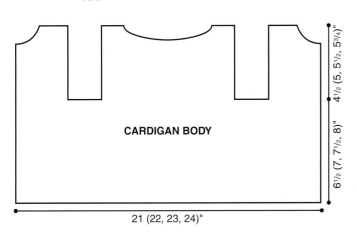

CARDIGAN BODY

21 (22, 23, 24)"

4½ (5, 5½, 5¾)"

6½ (7, 7½, 8)"

47

Leg
Make 2

With teal and smaller needles, cast on 43 (51, 55, 61) sts.

Work in k1, p1 rib for 1½ (1½, 2, 2) inches, inc 13 (15, 17, 19) sts on last WS row. (56, 66, 72, 80 sts)

Change to larger needles. Work Rows 1–4 of Raindrops pat.

Row 5: K1, M1, k2 (1, 4, 2), *cs, k4, rep from * to last 3 (2, 5, 2) sts, k2 (1, 4, 2), M1, k1.

Continue in established pat, [inc 1 st each end every 8th row] 4 (3, 4, 4) times, working added sts into pat. (66, 74, 82, 90 sts)

Work even until leg measures 7½ (9, 10, 11) inches, ending with a WS row.

Beg crotch shaping

Bind off 3 (5, 6, 7) sts at beg of next 2 rows.

[Dec 1 st each end every other row] 2 (3, 3, 4) times. (56, 58, 64, 68 sts)

Work even until leg measures 8½ (9, 9½, 10) inches above bound-off crotch sts, ending with a WS row.

Turning ridge (RS): Change to smaller needles and purl 1 row.

Work in St st for 1 inch. Bind off.

Finishing

Sew front and back center seams, ending at crotch.

Turn waist band facing to inside and sew in place, leaving a small opening at center back for inserting elastic.

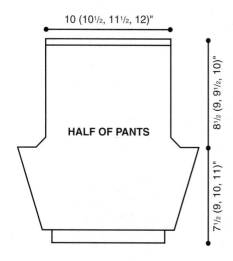

10 (10½, 11½, 12)"

HALF OF PANTS

8½ (9, 9½, 10)"

7½ (9, 10, 11)"

Sew inside leg seam, or apply snap tape as directed on package.

Cut elastic to 1 inch more than desired waist measurement.

Thread elastic through waist casing. Overlap ends and sew securely.

Sew small waistband opening.

Hat

Materials

- 1 ball each white and teal, small amounts of yellow and orange.

Instructions

With yellow and 16-inch circular needle, cast on 90 (96) sts.

Join without twisting, pm between first and last st.

Work in k1, p1 rib for 2 rnds.

Change to teal and work even in Raindrops pat for approximately 4 (5) inches, ending with Row 5 or 11.

Shape top

Dec rnd 1: *K4, k2tog, rep from * around. (75, 80 sts)

Knit 1 rnd.

Dec rnd 2: *K3, k2tog, rep from * around. (60, 64 sts)

Knit 1 rnd.

Dec rnd 3: *K2, k2tog, rep from * around. (45, 48 sts)

Knit 1 rnd.

Dec rnd 4: *K1, k2tog, rep from *

around. (30, 32 sts)

Dec rnd 5: *K2tog around. (15, 16 sts)

Cut yarn leaving a 12-inch end.

Draw yarn through remaining sts twice and draw up tightly.

Brim

With white and 16-inch circular needle, pick up and k 90 (96) sts along cast-on edge of hat. Knit 2 rnds.

Inc rnd: Knit, inc 15 (16) sts evenly. (105, 112 sts)

Work in rows from this point.

Next row: Inc 1 st in first st, k1, [work Row 1 of Chart B over next 11 sts, k4 (5) MC] 6 times, work chart over 11 sts, with MC knit to end of row. (106, 113 sts)

Work in established pat, inc 1 st at beg of row and between each duck motif on Rows 4, 8 and 13. [7 sts inc each row (127, 134 sts)].

Cut all CC. With MC only, knit 1 row, purl 1 row.

Next row: Knit, inc 7 sts evenly. (134, 141 sts)

Change to yellow and work in k1, p1 rib for 1 row.

Change to teal and work in k1, p1 rib for 1 row.

Bind off loosely in rib.

Finishing

Sew brim seam.

Referring to photo, embroider

random raindrops with teal between duck motifs.

Romper

Materials

- 3 (3, 4, 4) balls white (MC), 1 ball teal, small amount yellow and orange.

Back

Left leg

With teal and smaller needles, cast on 25 (27, 27, 29) sts.

Work in k1, p1 rib for ¾ (¾, 1, 1) inch, inc 5 (7, 7, 7) sts evenly on last WS row. (30, 34, 34, 36 sts)

Change to larger needles and MC.

Work in St st, [inc 1 st each end every 4th (8th, 6th, 6th) row] 3 (2, 3, 3) times. (36, 38, 40, 42 sts)

Work even until leg measures 2¾ (3¾, 4½, 5) inches from beg, ending with a WS row. Mark last row.

Beg crotch shaping

Bind off 2 (3, 3, 3) sts at beg of next row. This is inside of leg.

[Dec 1 st at same edge every other row] 1 (1, 2, 2) times. (33, 34, 35, 37 sts)

Purl 1 row.

Cut yarn and sl sts to holder.

Work right leg as for left, reversing crotch shaping. Do not cut yarn.

Join for body

Next row (RS): K across sts of right leg, sl sts from holder to LH needle, k across sts of left leg. (66, 68, 70, 74 sts)

Work even until body measures 7 (7½, 8½, 9½) inches above crotch marker, dec 6 (6, 4, 2) sts evenly on last WS row. (60, 62, 66, 72 sts)

Change to smaller needles and work k1, p1 rib for 6 rows.

Change to larger needles and St st.

Work even until body measures 9½ (10½, 12, 14) inches above crotch markers.

Shape armholes

Bind off 4 (4, 4, 6) sts at beg of next 2 rows.

Work even until armhole measures 5 (5½, 5½, 5¾) inches, ending with a WS row.

Shape shoulders and back neck

Next row: Bind off 14 (14, 15, 15) sts, k 24 (26, 28, 30) sts and sl to holder for back neck, bind off remaining 14 (14, 15, 15) sts.

Front

Work legs as for back, working 11 sts of single duck motif on left leg. Beg motif 6 rows above ribbing and 8 sts from outside seam.

Join for body

Work as for back, pm between legs on first row. (66, 68, 70, 74 sts)

Continue working as for back until body measures 2 (2, 2½, 2½) inches above crotch marker.

Divide for fronts

Next row (RS): K 30 (31, 32, 34) sts, join 2nd ball of yarn and bind off next 6 sts, k to end of row.

Working on both sides of front opening with separate balls of yarn, work to waist, dec 3 (3, 2, 1) sts evenly, work waist ribbing and armhole shaping as for back until armhole measures 1 inch, ending with a WS row. (23, 24, 25, 27 sts remain each side)

Beg duck motif on next RS row, starting chart 5

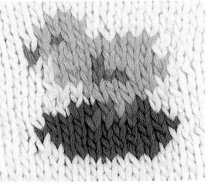

(5, 6, 6) sts from left armhole edge, *at the same time,* when armhole measures 3½ (4, 3½, 3¾) inches, shape neck.

49

Beg neck shaping

Bind off 6 (7, 7, 8) sts at each neck edge.

[Dec 1 st at each neck edge every other row] 3 (3, 4, 4) times.

Work even on remaining 14 (14, 15, 15) sts until armhole measures same as for back.

Bind off all sts.

Sew shoulder seams.

Neck band

With white and smaller needles, pick up and k 55 (59, 71, 73) sts around neck, including sts on back neck holder.

Work in k1, p1 ribbing for 3 rows.

Change to yellow and work in k1, p1 rib for 1 row.

Change to teal and work in k1, p1 rib for 1 row.

Bind off loosely in rib.

Front bands

Work as for button and buttonhole bands of cardigan, having 3 rows white after picked up row.

Make 5 (5, 6, 6) buttonholes on left band for boys and right band for girls. Buttonholes are made on Row 3.

Overlap front bands and sew lower edges to short side of front opening.

Sleeves

With yellow and smaller needles, cast on 43 (47, 47, 49) sts.

Work in k1, p1 rib for ¾ (¾, 1, 1) inch, inc 7 (9, 9, 9)

sts evenly on last WS row (50, 56, 56, 58 sts)

Change to teal and larger needles. Work Rows 1–4 of Raindrops pat.

Row 5: K 6 (3, 3, 4) sts, *cs, k4, rep from * across, end last rep k6 (3, 3, 4).

Work in established pat, [inc 1 st each end every 4th (6th, 6th, 6th) row] 3 (2, 2, 3) times. (56, 60, 60, 64) sts. Work even until sleeve measures 2¾ (2¾, 3½, 4) inches.

Mark each end st for underarm.

Work even for ¾ (¾, 1, 1) inch more. Bind off all sts.

Finishing

Sew sleeves into armholes, matching underarm markers to side seam.

Sew sleeve and side seams.

Sew short crotch seams and inside leg seams, or apply snap tape to inside leg seam as directed on package.

Sew on buttons. ✦

Cotton Candy Dress

Design by Celeste Pinheiro

Just as a bee is drawn to honey, a baby who is wearing this bright-colored lace dress will attract smiles from everyone.

Skill Level

Intermediate***

Size

6 (12, 18, 24) months
Instructions are given for smallest size, with larger sizes in parentheses. When only 1 number is given, it applies to all sizes.

Finished Measurements

Chest: 18 (20, 22, 24) inches

Length: 14 (15, 16, 18) inches

Materials

- Plymouth Fantasy Naturale 100 percent mercerized cotton worsted weight yarn (140 yds/ 100g per skein): 3 (3, 3, 4) skeins fuchsia #6092
- Size 6 (4mm) needles
- Size 8 (5mm) needles or size needed to obtain gauge
- 1 (⅝-inch) button
- 2 yds (³⁄₁₆-inch) double-faced satin picot-edge ribbon
- Size G/6 crochet hook
- Yarn needle
- Sewing needle and thread

Gauge

16 sts and 23 rows = 4 inches/10cm in St st with larger needles

To save time, take time to check gauge.

Pattern Stitches

A. Triangle Lace Border (multiple of 10 sts + 1)

Row 1 (WS): Knit.

Row 2: *K1, yo, k3, sl 1, k2tog, psso, k3, yo, rep from * across, end last rep k1.

Row 3 and all remaining WS rows: Purl.

Row 4: *K2, yo, k2, sl 1, k2tog, psso, k2, yo, k1, rep from * across, end last rep k2.

Row 6: *K3, yo, k1, sl 1, k2tog, psso, k1, yo, k2, rep from * across, end last rep k3.

Row 8: *K4, yo, sl 1, k2tog, psso, yo, k3, rep from * across, end last rep k4.

Row 10: *K5, yo, ssk, k3, rep from * across, end last rep k4.

B. Eyelet Lace Border (multiple of 2 sts +1)

Row 1 (WS): Knit.

Row 2: *K2tog, yo, rep from * across, end last rep k1.

Row 3: Knit.

Dress

Skirt

With larger needles, cast on 111 (121, 131, 141) sts.

Work 10 rows of Triangle Lace Border.

Change to smaller needles and work Eyelet Lace Border, ending with a WS row.

Change to larger needles and work even in St st until skirt measures 9½ (10½, 11½, 12½) inches from beg, ending with a WS row.

Next row: Dec 39 (39, 42, 45) sts

evenly across row. (72, 82, 89, 96 sts)

Change to smaller needles and work Eyelet Lace Border. Change to larger needles.

Divide for front & backs

Next row (RS): P2, k12 (14, 16, 18) and sl to holder for left back, bind off 8 sts for left underarm, k28 (34, 37, 40) and sl to holder for front, bind off 8 sts for right underarm, k12 (14, 16, 18), p2.

Right Back

Row 1 (WS): P2, pm, *k1, p2, rep from * across, end last rep p2 [(k1, p1) (k1), (p2)].

Row 2: Knit to last 2 sts, p2.

Keeping 2 edge sts in garter st and remaining sts in rib pat, work even until back measures 14 (15, 16, 18) inches from beg, ending with a WS row.

Shape neck

Next row: Work in pat across 6 (7, 9,

10) sts and sl to holder for shoulder, bind off 8 (9, 9, 10) sts for back neck.

Left Back

Sl sts from holder to needle. With WS facing, join arm at underarm.

Work as for right back, reversing shaping.

Front

Sl sts from holder to needle. With WS facing, join yarn at right underarm.

Set up rib pat

Row 1 (WS): P3, [k1, p2] 7 (9, 10, 11) times, k1, p3.

Row 2: Knit.

Work even in established pat until dress measures 12½ (13½, 14½, 16½) inches, ending with a WS row.

Neck shaping

Next row (RS): Work across 11 (13, 15, 16) sts, join 2nd ball of yarn and bind off 6 (8, 7, 8) sts for front neck, work to end of row.

Working on both sides of neck with separate balls of yarn, [bind off 2 sts at each neck edge] 2 (3, 3, 3) times, [then 1 st] 1 (0, 0, 0) times. (6, 7, 9, 10 sts remain for each shoulder)

Bind off front and back shoulder sts tog, using 3-needle bind-off method.

Sleeves

With smaller needles, cast on 25 sts.

Work 3 rows of Eyelet Lace Border.

Change to larger needles and work in St st until sleeve measures 5 (6, 7,

8) inches, *at the same time* [inc 1 st each end every 4th row] 4 (4, 6, 8) times. (33, 33, 37, 41 sts)

Bind off all sts.

Neck Band

With smaller needles, pick up and k 44 (46, 46, 48) sts evenly around neck edge,

Knit 1 row.

Bind off all sts.

Finishing

Sew sleeves into armholes. Sew sleeve seams.

Sew back seam, leaving 3 inches open at top of bodice.

With crochet hook, sl st in last row of left neck band, ch 8, sl st in next st to form button loop. Fasten off.

Sew on button.

Thread ribbon through eyelet border and tie in bow. ✦

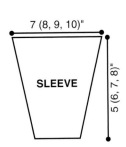

7 (8, 9, 10)"

SLEEVE

5 (6, 7, 8)"

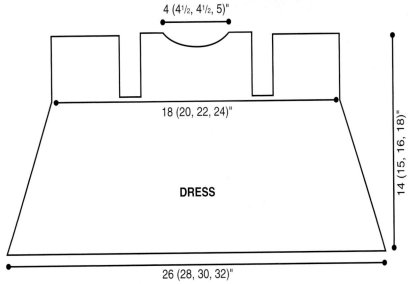

4 (4½, 4½, 5)"

18 (20, 22, 24)"

DRESS

14 (15, 16, 18)"

26 (28, 30, 32)"

Ocean Creatures Set

Designs by Celeste Pinheiro

Ocean creature appliqués enhance the components of a four-piece set. Make them for your favorite underwater fan.

Pullover

Skill Level
Intermediate***

Sizes
6 (12, 18, 24) months Instructions are given for smallest size, with larger sizes in parentheses. When only 1 number is given, it applies to all sizes.

Finished Measurements
Chest: 20 (22, 24, 26) inches

Length: 10 (11, 12, 13) inches

Sleeve length: 7 (8, 9, 10) inches

Armhole depth: 4 (4½, 5, 5½) inches

Materials
- Plymouth Fantasy Naturale 100 percent mercerized cotton worsted weight yarn (140 yds/100g per skein): 2 skeins sunset #9942 (MC), 1 skein each red #3611, gold #1404 and blue #8014 (enough for 1 sweater)
- Size 6 (4mm) needles
- Size 8 (5mm) straight and double-pointed needles or size needed to obtain gauge
- 2 (2, 3, 3) ⅝-inch white pearl buttons
- 6 (⅜-inch) white pearl buttons for fish sweater
- 2 (⅜-inch) white pearl buttons for octopus sweater
- Stitch holder
- Yarn needle

Gauge
16 sts and 20 rows = 4 inches/10cm in St st with larger needles

To save time, take time to check gauge.

Pattern Stitch
Body Pattern
Rows 1, 3, 5, 7 and 8 (RS): Knit.

Rows 2, 4 and 6: Purl.

Rep Rows 1–8 for pat.

Special Abbreviations
Sssk: Sl 2 sts individually knitwise, k1, pass 2 sl sts over.

Pattern Note
To avoid a choking hazard, you may want to substitute embroidery for the decorative buttons.

Back
With smaller needles and red, cast on 40 (44, 48, 52) sts.

Work in garter st in the following color sequence: 3 rows red, 2 rows gold, 2 rows red.

Change to larger needles and MC.

Work even in body pat until back measures 9½ (10½, 11½, 12½) inches, ending with a WS row.

SLEEVE

8 (9, 10, 11)"

7 (8, 9, 10)"

FRONT & BACK

4½ (5, 5½, 6)"

4 (4½, 5, 5½)"

10 (11, 12, 13)"

10 (11, 12, 13)"

COLOR KEY
☐ Blue
☒ Red
● Gold

BORDER CHART

Beg back neck shaping

Next row (RS): K11 (12, 13, 14), bind off next 18 (20, 22, 24) sts for back neck, k11 (12, 13, 14).

Work even on left shoulder sts only until back measures 10 (11, 12, 13) inches.

Bind off all sts.

With WS facing, rejoin yarn at neck edge.

Work right shoulder as for left.

Front

Work as for back until front measures 8½ (9½, 10½, 11) inches, ending with a WS row.

Beg front neck shaping

Next row (RS): Working in established pat, k17 (19, 20, 22), join 2nd ball of yarn and bind off next 6 (6, 8, 8) sts for front neck, k17 (19, 20, 22).

Working on both sides of neck with separate balls of yarn, bind off at each neck edge [2 sts] 3 times, then [dec 1 st] 0 (1, 1, 2) times. (11, 12, 13, 14 sts)

Work even until front measures same as for back.

Bind off all sts.

Sleeves

With smaller needles and red, cast on 24 (24, 28, 28) sts.

Work in garter st of 1 row red, 2 rows gold, 2 rows red.

Change to larger needles, blue and St st.

Work 4 rows in St st, then 7 rows of border chart, *at the same time* [inc 1 st each end every 6th row] 4 (6, 6, 8) times. (32, 36, 40, 44 sts)

Work even until sleeve measures 7 (8, 9, 10) inches.

Bind off.

Sew right shoulder seam.

Neck Band

With smaller needles and red, pick up and k 44 (48, 52, 56) sts evenly around neck.

Work in garter st of 1 row red, 2 rows gold, then 2 rows red.

Bind off.

Shoulder Placket

With smaller needles and red, pick up and k 13 (15, 16, 17) sts along left shoulder and neck band.

Knit 1 row.

Buttonhole row (RS): K4 (6, 2, 3), *bind off 2 sts, k3; rep from * once, bind off 2 sts, k2.

Next row: Knit, casting on 2 sts over bound-off sts of previous row.

Bind off.

Finishing

Measure down 4 (4½, 5, 5½) inches from each shoulder for armhole. Sew top of sleeve to armhole between markers.

Sew sleeve and side seams.

Sew ⅝-inch buttons to left shoulder placket.

Make 1 large fish or 1 small octopus appliqué and sew to front of sweater. For fish sweater sew five ⅜-inch pearl buttons on front of sweater and 1 button on fish for eye as shown in photo.

Blanket

Skill Level
Intermediate***

Size
Approximately 40 x 40 inches

Materials:
- Plymouth Fantasy Naturale 100 percent mercerized cotton worsted weight yarn (140 yds/100g per skein): 6 skeins sunset #9942 (MC), 3 skeins red #3611, 2 skeins sand #7360, 1 skein each gold #1404, blue #8014, lime #5228, and peach #4548
- Size 6 (4mm) needles
- Size 8 (5mm) straight and double-pointed needles or size needed to obtain gauge
- 31 (⁷⁄₁₆-inch) white pearl buttons
- Stitch holder
- Yarn needle

Gauge
16 sts and 20 rows = 4 inches/10cm in St st with larger needles

To save time, take time to check gauge.

Pattern Stitches

A. Seed Stitch

All rows: K1, *p1, k1, rep from * across row.

B. Main Pattern

Rows 1, 3, 5, 7, 9 and 10 (RS): Knit.

Rows 2, 4, 6 and 8: Purl.

Rep Rows 1–10 for pat.

Pattern Note
To avoid a choking hazard, you may want to substitute embroidery for the decorative buttons.

Blanket
With larger needles and sand, cast on 151 sts.

Work in Seed st for 5½ inches, ending with a WS row.

Change to MC and work even in Main pat until blanket measures approximately 38 inches, ending with row 9 of pat.

Bind off all sts.

Sew seams all on 3 sides, insert pillow form, sew remaining side.

Appliqués

Pattern Note
Make number of each as directed in individual instructions for pullover, blanket and pillow.

Seaweed
With dpn, cast on 4 sts.

*K4, sl sts back to LH needle, rep from * until cord is desired length.

Cut yarn and draw through all sts to fasten off. Hide end inside cord.

Make 3 cords 11 inches long, and one each measuring 17 and 20 inches respectively.

Small Fish
With larger needles, cast on 9 sts.

Rows 1, 3, 5 and 7: Knit.

Row 2: K2tog, k5, ssk.

Row 4: K2tog, k3, ssk.

Row 6: K2tog, k1, ssk.

Row 8: P1, yo, k1, yo, p1.

Row 9 and all following WS rows: Purl.

Row 10: P1, yo, k3, yo, p1.

Row 12: P1, yo, k5, yo, p1.

Rows 14, 16 and 18: P1, k7, p1.

Row 20: Purl.

Row 22: P1, k2tog, k3, ssk, p1.

Row 24: P1, k2tog, k1, ssk, p1.

Row 26: P1, sl 1, k2tog, psso, p1.

Cut yarn and pull end through all sts.

Border
*With smaller needles and red, pick up and k 144 sts along right edge of blanket.

Work in garter st sequence of 3 rows red, 2 rows gold, 2 rows red.

Bind off.

Rep from * for left side.

With smaller needles and red, pick up and k 152 sts along top edge including borders.

Work border as above.

Repeat for bottom edge.

Make 1 large and 1 small starfish; 1 large, 5 small gold and 3 small blue fish; 1 large octopus; and seaweed.

Sew on appliqués and buttons as shown in photo.

Pillow

Size
Approximately 12 inches square

Materials
• Plymouth Fantasy Naturale 100 percent mercerized cotton worsted weight yarn (140 yds/100g per skein): 2 skeins sunset #9942 (MC), small amount red #3611 and peach #4548
• Size 8 (5mm) straight and double-pointed needles or size needed to obtain gauge
• 12-inch square pillow form
• Yarn needle

Front & Back
Make 1 for each side

With MC, cast on 48 sts.

Work even in Body pat as for pullover until piece measues 12 inches.

Bind off.

Finishing
Make 1 large and 1 small starfish appliqué and sew to front.

Large Fish

With larger needles and blue, cast on 21 sts.

Work in garter st for 13 rows, *at the same time* [dec 1 st each side every other row] 6 times. (9 sts)

Row 14 (RS): P1, yo, k7, yo, p1.

Row 15 and all WS rows: Purl.

Row 16: P1, yo, k9, yo, p1.

Row 18: P1, yo, k11, yo, p1.

Row 20: P1, yo, k13, yo, p1.

Row 22: With gold, purl.

Row 24: P1, k15, p1.

Row 26: With blue, purl.

Row 28: P1, k15, p1.

Rep Rows 22–29.

Row 38: With gold, purl.

Row 40: P1, k2tog, k11, ssk, p1.

Row 42: P1, k2tog, k9, ssk, p1.

Row 44: P1, k2tog, k7, ssk, p1.

Row 46: P1, k2tog, k5, ssk, p1.

Row 48: P1, k2tog, k3, ssk, p1.

Row 50: P1, k2tog, k1, ssk, p1.

Row 52: P1, sl 1, k2tog, psso, p1.

Cut yarn and pull end through all sts.

Fins
Make 2

With larger needles and light blue, cast on 3 sts.

Row 1 and all WS rows: Purl.

Row 2: K1, yo, k1, yo, k1.

Row 4: K2, yo, k1, yo, k2.

Row 6: K3, yo, k1, yo, k3.

Row 8: K2tog, k5, ssk.

Row 10: K2tog, k3, ssk.

Row 12: K2tog, k1, ssk.

Row 14: Sl 1, k2tog, psso.

Cut yarn and pull end through all sts. Sew fins to body.

Small Starfish
Arm
Make 5

With larger dpn and red, cast on 4 sts.

Work in I-cord as for seaweed until arm measures 2½ inches, place sts on holder.

Sl all sts from holders to LH needle.

Next row: K2tog across row.

Knit 1 row.

Cut yarn and run end through remaining sts.

Large Starfish

With larger needles and peach, cast on 15 sts.

Row 1 (WS): Knit.

Row 2: K1, *yo, k1, yo, k2; rep from * across, end last rep yo, k1, yo, k1.

Row 3 and all remaining WS rows: Purl.

Row 4: K2, *yo, k1, yo, k4; rep from * across, end last rep yo, k1, yo, k2.

Row 6: K3, *yo, k1, yo, k6; rep from * across, end last rep yo, k1, yo, k3.

Row 8: K4, *yo, k1, yo, k8; rep from * across, end last rep yo, k1, yo, k4. (55 sts)

Row 9: Purl.

Divide for arms

Each arm is worked over 11 sts for a total of 5 arms in all.

Row 10: P1, k4, yo, k1, yo, k4, p1.

Row 12: P1, k2tog, k7, ssk, p1.

Row 14: P1, k2tog, k5, ssk, p1.

Row 16: P1, k2tog, k3, ssk, p1.

Row 18: P1, k2tog, k1, ssk, p1.

Row 20: P1, sl 1, k2tog, psso, p1.

Cut yarn and run end through remaining sts.

Rep Rows 10–20 for remaining 4 arms.

Sew first and last arms tog through Row 9.

Run yarn end through cast-on sts and pull tightly.

Small (Large) Octopus
Legs
Make 5 (8)

With dpn and red, cast on 4 sts.

Work in I-cord as for seaweed until leg measures 4 (7) inches, place sts on holder.

Head

Sl all sts from holders to LH needle.

Row 1 (RS): K2tog across row. (10, 16 sts)

Working in St st, [inc 1 st each end every other row] 3 times. (16, 22 sts)

Work even for 4 (8) rows.

Shape top of head

Next row (RS): K2tog, k to last 2 sts, ssk.

Purl 1 row.

[Rep last 2 rows] once (twice).

Next row: K3tog, k to last 3 sts, sssk.

[Rep last 2 rows] once (twice).

Cut yarn and draw end through remaining sts.

With gold embroider French knot spots on head.

With a dark blue section of MC, embroider mouth in running st.

Sew on pearl buttons for eyes. ✦

One Fish, Two Fish

Designs by Diane Zangl

Traditional sailor's suits are dressed up with the addition of a small school of fish. Make a matching set for brother and sister.

Skill Level

Intermediate***

Size

Infant's 6 (12, 18, 24) months
Instructions are given for smallest size, with larger sizes in parentheses. When only 1 number is given, it applies to all sizes.

Finished Measurements

Chest: 22 (23, 24, 26) inches

Side from waist to underarm: 4 (4½, 5, 5½) inches

Pants length: 15 (16½, 18, 19½) inches

Skirt length: 9 (9½, 10, 11½) inches

Sleeve length: 3½ (3½, 4½, 5) inches

Boy's Romper

Materials

- Plymouth Dreambaby D.K. 50 percent acrylic microfiber/50 percent nylon DK weight yarn (183 yds/50g per ball): 2 (3, 3, 3) balls blue #109, 2 balls white #100, 1 ball red #108
- Size 2 (3mm) needles
- Size 3 (3.25mm) needles or size needed to obtain gauge
- Stitch markers
- Stitch holders
- Tapestry needle
- 10 (⅜-inch) blue buttons
- Snap tape (optional)
- K1C2 Rainbow® Elastic Thread

Gauge

23 sts and 32 rows = 4 inches/10cm in St st with larger needles

To save time, take time to check gauge.

Special Abbreviations

M1 (Make 1): Make a backwards loop and place on RH needle.

Pattern Stitches

A. 1/1 Twisted Rib (odd number of sts)

Row 1 (RS): K1-tbl, *p1, k1-tbl, rep from * across row.

Row 2: P1-tbl, *k1, p1-tbl, rep from * across row.

Rep Rows 1 and 2 for pat.

B. Stripe Sequence Work in sequence of 2 rows red, then 8 rows white.

Pattern Notes

Romper features ribbed cuffs on the pants and sleeves.

Fish are worked in duplicate st after the romper is completed.

For collar, wind separate bobbins of each color. To avoid holes when changing colors, always bring new color up over old.

On collar, sl first edge st of each blue section to maintain a chained edge.

Pants Leg

With white and smaller needles, cast on 43 (51, 57, 61) sts.

Work in 1/1 Twisted Rib for 1 row, change to blue.

Continue in 1/1 Twisted Rib until cuff measures 2 inches, inc 14 (18, 18, 20) sts

on last WS row. (57, 69, 75, 81 sts)

Change to larger needles and St st.

[Inc 1 st each end every 4th (6th, 8th, 10th) row] 7 (4, 6, 6) times. (71, 77, 87, 93 sts)

Work even until leg measures 7 (8, 9, 10) inches. Mark last row.

Shape crotch

Bind off 0 (0, 4, 4) sts at beg of next 2 rows.

[Dec 1 st each end every other row] 4 (5, 5, 5) times. (63, 67, 69, 75 sts)

Work even until leg measures 7 (7½,

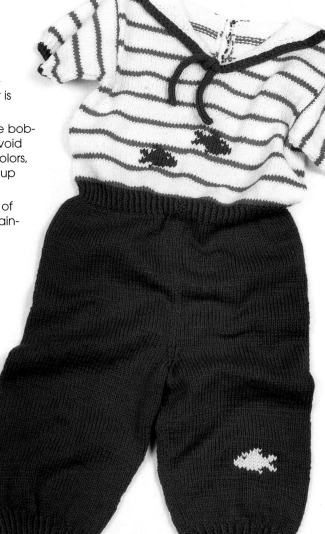

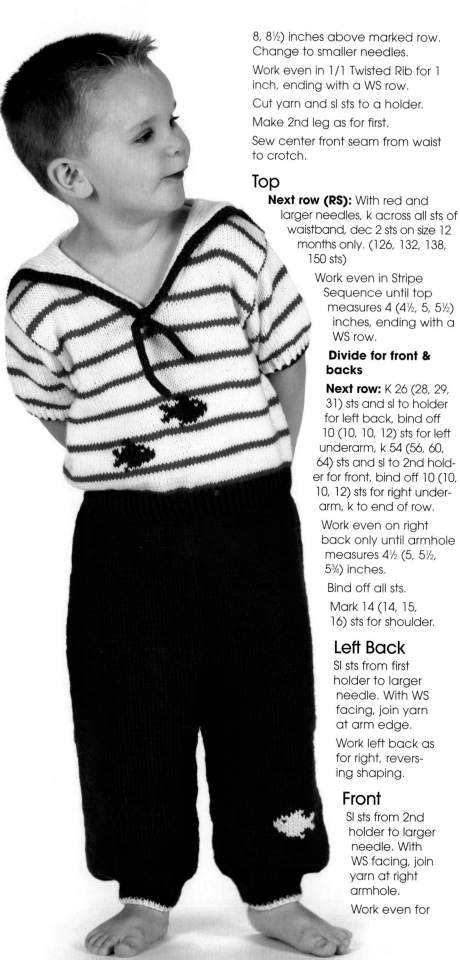

8, 8½) inches above marked row. Change to smaller needles.

Work even in 1/1 Twisted Rib for 1 inch, ending with a WS row.

Cut yarn and sl sts to a holder.

Make 2nd leg as for first.

Sew center front seam from waist to crotch.

Top

Next row (RS): With red and larger needles, k across all sts of waistband, dec 2 sts on size 12 months only. (126, 132, 138, 150 sts)

Work even in Stripe Sequence until top measures 4 (4½, 5, 5½) inches, ending with a WS row.

Divide for front & backs

Next row: K 26 (28, 29, 31) sts and sl to holder for left back, bind off 10 (10, 10, 12) sts for left underarm, k 54 (56, 60, 64) sts and sl to 2nd holder for front, bind off 10 (10, 10, 12) sts for right underarm, k to end of row.

Work even on right back only until armhole measures 4½ (5, 5½, 5¾) inches.

Bind off all sts.

Mark 14 (14, 15, 16) sts for shoulder.

Left Back

Sl sts from first holder to larger needle. With WS facing, join yarn at arm edge.

Work left back as for right, reversing shaping.

Front

Sl sts from 2nd holder to larger needle. With WS facing, join yarn at right armhole.

Work even for

1½ (2, 2, 1¾) inches, ending with a WS row.

Beg neck shaping

K 25 (26, 28, 30) sts, k2tog, join 2nd ball of yarn and k2tog, k to end of row.

Working on both sides of neck with separate balls of yarn, [dec 1 st each side of neck every other row] 12 (13, 14, 15) times more. (14, 14, 15, 16 sts on each side)

Work even until armhole measures same as for back.

Bind off all sts.

Sew shoulder seams. Sew center back seam from crotch to bottom of waist rib.

Sew leg seams or apply snap tape as directed on package.

Back Bands

With RS facing, join white at back neck edge.

With smaller needles, pick up and k 3 sts for every 4 rows along right edge to bottom of opening, pm, pick up and k same number of sts along left edge.

Work in 1/1 Twisted Rib for 1 row, dec 1 st each side of marker.

Buttonhole row: At each red stripe of left edge, make 1 buttonhole by working yo, k2tog and dec each side of marker as before.

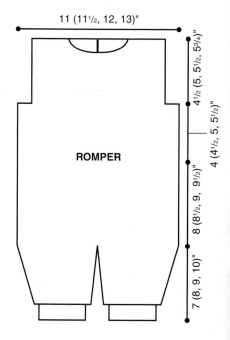

11 (11½, 12, 13)"

4½ (5, 5½, 5¾)"

4 (4½, 5, 5½)"

ROMPER

8 (8½, 9, 9½)"

7 (8, 9, 10)"

Work 1/1 Twisted Rib for 1 more row, dec 1 st each side of marker.

Bind off in pat.

Sleeves

With blue and smaller needles, cast on 41 (45, 45, 51) sts.

Work in 1/1 Twisted Rib for 1 row, change to white.

Work even in established pat until cuff measures ¾ (¾, 1, 1) inch, inc 10 (12, 12, 10) sts evenly on last WS row. (51, 57, 57, 61 sts)

Change to larger needles.

Work in Stripe Sequence, [inc 1 st each end every 4th (4th, 6th, 8th) row] 3 times. (57, 63, 63, 67 sts)

Work even until sleeve measures 2¾ (2¾, 3½, 4) inches. Mark each end st for underarm.

Continue to work even in established pat for ¾ (¾, 1, 1) inch more.

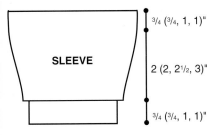

SLEEVE

3/4 (3/4, 1, 1)"

2 (2, 2½, 3)"

3/4 (3/4, 1, 1)"

Bind off all sts.

Sew sleeve into armhole, matching underarm markers to center of bound-off underarm sts.

Sew sleeve seams.

Left Half of Collar

Tie

With blue and smaller needles, cast on 4 sts.

*K4, sl sts back to LH needle. Rep from * until tie measures 3 (3, 4, 4) inches. Change to larger needles.

Beg neck shaping

Next row (RS): K 3 blue, join white and inc 1 st in last st.

Keeping blue sts in garter st and white in St st, [inc 1 st in first white st every other row] 12 (12, 14, 16) times, and *at the same time,* [dec 1 st at neck edge every 4th row] 6 (6, 7, 8) times. (11, 11, 12, 13 sts)

Work even for 1 inch, ending with a WS row.

Back neck shaping

Next row (RS): K 3 blue, k 8 (8, 9, 10) white, cast on 9 (11, 11, 12) white, cast on 3 blue. (23, 25, 26, 28 sts)

Keeping first and last 3 sts in blue garter st and remaining white sts in St st, work even until collar measures

2½ (2½, 3, 3) inches above cast-on neck sts, ending with a RS row.

With blue only, knit 4 rows.

Bind off all sts.

Make right half of collar as for left, reversing shaping.

Sew each half of collar to corresponding neckline.

Referring to charts and working in duplicate st, embroider 1 white fish on lower left leg and 2 blue fish on front of body as shown in photo.

Sew on buttons.

Girl's Dress

Materials

- Plymouth Dreambaby D.K. 50 percent acrylic microfiber/50 percent nylon DK weight yarn (183 yds/50g per ball): 2 (2, 2, 3) balls blue #109, 2 balls white #100, 1 ball red #108
- Size 2 (3mm) needles
- Size 3 (3.25mm) straight and 16-inch circular needles or size needed to obtain gauge
- Stitch markers
- Stitch holders
- Tapestry needle
- 10 (⅜-inch) red buttons
- K1C2 Rainbow® Elastic Thread

Gauge

23 sts and 32 rows = 4 inches/10cm in St st with larger needles

To save time, take time to check gauge.

Special Abbreviations

M1 (Make 1): Make a backwards loop and place on RH needle.

Pattern Stitches

A. 1/1 Twisted Rib (odd number of sts)

Row 1 (RS): K1-tbl, *p1, k1-tbl, rep from * across row.

Row 2: P1-tbl, *k1, p1-tbl, rep from * across row.

Rep Rows 1 and 2 for pat.

B. Stripe Sequence

Work in sequence of 2 rows red, then 8 rows white.

Pattern Notes

Sister's dress is styled in the same manner as boy's romper, replacing the pants with a short skirt.

White garter st trims the lower edge.

Fish are worked in duplicate st after the dress is completed.

For collar, wind separate bobbins of each color. To avoid holes when changing colors, always bring new color up over old.

On collar, sl first edge st of each blue section to maintain a chained edge.

Skirt

Beg at waistband with blue and smaller needles, cast on 127 (133, 139, 151) sts.

Work in 1/1 Twisted Rib for 1 inch, ending with a WS row.

Change to larger needles, join and work in rnds from this point, pm between first and last st.

Next rnd: Knit, inc 5 (3, 5, 5) sts

evenly (132, 136, 144, 156 sts)

Pm after every 33 (34, 36, 39) sts.

Work even in St st for 7 rnds.

Inc rnd: [K1, M1, k to 1 st before marker, M1, k1] 4 times.

Rep last 8 rnds 4 (5, 6, 6) times more. (172, 184, 200, 212 sts)

Work even in St st until skirt measures 9½ (10, 10½, 11) inches from beg.

Change to white and work in garter st for 4 rnds.

Bind off all sts.

Top

With red and larger needles, pick up and k 126 (132, 128, 150) sts along cast-on edge of waistband. Do not join.

Work even in Stripe Sequence until top measures 4 (4½, 5, 5½) inches, ending with a WS row.

Divide for front & backs

Next row: K 26 (28, 29, 31) sts and sl

to holder for left back, bind off 10 (10, 10, 12) sts for left underarm, k 54 (56, 60, 64) sts and sl to 2nd holder for front, bind off 10 (10, 10, 12) sts for right underarm, k to end of row.

Work even on right back only until armhole measures 4½ (5, 5½, 5¾) inches.

Bind off all sts.

Mark 14 (14, 15, 16) sts for shoulder.

Left Back

Sl sts from first holder to larger needle. With WS facing, join yarn at arm edge.

Work left back as for right, reversing shaping.

Front

Sl sts from 2nd holder to larger needle. With WS facing, join yarn at right armhole.

Work even for 1½ (2, 2, 1¾) inches, ending with a WS row.

Beg neck shaping

K 25 (26, 28, 30) sts, k2tog, join 2nd ball of yarn and k2tog, k to end of row.

Working on both sides of neck with separate balls of yarn, [dec 1 st each side of neck every other row] 12 (13, 15, 15) times more. (14, 14, 15, 16 sts on each side)

Work even until armhole measures same as for back.

Bind off all sts.

Sew shoulder seams. Sew center back

11 (11½, 12, 13)"

4½ (5, 5½, 5¾)"

4 (4½, 5, 5½)"

9 (9½, 10, 11½)"

DRESS

seam from just below waistband to lower edge of skirt.

Back Bands

With RS facing, join white at back neck edge.

With smaller needles, pick up and k 3 sts for every 4 rows along right edge to bottom of opening, pm, pick up and k same number of sts along left edge.

Work in 1/1 Twisted Rib for 1 row, dec 1 st each side of marker.

Buttonhole row: At each red stripe of left edge, make 1 buttonhole by working yo, k2tog and dec each side of marker as before.

Work 1/1 Twisted Rib for 1 more row, dec 1 st each side of marker.

Bind off in pat.

Sleeves

With blue and smaller needles, cast on 41 (45, 45, 51) sts.

Work in 1/1 Twisted rib for 1 row, change to white.

Work even in established pat until cuff measures ¾ (¾, 1, 1) inch, inc 10 (12, 12, 10) sts evenly on last WS row. (51, 57, 57, 61 sts)

Change to larger needles.

Work in Stripe Sequence, [inc 1 st each end every 4th (4th, 6th, 8th) row] 3 times. (57, 63, 63, 67 sts)

Work even until sleeve measures 2¾ (2¾, 3½, 4) inches. Mark each end st for underarm.

Continue to work even in established pat for ¾ (¾, 1, 1) inch more.

Bind off all sts.

Sew sleeve into armhole, matching underarm markers to center of bound-off underarm sts.

Sew sleeve seams.

Left Half of Collar
Tie

With blue and smaller needles, cast on 4 sts.

*K4, sl sts back to LH needle. Rep from * until tie measures 3 (3, 4, 4) inches. Change to larger needles.

Beg neck shaping

Next row (RS): K 3 blue, join white and inc 1 st in last st.

Keeping blue sts in garter st and white in St st, [inc 1 st in first white st every other row] 12 (12, 14, 16) times, and *at the same time*, [dec 1 st at neck edge every 4th row] 6 (6, 7, 8) times. (11, 11, 12, 13 sts)

Work even for 1 inch, ending with a WS row.

Back neck shaping

Next row (RS): K 3 blue, k 8 (8, 9, 10) white, cast on 9 (11, 11, 12) white, cast on 3 blue. (23, 25, 26, 28 sts)

Keeping first and last 3 sts in blue garter st and remaining white sts in St st, work even until collar measures 2½ (2½, 3, 3) inches above cast-on neck sts, ending with a RS row.

With blue only, knit 4 rows.

Bind off all sts.

Make right half of collar as for left, reversing shaping.

Sew each half of collar to corresponding neckline.

Referring to charts and working in duplicate st, embroider 1 white fish on lower skirt and 2 blue fish on front of body as shown in photo.

Sew on buttons. ✦

COLOR KEY	
■	Red
□	White
■	Blue

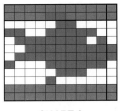

CHART A
BODICE

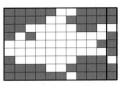

CHART B
PANTS LEG OR SKIRT

Goose in the Flowers Hat

Design by Jacqueline Hoyle

Make a cheerful hat that features a goose munching on nearby flowers.

Skill Level
Intermediate***

Size
Infant's 6 (12, 18, 24) months. Instructions are given for smallest size, with larger sizes in parentheses. When only 1 number is given, it applies to all sizes.

Finished Measurements
Circumference: 16 (16, 16½, 17) inches

Length: 8½ inches

Materials
- Plymouth Dreambaby D.K. 50 percent acrylic microfiber/50 percent nylon DK weight yarn (183 yds/50g per ball): 1 ball royal #109 (MC), small amounts orange #108, yellow #110, green #111
- Plymouth Encore D.K. 75 percent acrylic/25 percent wool DK weight yarn (150 yds/50g per ball): small amount magenta #1385
- Size 5 (3.75mm) needles or size needed to obtain gauge
- Tapestry needle

Gauge
22 sts and 34 rows = 4 inches/10cm in St st

To save time, take time to check gauge.

Pattern Note
Flowers are embroidered in a random pattern after hat is completed.

Hat
With MC, cast on 88 (88, 92, 96) sts. Knit 4 rows.

Work even in k2, p2 ribbing for 6 rows.

Knit 8 rows.

Set up pat
Next row (RS): K 23 (23, 25, 27) MC, work Row 1 of chart over next 42 sts, k 23 (23, 25, 27) MC.

Work even in established pat through Row 22 of chart.

Shape top
Dec row: K1, k2tog around, leaving 3 sts before neck, across neck area, and after neck untouched. (60, 60, 63, 63 sts)

Work 2 rows even.

Rep dec row, leaving 4 sts before neck, across neck area, and after neck untouched. (40, 40, 42, 42 sts)

Work even until chart is completed.

With MC only, knit 1 row, purl 1 row.

Dec row 2: *K1, k2tog, rep from * around. (27, 27, 28, 28 sts)

Work 1 row even.

Rep dec row 2. (18, 18, 19, 19 sts)

Work even for 3 rows.

Rep dec row 2. (12, 12, 13, 13 sts)

Work even for 3 rows.

Next row: K2tog around. (6, 6, 7, 7 sts)

Cut yarn, leaving a 12-inch end. Draw yarn through remaining sts twice.

Bobble
With yellow, cast on 9 sts.

Work in St st for 8 rows.

Next row: *K1, k2tog, rep from * across. (6 sts)

Row 2: P2tog across. (3 sts)

Row 3: K2tog, k1, pass 2nd st over first.

Cut yarn, leaving a 12-inch end. Draw end through final st.

Continued on page 189

ARAN ANYONE?

Baby Aran

Design by Lois S. Young

Aran sweaters aren't just for big guys. Here are two pared-down versions for the younger set.

Skill Level
Intermediate***

Size
Infant's 6 (12, 18, 24) months
Instructions are given for smallest size, with larger sizes in parentheses.

When only 1 number is given, it applies to all sizes.

Finished Measurements
Chest: 20 (21, 22, 23) inches
Length: 10½ (11¼, 12, 13) inches

Materials
- Plymouth Encore D.K. 75 percent acrylic/25 percent wool DK weight yarn (150 yds/50g per ball): 2 (3, 3, 4) balls Aran #256
- Size 4 (3.5mm) straight and 16-inch circular needles
- Size 5 (3.75 mm) needles or size needed to obtain gauge
- Cable needle
- Stitch holders
- Stitch markers
- Yarn needle

Gauge
28 sts and 36 rows = 4 inches/10cm in pat with larger needles

To save time, take time to check gauge.

Special Abbreviations
DC (double cable): Sl 2 to cn and hold in back, k1, k 2nd st from cn, k first st, sl 1 to cn and hold in front, k 2nd st of LH needle, k first st, k2 from cn.

C3L (cable 3 left): Sl 1 to cn and hold in front, k 2nd st of LH needle, k first st, k2 from cn.

RKC (right knit cross): Sl 1 to cn and hold in back, k1, k1 from cn.

LKC (left knit cross): Sl 1 to cn and hold in front, k1, k1 from cn.

RPC (right purl cross): Sl 1 to cn and hold in back, p1, k1 from cn.

LPC (left purl cross): Sl 1 to cn and hold in front, p1, k1 from cn.

Back
With smaller needles, cast on 69 (73, 77, 81) sts.

Work in k1, p1 ribbing for 10 rows. Change to larger needles.

Referring to Chart A, work even until back measures 7 (7½, 8, 8½) inches, ending with a WS row.

Shape underarm
Bind off 4 (5, 5, 5) sts at beg of next 2 rows.

[Dec 1 st at each end] twice. (57, 59, 63, 67 sts).

Work even until back measures 10½ (11¼, 12, 13) inches, ending with a WS row.

Shape shoulders

Bind off 11 (12, 14, 15) sts for right shoulder, work across 35 (35, 35, 37) sts and sl to holder for back neck, bind off remaining 11 (12, 14, 15) sts for left shoulder.

Front

Work as for back until armhole measures 2 (2¼, 2½, 3) inches, ending with a WS row.

Shape front neck

Work 17 (18, 20, 21) sts, join 2nd ball of yarn and work across 23 (23, 23, 25) sts, sl these sts to holder for front neck, work across remaining 17 (18, 20, 21) sts.

Working on both sides of neck with separate balls of yarn, [dec 1 st each side of neck on every RS row] 6 times (11, 12, 14, 15 sts).

Work even until armhole is same as for back.

Bind off.

Sew shoulder seams.

Sleeves

With smaller needles, cast on 35 (37, 37, 39) sts.

Work even in k1, p1 ({k1, p1}, {p1, k1} {p1, k1}) ribbing for 12 (14, 16, 20) rows, inc 0 (0, 1, 1) st at beg and end of last row. (35, 37, 39, 41 sts)

Change to larger needles.

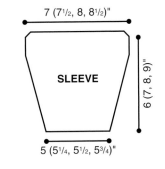

SLEEVE

7 (7½, 8, 8½)"

6 (7, 8, 9)"

5 (5¼, 5½, 5¾)"

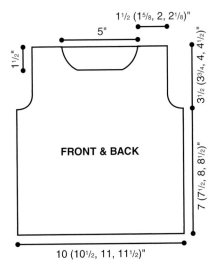

1½ (1⅝, 2, 2⅛)"

5"

1½"

3½ (3¾, 4, 4½)"

7 (7½, 8, 8½)"

FRONT & BACK

10 (10½, 11, 11½)"

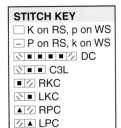

STITCH KEY

☐ K on RS, p on WS
⊟ P on RS, k on WS
▧▪▪▪▫▱ DC
▧▪▪▪ C3L
▪▱ RKC
▨▪ LKC
▲▱ RPC
▱▲ LPC

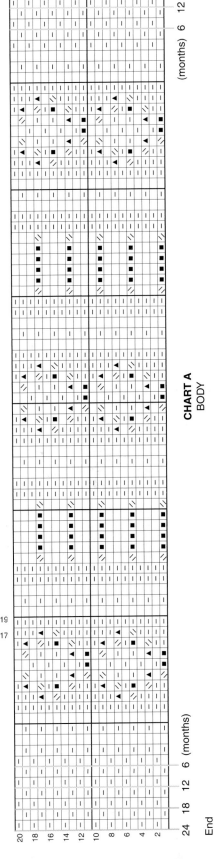

CHART A
BODY

19 17 15 13 11 9 7 5 3 1

24 18 12 6 (months) Beg

24 18 12 6 (months)

24 18 12 6 (months) End

20 18 16 14 12 10 8 6 4 2

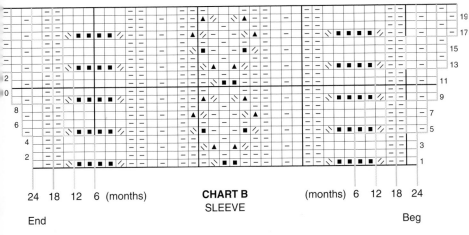

24 18 12 6 (months)

CHART B
SLEEVE

(months) 6 12 18 24

End

Beg

Referring to Chart B and continuing in pat as established, [inc 1 st each end every 4th row] 5 (5, 6, 7) times, then [every 6th row] 2 (3, 3, 4) times. (49, 53, 57, 63 sts)

Work even until sleeve measures 6 (7, 8, 9) inches. Mark each end of last row for underarm.

Shape cap
Bind off 1 st at beg of next 2 (4, 4, 6) rows, bind off rem 47 (49, 53, 57) sts.

Neck Band
With smaller circular needle and RS facing, join yarn at right back neck.

Work in pat on 35 (35, 35, 37) sts of back neck, pick up and k 13 sts along left neck, work in pat on 23 (23, 23, 25) sts of front neck, pick up and k 13 sts along right neck, pm between first and last st. (84, 84, 84, 88 sts)

Work in k1, p1 ribbing for 8 rnds, lining up k sts of ribbing with k sts at center front of body.

Bind off in rib.

Finishing
Sew sleeve into armhole, matching underarm markers to underarm seam of body.

Sew sleeve and side seams. ✦

Big Kid Aran

Design by Lois S. Young

Here is the second Aran—this time for bigger kids.

Skill Level

Intermediate***

Size

Child's 4 (6, 8, 10) Instructions are given for smallest size, with larger sizes in parentheses. When only 1 number is given, it applies to all sizes.

Finished Measurements

Chest: 23 (25, 26, 28) inches

Length: 14 (15½, 17, 18½) inches

Materials

- Plymouth Encore Worsted 75 percent acrylic/25 percent wool worsted weight yarn (200 yds/ 100g per skein): 3 (3, 4, 4) skeins Aran #256
- Size 5 (3.75mm) straight and 16-inch circular needles
- Size 6 (4mm) needles or size needed to obtain gauge
- Cable needle
- Stitch holder
- Stitch markers
- Yarn needle

Gauge

25 sts and 30 rows = 4 inches/10cm in pat with larger needles

To save time, take time to check gauge.

Special Abbreviations

DC (double cable): Sl 2 to cn and hold in back, k1, k 2nd st from cn, k first st, sl 1 to cn and hold in front, k 2nd st of LH needle, k first st, k2 from cn.

C3L (cable 3 left): Sl 1 to cn and hold in front, k 2nd st of LH needle, k first st, k2 from cn.

RKC (right knit cross): Sl 1 to cn and hold in back, k1, k1 from cn.

LKC (left knit cross): Sl 1 to cn and hold in front, k1, k1 from cn.

RPC (right purl cross): Sl 1 to cn and hold in back, p1, k1 from cn.

LPC (left purl cross): Sl 1 to cn and hold in front, p1, k1 from cn.

Back

With smaller needles, cast on 73 (77, 81, 85) sts.

Work in k1, p1 ribbing for 10 rows.

Change to larger needles.

Referring to Chart A, work even until back measures 9 (10, 11, 11½) inches, ending with a WS row.

Shape underarm

Bind off 5 sts at beg of next 2 rows. (63, 67, 71, 75 sts)

[Dec 1 st each end] twice. (59, 63, 67, 71 sts)

Work even until back measures 14 (15½, 17, 18½) inches, ending with a WS row.

Shape shoulders

Bind off 11 (13, 14, 15) sts for right shoulder, work across 37 (37, 39, 41) sts and sl to holder for back neck,

bind off remaining 11 (13, 14, 15) sts for left shoulder.

Front

Work as for back until armhole measures 3¼ (3½, 3¾, 4¼) inches, ending with WS row.

Shape front neck

Work across 16 (18, 20, 21) sts, join 2nd ball of yarn and work across 27 sts, sl these sts to holder for front neck, work across remaining 16 (18, 20, 21) sts.

Working on both sides of neck with separate balls of yarn, [dec 1 st at each neck edge on every RS row] 5 (5, 6, 6) times. (11, 13, 14, 15 sts)

Work even until armhole measures same as for back.

Bind off.

Sew shoulder seams.

Sleeves

With smaller needles, cast on 35 (3 39, 41) sts.

Work even p1, k1 ribbing for 12 (14 16, 20) rows, inc 1 st at beg and er of last row (37, 39, 41, 43 sts)

Change to larger needles.

Referring to Chart B and continuing in pat as established, [inc 1 st each end every 4th row] 5 (6, 7, 8) times then [every 6th row] 3 (3, 4, 4) time (53, 57, 63, 67 sts)

Work even until sleeve measures 11½ (12¾, 14, 15¼) inches. Mark each end of last row for underarm

Shape cap

Bind off 1 st at beg of next 4 (4, 6, rows, bind off remaining 49 (53, 57, 61) sts.

Neck Band

With smaller circular needle and R facing, join yarn at right back necl

Work in pat on 37 (37, 39, 41) sts of back neck, pick up and k 13 (15, 17, 19) sts along left neck, work in pat on 27 sts of front neck, pick up and k 13 (15, 17, 19) sts along right neck, pm between first and last st. (90, 94, 100, 106 sts)

Work in k1, p1 ribbing for 8 rnds, lin ing up k sts of ribbing with k sts at center front of body.

Bind off in rib.

Finishing

Sew sleeve into armhole, matching underarm markers to underarm seam of body.

Sew sleeve and side seams. ✦

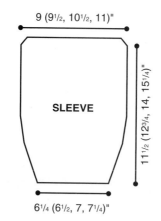

9 (9½, 10½, 11)"

SLEEVE

11½ (12¾, 14, 15¼)"

6¼ (6½, 7, 7¼)"

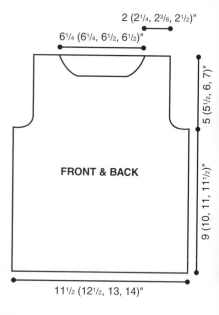

2 (2¼, 2⅜, 2½)"

6¼ (6¼, 6½, 6½)"

5 (5½, 6, 7)"

FRONT & BACK

9 (10, 11, 11½)"

11½ (12½, 13, 14)"

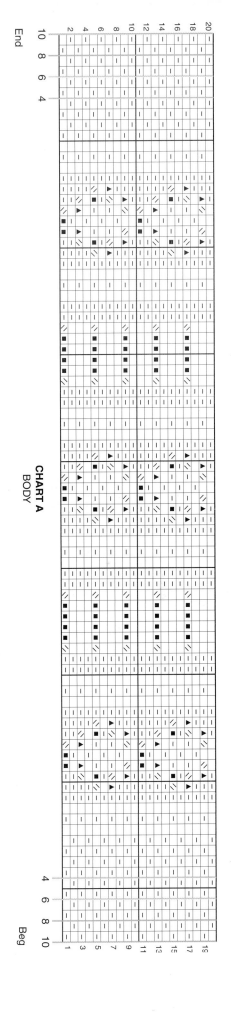

CHART A
BODY

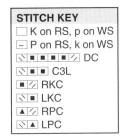

STITCH KEY
- ☐ K on RS, p on WS
- − P on RS, k on WS
- DC
- C3L
- RKC
- LKC
- RPC
- LPC

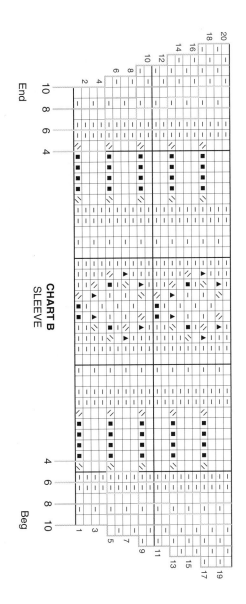

CHART B
SLEEVE

Bam-Bam Balls

Design by Cindy Polfer

Soft balls in three sizes will fit any little hand in a game of catch. Because they are so soft, they can even be tossed in the house.

Skill Level
Easy**

Size
Small (medium, large) Instructions are given for smallest size, with larger sizes in parentheses. When only 1 number is given, it applies to all sizes.

Finished Measurements
Approximately 5 (6, 7) inches in diameter; 15½ (18½, 21½)-inch circumference

Materials
- Plymouth BAM 42 percent acrylic/40 percent nylon/18 percent wool novelty yarn (60 yds/50g per ball): 1 (1, 2) balls #3459 (#3461, #3458)
- Size 10 (6mm) needles
- Stitch markers
- Yarn needle
- Polyester fiberfill

Gauge
12 sts and 24 rows = 4 inches/10cm in garter st

Gauge is not critical for this project, but sts should be worked tightly so fiberfill does not show through.

Pattern Notes

Ball is knit in 2 separate pieces.

Incs are worked by knitting into the front then back of st.

When instructed to inc 1 st on each side of a row, work as follows: Inc in first st, k to last 2 sts, inc in next st, k1.

When instructed to dec on each side of row, work as follows: Work a ssk on first 2 sts, k to last 2 sts, k2tog.

Ball

Make 2 pieces

Cast on 3 (4, 5) sts. Mark center st.

Row 1: Knit.

Inc row: Inc in first st, k to last 2 sts, inc in next st, k1. (5, 6, 7 sts)

Row 3: Knit (work inc row, work inc row). (5, 8, 9 sts)

Row 4: Work inc row (knit, knit). (7, 8, 9 sts)

Row 5: Knit (work inc row, work inc row). (7, 10, 11 sts)

Row 6: Work inc row (knit, knit). (9, 10, 11 sts)

Row 7: Knit (work inc row, work inc row). (9, 12, 13 sts)

Rows 8-14 (8-16, 8-20): Knit.

Dec row 15 (17, 21): Ssk, k to last 2 sts, k2tog. (7, 10, 11 sts)

Rows 16-20 (18-22, 22-26): Knit.

Row 21 (23, 27): Rep dec row. (5, 8, 9 sts)

Sizes medium & large only:

Rows (24-30, 28-32): Knit.

Row (31, 33): Work dec row. (6, 7 sts)

All sizes

Rows 22-40 (32-42, 34-52): Knit, marking beg and end of row 36 (37, 43).

Row 41 (43, 53): Work inc row. (7, 8, 9 sts)

Rows 42-46 (44-50, 54-58): Knit.

Row 47 (51, 59): Work inc row. (9, 10, 11 sts)

Rows 48-55 (52-56, 60-64): Knit.

Sizes medium & large only

Row (57, 65): Work inc row. (12, 13 sts)

Rows (58-66, 66-78): Knit.

All sizes

Row 56 (67, 79): Work dec row. (7, 10, 11 sts)

Row 57 (68, 80): Knit.

Row 58 (69, 81): Work dec row. (5, 8, 9 sts)

Row 59 (70, 82): Knit.

Row 60 (71, 83): Work dec row. (3, 6, 7 sts)

Sizes medium & large only

Row (72, 84): Work dec row. (4, 5 sts)

Bind off all sts.

Mark center st of bound-off row.

Finishing

Steam pieces to set sts.

Matching marker of cast-on or bound-off row to marker placed at Row 36 (37, 43), sew pieces tog to form ball as shown in Fig 1.

Before entire seam is completely sewn, stuff ball to desired firmness and close seam. Weave in ends. ✦

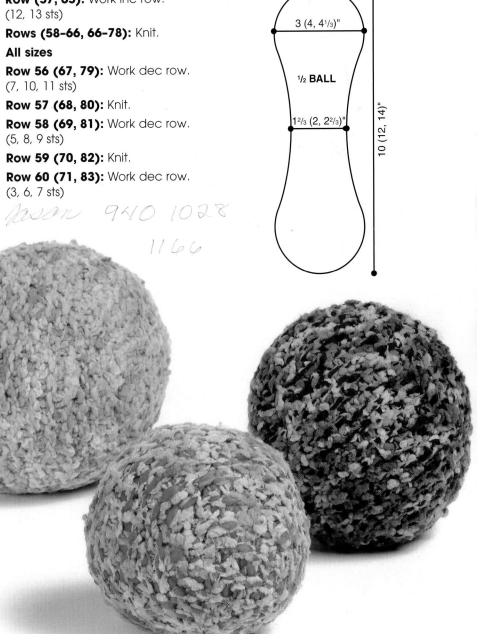

3 (4, 4⅓)"

½ BALL

1⅔ (2, 2⅔)"

10 (12, 14)"

Fig. 1

Play Ball Short Overall

Design by Joan McGowan-Michael

*Hot summer days and kids seem to go together.
This short overall is perfect for outdoor play.*

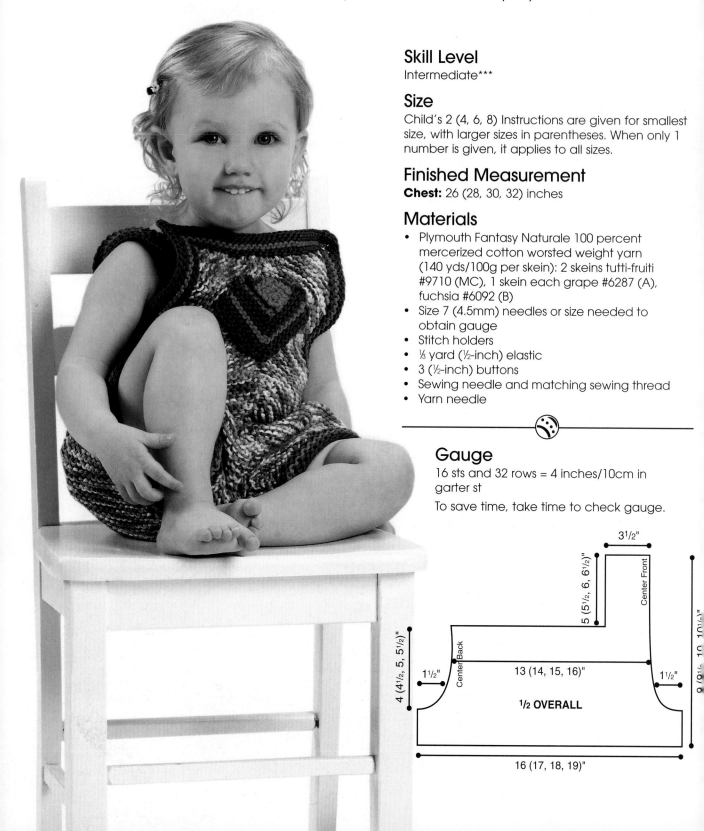

Skill Level
Intermediate***

Size
Child's 2 (4, 6, 8) Instructions are given for smallest size, with larger sizes in parentheses. When only 1 number is given, it applies to all sizes.

Finished Measurement
Chest: 26 (28, 30, 32) inches

Materials
- Plymouth Fantasy Naturale 100 percent mercerized cotton worsted weight yarn (140 yds/100g per skein): 2 skeins tutti-fruiti #9710 (MC), 1 skein each grape #6287 (A), fuchsia #6092 (B)
- Size 7 (4.5mm) needles or size needed to obtain gauge
- Stitch holders
- ⅛ yard (½-inch) elastic
- 3 (½-inch) buttons
- Sewing needle and matching sewing thread
- Yarn needle

Gauge
16 sts and 32 rows = 4 inches/10cm in garter st

To save time, take time to check gauge.

Special Abbreviations

M1 (Make 1): Make a backwards loop and place on RH needle.

Sk2p (a decrease): Sl 1, k2tog, pass sl st over.

Pattern Note

Incs and decs are made on RS of work unless otherwise stated.

Overall

Right Half

Beg at crotch with MC, cast on 2 sts.

Working in garter st, [inc 1 st at each end of needle every other row] 7 (7, 8, 8) times. (16, 16, 18, 18 sts)

Continue to inc at left edge as established, *at the same time* [dec 1 st every other row at right edge] 3 times.

Inc on both edges as before every other row until there are 55 (57, 59, 61) sts.

Shape bib

Next row (RS): K1, M1, k14, k2tog, place remaining sts on holder. Turn, k17.

Continue as established, inc 1 st at beg of every RS row and dec 1 st at end of row until bib area measures 5 (5½, 6, 6½) inches from waist.

Dec 1 st at each end every other row until 1 st remains. Fasten off.

Sides & Back

Sl sts from holder to needle. With RS facing, join yarn at bib edge.

Continue working over 38 (40, 42, 44) sts, dec 1 st at beg and inc 1 st at end of every RS row until bottom edge of overall measures 16 (17, 18, 19) inches, ending with a RS row.

Shape crotch

Next row (WS): K 16 (16, 18, 18) sts, sl remaining sts to holder. Turn.

Dec 1 st each end of this and every other RS row until 1 st remains. Fasten off.

Complete back

Sl sts from holder to needle.

With WS facing, attach yarn and k across 22 (24, 24, 26) sts.

Dec 1 st at beg and end of every RS row until 1 st remains. Fasten off.

Left Half

Work as for right side. Turn piece over; WS becomes RS.

Leg Bands

With A, pick up 1 st in every ridge along bottom of leg.

Knit 2 rows A, 2 rows B, and 2 rows A.

Bind off all sts.

Waist & Bib Band

Sew center front seam.

With A, and RS facing, pick up 1 st in every ridge all along right waist, around bib and along left waist.

Knit 1 row.

Next row: Change to B and k to within 1 st of waist/bib intersection, k3 tog for mitered corner, work to corner st at top edge of bib, M2 in this st for miter, rep at other corner, knit to within 1 st of waist/bib intersection, sk2p, work to end.

Knit 1 row.

Change to A and rep last 2 rows.

Bind off all sts.

Straps
Make 2

With A, cast on 50 (54, 58, 60) sts and work in color sequence as for leg bands, making a buttonhole by working (yo, k2tog) on first row of color B 4 sts from end.

Pocket

With A, cast on 25 sts.

Mark center st.

Row 1 (RS): K to 1 st before marker, remove marker, k3tog, replace marker in new center st, k to end.

Row 2: Knit.

Rep these 2 rows until 1 st remains, working in color sequence of [4 rows A, 2 rows B] twice, then 2 rows A, finish with B.

Finishing

Referring to photo, sew pocket to front of bib, turning down edge and sewing on button.

Sew center back and crotch seam.

Sew leg seams.

Sew straps to back of overalls, having buttonholes at front of bib.

Sew two buttons to inside of bib.

Make casing for elastic on inside of back waistband, by sewing cross-sts with MC across center ⅔ of waistband.

Cut elastic to size and run through casing, securing ends with sewing thread. ✦

Furry Friends Pullovers

Designs by Uyvonne Bigham

Take your pick of a cat, dog or bear pocket to hold a child's treasures and keep little hands warm. Any of them are sure to delight.

Skill Level
Beginner*

Size
Child's 2 (3, 4, 5, 6) years Instructions are given for smallest size, with larger sizes in parentheses. When only 1 number is given, it applies to all sizes.

Finished Measurements
Chest: 25½ (28, 30, 32, 34) inches

Length: 14 (15, 16, 17, 17½) inches

Sleeve width at upper arm: 12 (12½, 13, 14, 15) inches

Materials
- Plymouth Encore Worsted 75 percent acrylic/25 percent wool worsted weight yarn (220 yds/100g per skein): 2 (3, 3, 4, 4) skeins MC Bear: off-white #256, Cat: dark red #9601, Dog: royal blue #133; 1 ball CC Bear: brown #1204, Cat: caramel tweed #7172, Dog: off-white #256; small amounts black #217, pink #029, green #054 for face features
- Size 7 (4.5mm) needles
- Size 8 (5mm) needles or size needed to obtain gauge

Gauge
20 sts and 28 rows = 4 inches/10cm in St st with larger needles

To save time, take time to check gauge.

Special Abbreviations
M1 (Make 1): Make a backwards loop and place on LH needle.

Sssk (a double decrease): Sl next 2 sts purlwise, k1, pass 2 sl sts over.

Pattern Note
Face appliqué is the same for all animals.

Back
With smaller needles and MC, cast on 58 (63, 68, 72, 74) sts.

Work in k2, p2 rib for 1 inch, ending with a WS row.

Change to larger needles.

Next row (RS): Knit, inc 6 (7, 8, 8, 10) sts evenly. (64, 70, 76, 80, 84 sts)

Work even in St st until back measures 8 (8¾, 9½, 10, 10½) inches.

Mark each end st for underarm.

Continue to work even until back measures 14 (15, 16, 17, 18) inches.

Bind off all sts.

Mark center 30 sts for back neck.

Front

Work as for back until front measures 11 (12, 13, 14, 14½) inches, ending with a WS row.

Neck shaping

Next row (RS): K 27 (30, 33, 35, 37) sts, join 2nd ball of yarn and bind off 10 sts for front neck, k to end of row.

Working on both sides of neck with separate balls of yarn, bind off at each neck edge [3 sts once], then [2 sts] twice.

[Dec 1 st side of neck every row] 3 times. (17, 20, 23, 25, 27 sts remain for each shoulder)

Work even until front measures same as for back.

Sleeves

With smaller needles and MC, cast on 32 (36, 38, 40, 42) sts.

Work in k2, p2 rib for 1 inch, ending with a WS row.

Change to larger needles and St st.

[Inc 1 st each end every 4th row] 8 (7, 7, 8, 9,) times. (48, 50, 52, 56, 60 sts)

Work even until sleeve measures 11 (12, 13, 14, 14½) inches.

Bind off all sts.

Neck Band

Sew right shoulder seam.

With RS facing, join yarn at left front neck.

With smaller needles and MC, pick up and k 72 sts evenly around neck edge.

Work even in k2, p2 rib for 8 rows.

Bind off loosely in rib.

Finishing

Sew left shoulder and neck band seam.

Sew sleeves between underarm markers.

Face Appliqué

With smaller needles and CC, cast on 22 sts.

Row 1 (WS): P2 *k2, p2, rep from * across row.

Row 2: K2, *p2, k2, rep from * across row.

[Rep Rows 1 and 2] twice.

Rep Row 1. Change to larger needles.

Shape end

Row 1 (RS): K4, M1, k17. (23 sts)

Row 2 and all even-numbered rows: Purl.

Row 3: K4, M1, k13, M1, k4. (25 sts)

Row 5: K4, M1, k20. (26 sts)

Row 7: K4, M1, k17, M1, k3. (28 sts)

Row 9: K4, M1, k23. (29 sts)

Row 11: K4, M1, k20, M1, k3. (31 sts)

Row 13: K4, M1, k26. (32 sts)

Row 15: K4, M1, k23, M1, k3. (34 sts)

Row 17: K4, M1, k29. (35 sts)

Row 18: Purl.

Work even in St st for 16 (16, 18, 18, 20) rows.

Shape second end

Row 1: K3, k2tog, k25, ssk, k3. (33 sts)

Row 2 and all even-numbered rows: Purl.

Row 3: K3, k2tog, k28, k3. (32 sts)

Row 5: K3, k2tog, k22, ssk, k3. (30 sts)

Row 7: K3, k2tog, k25. (29 sts)

Row 9: K3, k2tog, k19, ssk, k3. (27 sts)

Row 11: K3, k2tog, k22. (26 sts)

Row 13: K3, k2tog, k17, ssk, k3. (24 sts)

Row 15: K3, k2tog, k19. (23 sts)

Row 17: K3, k2tog, k13, k3. (22 sts)

Row 18: Purl.

Change to smaller needles.

Work even in k2, p2 rib for 8 rows.

Bind off.

Bear Ears

With larger needles and black, cast on 12 sts.

Work in St st for 2½ inches, ending with a WS row.

Shape top of ear

Next row (RS): Ssk, k to last 2 sts, k2tog. Purl 1 row.

Rep these 2 rows until 6 sts remain.

Bind off.

Dog Ears

With white and larger needles, cast on 11 sts.

Row 1 (WS): K3, p5, k3.

Row 2: Knit.

[Rep Rows 1 and 2] 6 times.

Shape top of ear

Next row (WS): K2, k2tog, p3, k2tog, k2. (9 sts)

Row 2: Knit.

Row 3: K2, k2tog, p1, k2tog, k2. (7 sts)

Knit 3 rows.

Next row: K1, k2tog, k to end of row.

[Rep last row] once. (5 sts)

Bind off.

Cat Ears

With CC and larger needles, cast on 11 sts.

Knit 3 rows.

Row 4: K4, sssk, k4. (9 sts)

Rows 5–7: Knit.

Row 8: K3, sssk, k3. (7 sts)

Rows 9–11: Knit.

Row 12: K2, sssk, k2. (5 sts)

Rows 13–14: Knit.

Row 15: K1, sssk, k1. (3 sts)

Row 16: K3tog.

Bind off remaining st.

Dog Tongue

With pink and smaller needles, cast on 5 sts.

Row 1: Knit.

Row 2: K1, M1, k1, M1, k1. (7 sts)

Row 3–5: Knit.

Row 6: K1, M1, k3, M1, k1. (9 sts)

Row 7–14: Knit.

Bind off.

Finishing

Refer to photo for placement of all features.

Bear

With black, duplicate st eyes, nose and mouth onto face appliqué.

Sew face appliqué onto sweater

along top and bottom edge, leaving ribbed ends open.

Sew ears in position.

Dog

Sew tongue to face appliqué.

With black, duplicate st nose, right eye and left eye circle onto face appliqué.

With black, duplicate st over center sts of one ear.

Sew face appliqué onto sweater along top and bottom edge, leaving ribbed ends open.

Sew ears in position.

Cat

With black, duplicate st nose and nose line onto face appliqué.

With pink, duplicate st mouth onto face appliqué.

With white, embroider whiskers on face appliqué using 3 long straight sts for each set of whiskers.

With green, embroider eyes.

Sew face appliqué onto sweater along top and bottom edge, leaving ribbed ends open.

Sew ears in position.

Sew side and sleeve seams. ✦

VESTED INTEREST

Primary Colors Vest

Design by Lois S. Young

Primary colors combine with a basic silhouette to produce a vest for the young gentleman.

Skill Level
Intermediate***

Size
Child's 2 (4, 6, 8) Instructions are given for smallest size, with larger sizes in parentheses. When only 1 number is given, it applies to all sizes.

Finished Measurements
Chest: 22 (23, 24½, 26) inches

Length: 12 (13, 15, 16½) inches

Materials
- Plymouth Encore D.K. 75 percent acrylic/25 percent wool DK weight yarn (150 yds/50g per ball): 2 (2, 3, 4) balls royal #133 (MC), 1 ball dark red #9601 (CC)
- Size 4 (3.5mm) straight and 16-inch circular needles
- Size 5 (3.75mm) needles or size needed to obtain gauge
- Stitch holders
- Stitch markers
- Tapestry needle

Gauge
23 sts and 31 rows = 4 inches/10cm in St st

To save time, take time to check gauge.

Special Abbreviation
Cdd (centered double decrease): Slip 2 sts tog knitwise, k1, pass 2 slipped sts. Center st will lie on top.

Back
With smaller needles and MC, cast on 61 (65, 69, 73) sts.

Work in k1, p1 ribbing for 8 (8, 10, 10) rows.

Change to larger needles.

Work 7 rows of Chart A.

Work in St st until back measures 7 (8, 9, 10) inches, ending with a WS row.

Shape underarms
Bind off 8 sts at beg of next 2 rows. (45, 49, 51, 57 sts)

[Dec 1 st each end every other row] 4 times. (37, 41, 45, 49 sts)

Work even until armhole measures 4½ (4¾, 5¼, 5¾) inches, ending with a WS row.

Work Rows 3–7 of Chart A.

Shape shoulders
Bind off 7 (8, 9, 10) sts at beg of next 2 rows.

Put remaining 23 (25, 27, 29) sts on holder for neck back.

Front
Work as for back until armhole decs are finished, ending with a WS Row.

Begin neck border
K18 (20, 22, 24) MC, k1 CC, this

s Row 1 of Chart B, k18 (20, 22, 24) MC.

Continue in pat from chart through Row 6 of chart.

Row 7: Working in established pat, k18 (20, 22, 24), sl next st to holder, join 2 additional balls of yarn and k to end of row.

Working on both sides of neck with separate balls of yarn and keeping 6 sts at each side of neck in established color pat, rep Rows 8–11 of Chart B, *at the same time* [dec 1 st at each neck edge every other row 11 (12, 13, 14) times, working decs next to color border. (7, 8, 9, 10 sts)

Work even until armhole measures same as for back.

Bind off all shoulder sts.

Neck Band

With RS facing, using smaller circular needle and MC, pick up and k 24 (26, 28, 30) sts along left side of neck, pm, k center st and mark it, pick up and k 24 (26, 28, 30 sts) along left side of neck, k 23 (25, 27, 29) sts of back neck. (72, 78, 84, 90 sts)

Pm between first and last st.

Work even in k1, p1 ribbing for 6 (6, 8, 8) rnds, dec for V-neck shaping on every even-numbered rnd as follows:

Dec rnd: Work to 1 st before center st, cdd, remark new st as center, work to end of row.

Bind off loosely in rib.

Armband

With RS facing using smaller circular needle join MC at end of underarm.

Pick up and k 74 (78, 86, 94) sts around armhole, and 16 sts along bound-off underarm sts. (90, 94, 102, 110 sts)

Pm between first and last st.

Work in k1, p1 ribbing for 6 (6, 8, 8) rnds.

Bind off. ✦

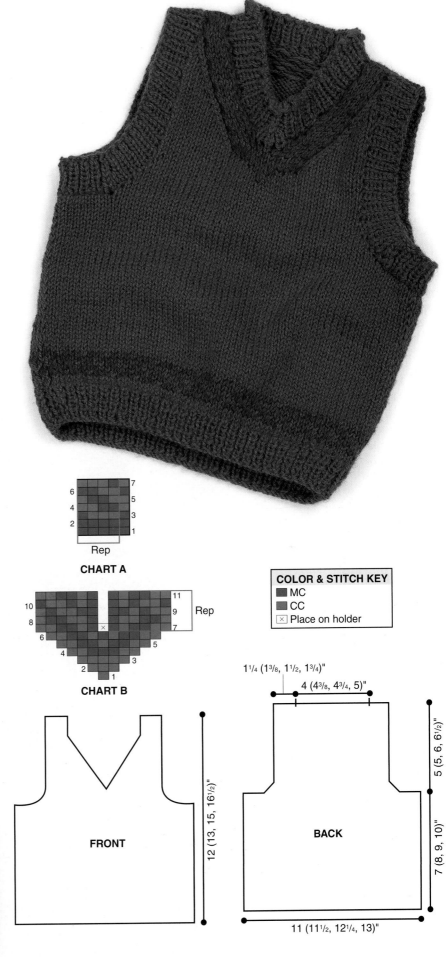

CHART A

CHART B

COLOR & STITCH KEY
- ■ MC
- ■ CC
- ☒ Place on holder

Rep

FRONT

BACK

12 (13, 15, 16½)"

1¼ (1³⁄₈, 1½, 1¾)"

4 (4³⁄₈, 4¾, 5)"

5 (5, 6, 6½)"

7 (8, 9, 10)"

11 (11½, 12¼, 13)"

Flower Power Vest

Design by Lois S. Young

Tiny flowers trim the edges of this vest. Faux pockets add a refined touch.

Skill Level
Intermediate***

Size
Child's 2 (4, 6, 8) Instructions are given for smallest size, with larger sizes in parentheses. When only 1 number is given, it applies to all sizes.

Finished Measurements
Chest: 23 (24½, 26, 27½) inches
Length: 13 (14½, 16, 17½) inches

Materials
* Plymouth Encore D.K. 75 percent acrylic/25 percent wool DK weight yarn (150 yds/50g per ball): 2 (2, 3, 4) balls dark red #9601 (MC) 1 ball royal #133 (CC)
* Size 4 (3.5 mm) 24-inch circular needle
* Size 5 (3.75mm) 24-inch circular needle or size needed to obtain gauge
* Stitch markers
* Stitch holders
* Tapestry needle

Gauge
23 sts and 31 rows = 4 inches/10cm in St st

To save time, take time to check gauge.

Pattern Stitch
Seed Stitch

Row 1 (RS): *K1, p1, rep from * across, ending with k1 if an odd number of sts in row.

Row 2: P the k sts and k the p sts.

Rep Rows 1–2 for pat.

Pattern Notes
Vest is worked in one piece with borders knit on as you go.

Wind separate balls or bobbins of CC for each front border and mock pocket.

For front edges, sl first st of each row purlwise if the last st of the preceding row was k; sl it knitwise if the last st was p.

Body
With smaller needle and MC, cast on 143 (151, 159, 167) sts.

Work even in Seed st for 6 rows. Change to larger needles.

Set up pat: Seed st over 6 sts, work Row 1 of Chart C to last 6 sts, Seed st over 6 sts.

Work in established pat through Row 9 of chart, then rep Rows 10–19 only for front borders.

Work even in established pats, until body measures 2 (3, 3¼, 4½, 4¾) inches, ending with a WS row.

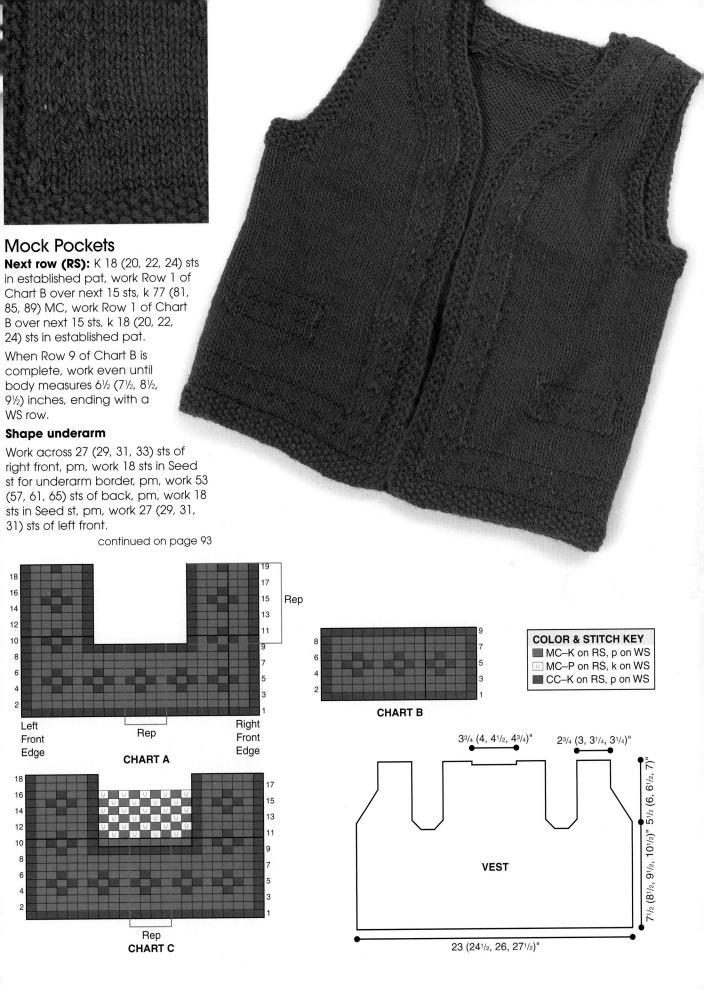

Mock Pockets

Next row (RS): K 18 (20, 22, 24) sts in established pat, work Row 1 of Chart B over next 15 sts, k 77 (81, 85, 89) MC, work Row 1 of Chart B over next 15 sts, k 18 (20, 22, 24) sts in established pat.

When Row 9 of Chart B is complete, work even until body measures 6½ (7½, 8½, 9½) inches, ending with a WS row.

Shape underarm

Work across 27 (29, 31, 33) sts of right front, pm, work 18 sts in Seed st for underarm border, pm, work 53 (57, 61, 65) sts of back, pm, work 18 sts in Seed st, pm, work 27 (29, 31, 31) sts of left front.

continued on page 93

CHART A

Left Front Edge — Rep — Right Front Edge

CHART B

CHART C

Rep

COLOR & STITCH KEY
- ■ MC–K on RS, p on WS
- Ⴟ MC–P on RS, k on WS
- ■ CC–K on RS, p on WS

VEST

3¾ (4, 4½, 4¾)" 2¾ (3, 3¼, 3¼)"

5½ (6, 6½, 7)"

7½ (8½, 9½, 10½)"

7½ (8½, 9½, 10½)"

23 (24½, 26, 27½)"

Dapple Gray Vest

Design by Kennita Tully

This classic vest, worked in a broken rib pattern, will make your child standout during any special occasion.

Skill Level
Beginner*

Size
Child's 2 (4, 6, 8) Instructions are given for smallest size, with larger sizes in parentheses. When only 1 number is given, it applies to all sizes.

Finished Measurements
Chest: 26 (28, 30, 32) inches
Length: 13 (14, 15, 16) inches

Materials
- Plymouth Encore Worsted 75 percent acrylic/25 percent wool worsted weight yarn (200 yds/100g per skein): 2 (2, 3, 4) skeins gray heather #153

- Size 4 (3.5mm) needles
- Size 5 (3.75) needles or size needed to obtain gauge
- Stitch holders
- Tapestry needle
- 4 (4, 5, 5) ¾-inch buttons

Gauge
18 sts and 28 rows = 4 inches/10cm in Broken Rib pat with larger needles

To save time, take time to check gauge.

Pattern Stitch
Broken Rib
Rows 1 (RS) and 2: Knit.
Row 3: P1, *k1, p1; rep from * across row.
Row 4: K1, *p1, k1; rep from * across row.
Rep Rows 1–4 for pat.

Pattern Note
Sweater is knit in one

piece to underarm, then divided for fronts and back.

Body
With smaller needles, cast on 119 (127, 135, 143) sts.

Knit 4 rows, changing to larger needles on last row.

Work even in Broken Rib Pat until body measures 7 (7½, 8, 8½) inches, ending with a WS row.

Divide for fronts & back
Next row (RS): Work across 27 (29, 31, 33) sts and sl to holder for right front, bind off 6 sts for underarm, knit across next 53 (57, 61, 65) sts for back, sl remaining 33 (35, 37, 39) sts to 2nd holder for left front.

Armhole shaping
Working on back sts only, [dec 1 st each end every other row] twice. (49, 53, 57, 61 sts)

Work even until armhole measures 6 (6½, 7, 7½) inches, ending with a WS row.

Shape shoulders
Bind off 4 (4, 5, 5) sts at beg of next 4 rows, then 4 (5, 4, 5) sts at beg of next 2 rows.

Bind off remaining 25 (27, 29, 31) back neck sts.

Left Front
Sl sts from 2nd holder to LH needle.

With RS facing, join yarn at back armhole.

Next row (RS): Bind off 6 sts, work to end of row.

[Dec 1 st at arm edge every other row] twice. (25, 27, 29, 31 sts)

Work even in established pat until armhole measures 4½ (5, 5½, 6) inches, ending with a RS row.

Shape front neck
Bind off 6 (7, 8, 9) sts at beg of next

Right Front

Sl sts from first holder to LH needle.

With WS facing, join yarn at underarm.

Work right front as for left, reversing shaping.

Sew shoulder seams.

Armband

Beg at underarm with smaller needles, pick up and k 67 (72, 77, 81) sts around entire armhole.

Knit 6 rows.

Bind off.

Right Front Band

With smaller needles, pick up and knit 58 (66, 70, 74) sts along right front edge.

Knit 8 rows.

Bind off.

Left Front Band

Mark band for 4 (4, 5, 5) buttonholes, evenly spaced.

With smaller needles, pick up and knit 58 (66, 70, 74) sts along left front edge.

Knit 3 rows.

Buttonhole row (RS): [K to marker, bind off next 3 sts] 4 (4, 5, 5) times, k to end of row.

Knit 4 more rows, casting on 3 sts over each buttonhole area on first row only.

Bind off.

Neck Band

With RS facing, join yarn at right front edge.

Pick up and k 23 (25, 27, 29) sts to right shoulder seam, 23 (25, 27, 29) sts along back neck and 23 (25, 27, 29) sts along left front from shoulder seam to edge. (69, 75, 81, 87 sts)

Knit 6 rows.

Bind off. ✦

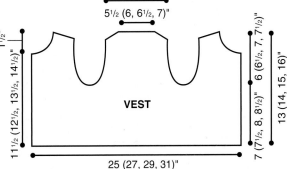

row, then [bind off 2 sts at neck edge] twice.

[Dec 1 st at neck edge every other row] 3 times. (12, 13, 14,15 sts)

Work even until armhole measures same as for back, ending with a WS row.

Shape shoulders

[Bind off 4 (4, 5, 5) sts at arm edge] twice, then bind off 4 (5, 4, 5) sts at same edge.

Flower Power Vest

continued from page 91

Work even for 5 more rows, keeping underarm sts in Seed st.

Divide for fronts & back

Next row (RS): Work across 31 (33, 35, 37) sts and sl to holder for right front, bind off 10 (10, 10, 12) sts for underarm, work 61 (65, 69, 71) sts and sl to 2nd holder for back, bind off 10 sts for underarm, work across remaining 31 (33, 35, 37) sts.

Left Front

Keeping front border in established pats, and 4 sts at armhole edge in Seed st, [dec 1 st in St st area inside armhole every other row] 3 times. (28, 30, 32, 34 sts)

[Dec 1 st inside color border at front edge every other row] 12 times.

(16, 18, 20, 22 sts)

Work even until armhole measures 5½ (6, 6½, 7) inches.

Bind off.

Right Front

Sl sts from holder to needle. With WS facing, join yarn at underarm. Work right front as for left front, reversing shaping.

Back

Sl sts from 2nd holder to needle. With WS facing, join yarn at underarm.

Keeping first and last 4 sts in Seed st, [dec 1 st each end inside Seed st border every other row] 3 times. (55, 59, 63, 65 sts)

Work even until back is 18 rows shorter than fronts, dec 2 (2, 2, 0) sts on last row. (53, 57, 61, 65 sts)

Shape shoulders

Next row (RS): Work across 5 (7, 9, 9) sts in established pat, work Row 1 of Chart C on next 43 (43, 43, 47) sts, work 5 (7, 9, 9) sts in established pat.

Work even in established pats through Row 16 of chart.

Next row: Work across 16 (18, 20, 20) sts, bind off 21 (21, 21, 25) sts for back neck, work to end of row.

Work 1 more row on left shoulder, bind off.

Attach yarn to WS of right shoulder, work 1 more row, bind off.

Sew shoulder seams. ✦

Rickrack Stripes

Designs Barbara Venishnick

The V-neck pullover in this set is made for the young man in your life. The crew-neck cardigan is made for the young lady. By changing the colors the reverse would work just as well.

Skill Level
Intermediate***

Size
Child's 2 (4, 6, 8) Instructions are given for smallest size, with larger sizes in parentheses. When only 1 number is given, it applies to all sizes.

Boy's Pullover

Finished Measurements
Chest: 24 (28, 32, 36) inches
Length: 14 (15, 16, 17) inches

Materials
- Plymouth Encore Worsted 75 percent acrylic/25 percent wool worsted weight yarn (200 yds/100g per ball): 1 ball each gray #194 (MC), gold #1014 (A), green #1232 (B), yellow #1382 (C), blue #515 (D)
- Size 5 (3.75mm) straight and 16-inch circular needles or size needed to obtain gauge
- Tapestry needle
- Crochet hook (optional)

Gauge
18 sts and 32 rows = 4 inches/10cm in Stripe pat

To save time, take time to check gauge.

Pattern Stitch
Rickrack Stripe (multiple of 4 sts + 1)

Set-up row (WS): With MC, purl.

Row 1: With A, k1, *sl 3 wyib, k1, rep from * across row.

Row 2: With A, p2, *sl 1 wyif, p3, rep from * across, end last rep sl 1, p2.

Row 3: With A, knit.

Row 4: With A, purl.

Rep Rows 1–4 for pat, using colors B, C and D in order.

Pattern Notes
Colors not in use may be carried up side of work. Take care to keep tension even.

Neck decs and sleeve incs are best worked on Row 3 of pat.

When joining pieces, crochet hook may be used to pick up sts through both layers. Place each loop as it is made onto knitting needle.

Back
With MC, cast on 57 (65, 73, 81) sts.

Work in garter st for 7 rows.

Work even in Rickrack Stripe pat until back measures 7½ (8, 8½, 9) inches.

Mark each end st of last row for underarm.

Continue to work even until back measures 13 (14, 15, 16) inches, ending with a WS row.

Shape shoulders
Bind off 4 (5, 6, 7) sts at beg of next 6 (6, 6, 4) rows, then 5 (5, 5, 6) sts at beg of next 2 (2, 2, 4) rows.

Place remaining 23 (25, 27, 29) sts on holder for back neck.

Front
Work as for back until front measures 8½ inches, ending with a WS row.

about every 3rd row on body for correct fit.

Work as for shoulder trim, and sew in place on sleeve side of seam.

Neck Band

With RS facing, using MC and circular needle, pick up and k 38 (40, 42, 44) sts along right side of neck, knit 23 (25, 27, 29) sts of back neck, pick up and k 38 (40, 42, 44) sts along left side of neck. (99, 105, 111, 117 sts)

Next row: Knit.

Dec row: Knit, working k3tog at each end of back neck.

[Rep last 2 rows] twice. (87, 93, 99, 105 sts)

Bind off all sts knitwise.

Overlap ends of neck trim at bottom of neck and sew in place.

Finishing

Sew sleeve and underarm seams.

Girl's Cardigan

Materials

- Plymouth Encore Worsted 75 percent acrylic/25 percent wool worsted weight yarn (200 yds/100g per ball): 1 ball each gray #194 (MC), gold #1014 (A), green #1232 (B), yellow #1382 (C), lavender #1033 (D)
- Size 5 (3.75mm) straight and 16-inch circular needles or size needed to obtain gauge
- 6 (¾-inch) buttons
- Tapestry needle
- Crochet hook (optional)

Back

Work as for boy's pullover.

Right Front

With MC cast on 26 (30, 34, 38) sts.

Work in garter st for 7 rows

Work even in Rickrack Stripe pat, keeping 1 st in St st at beg of all RS rows and end of all WS rows.

Mark underarm as for back.

Work even until front measures 11 (12, 13, 14) inches, ending with a WS row.

16, 16) times. (57, 59, 65, 69 sts)

Work even until sleeve measures 7½ (8½, 9½, 10½) inches.

Bind off loosely.

Shoulder Trim & Join

Place back and front tog, with RS facing out.

With front facing using MC, pick up and k 1 st in each bound-off left shoulder st through both layers of front and back. (17, 20, 23, 26 sts) Purl 1 row, knit 1 row, purl 1 row.

Bind off all sts loosely.

Allow trim to roll over shoulder seam. Sew trim in place, stitching purl bumps of picked-up row to outside edge of bound-off row.

Rep for right shoulder.

Sleeve Trim & Join

Place sleeve and body tog, with RS facing out.

Holding work with body facing, with MC pick up and k 1 st in each bound-off sleeve st and in body sts. **Note:** It will be necessary to skip

---

Divide for neck

Work across 28 (32, 36, 40) sts, join 2nd ball of yarn and bind off center st, work to end of row.

Working on both sides of neck in established pat with separate balls of yarn, [dec 1 st each side of neck every 4th row] 11 (12, 13, 14) times. (17, 20, 23, 26 sts)

Work even until armhole measures same as for back.

Shape shoulders as for back.

Sleeves

With MC, cast on 29 (29, 33, 37) sts.

Work in garter st for 7 rows.

Working in Rickrack Stripe pat, [inc 1 st each end every 4th row] 14 (15,

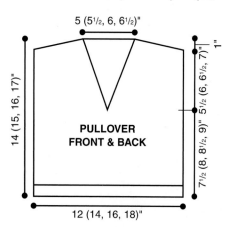

5 (5½, 6, 6½)"

1"

PULLOVER FRONT & BACK

14 (15, 16, 17)"

7½ (8, 8½, 9)"

5½ (6, 6½, 7)"

12 (14, 16, 18)"

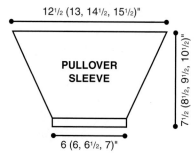

12½ (13, 14½, 15½)"

PULLOVER SLEEVE

7½ (8½, 9½, 10½)"

6 (6, 6½, 7)"

Shape neck

Next row (RS): Work across 4 (5, 6, 7) sts and place on holder for front neck, work to end of row. (22, 25, 28, 31 sts)

[Dec 1 st at neck edge every RS row] 5 times. (17, 20, 23, 26 sts)

Work shoulder shaping as for back, binding off at beg of every WS row.

Left Front

Work as for right front, reversing shaping.

Sleeves

Work as for boy's pullover.

Work shoulder and sleeve trims and join as for boy's pullover.

Neck Band

With RS facing using MC, beg at right front neck k 4 (5, 6, 7) sts from holder, pick up and k 16 sts along

right side of neck, k 23 (25, 27, 29) sts of back neck, pick up and k 16 sts along left side of neck, k 4 (5, 6, 7) sts from holder. (63, 67, 71, 75 sts)

Knit 1 row.

Next row: Knit, working k2tog at beg of neck shaping and at each shoulder seam. (59, 63, 67, 71 sts)

Knit 4 rows.

Bind off knitwise.

Button Band

With RS facing using MC, pick up and k 50 (55, 60, 65) sts along left front edge, including neck and bottom bands.

Knit 6 rows.

Bind off knitwise.

Buttonhole Band

Work as for button band, knitting 2 rows after picked-up row.

Mark band for 6 buttons evenly spaced.

Buttonhole row: [K to marker, bring yarn forward between needles and drop it. Sl 2 sts purl-wise from LH to RH needle, pass first st over 2nd, sl next st from LH to RH needle and pass 2nd st over this 3rd st, return 3rd st to LH needle. Turn work and cable cast on 2 sts, bring yarn to front between sts, cable cast on 1 st,

turn] 6 times, k to end of row.

Knit 3 rows.

Bind off knitwise.

Finishing

Sew sleeve and side seams. Sew on buttons. ✦

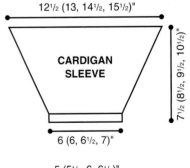

CARDIGAN RIGHT FRONT

3"

6 (7, 8, 9)"

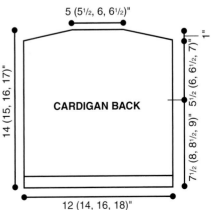

12½ (13, 14½, 15½)"

CARDIGAN SLEEVE

7½ (8½, 9½, 10½)"

6 (6, 6½, 7)"

5 (5½, 6, 6½)"

CARDIGAN BACK

14 (15, 16, 17)"

1"

5½ (6, 6½, 7)"

7½ (8, 8½, 9)"

12 (14, 16, 18)"

Jellybean Tee

Design by Barbara Venishnick

Jellybeans and colorful hearts enhance a playful summer top.

Skill Level

Intermediate***

Size

Girl's 2 (4, 6, 8) Instructions are given for smallest size, with larger sizes in parentheses. When only 1 number is given, it applies to all sizes.

Finished Measurements

Chest: 24 (26, 28, 30) inches
Length: 12 (13, 14, 15) inches

Materials

- Plymouth Wildflower D.K. 51 percent cotton/49 percent acrylic DK weight yarn (137 yds/50g per ball): 2 (2, 3, 3) balls turquoise #55 (MC), 1 ball each yellow #48 (A), hot pink #59 (B), lime #58 (C), purple #45 (D)
- Size 4 (3.5mm) needles
- Size 5 (3.75) needles or size needed to obtain gauge
- Bobbins
- Stitch markers
- Stitch holder

Gauge

20 sts and 42 rows = 4 inches/10cm in Jelly Bean pat with larger needles

22 sts and 32 rows = 4 inches/10cm in St st with larger needles

To save time, take time to check gauge.

Special Abbreviations

K1BL (knit 1 below): Drop next st off needle and unravel 4 rows down, insert RH needle from front into MC st in 5th row below and knit it

SUMMER TOPS

catching all dropped strands in this st.

M1 (Make 1): Inc by lifting running thread between needles and placing on LH needle, k new st tbl.

K5tog: Sl 3 sts wyib to RH needle, *pass 2nd st on RH needle over first (center) st, sl center st back to LH needle and pass 2nd st on LH needle over it,* sl center st back to RH needle, rep from * to *. Center sts will remain, k this st.

Pattern Stitches

A. Embossed Hearts Panel of 15 sts (Increases to 21 sts at widest part of heart)

Row 1 (RS): P7 MC, k1 A, p7 MC.

Row 2: K7 MC, p1 A, k7 MC.

Row 3: P7 MC, with A (M1, k1, M1), p7 MC.

Row 4: K7 MC, p3 A, k7 MC.

Row 5: P6 MC, with A (k2tog, M1, k1, M1, ssk), p6 MC.

Row 6: K6 MC, p5 A, k6 MC.

Row 7: P5 MC, with A (k2tog, [k1, M1] twice, k1, ssk), p5 MC.

Row 8: K5 MC, p7 A, k5 MC.

Row 9: P4 MC, with A (k2tog, k2, M1, k1, M1, k2, ssk), p4 MC.

Row 10: K4 MC, p9 A, k4 MC.

Row 11: P4 MC, with A (k4, M1, k1, M1, k4), p4 MC.

Row 12: K4 MC, p5 A, k1 MC, p5 A, k4 MC.

Row 13: P4 MC, k5 A, with MC [k1, yo, k1] in next st, k5 A, p4 MC.

Row 14: K4 MC, p5 A, k3 MC, p5 A, k4 MC.

Row 15: P4 MC, k5tog A, with MC (p in front and back of next st, p1, p in front and back of next st), k5tog A, p4 MC.

Row 16: P15 MC.

Rep Rows 1–16 for pat.

B. Jellybean Pattern (Multiple of 4 sts + 3)

Rows 1 and 3 (RS): With A, knit.

Rows 2 and 4: With A, purl.

Row 5: With MC, k3 *K1BL, k3, rep from * across.

Row 6: With MC, purl.

Rows 7 and 9: With B, knit.

Rows 8 and 10: With B, purl.

Row 11: With MC, k1 *K1BL, k3, rep from * across, end last rep K1BL, k1.

Row 12: With MC, purl.

Rows 13–16: With C, rep Rows 1–4.

Rows 17 and 18: Rep Rows 5 and 6.

Rows 19–22: With D, rep Rows 7–10.

Rows 23 and 24: Rep Rows 11 and 12.

Rep Rows 1–24 for pat.

Pattern Notes

Embossed hearts are worked using intarsia technique. Wind a separate bobbin for each area of color. To avoid holes when changing colors, always bring new color up over old.

Color sequence for hearts: D, C, B, A.

Left Front

With larger needles and MC, cast on 21 (21, 24, 27) sts.

Plain Row 1 (RS): K4 (4, 7, 10), pm, p15, pm, k2.

Plain Row 2: P2, k15, p4 (4, 7, 10).

[Rep Rows 1 and 2] 1 (1, 0, 0) times more.

Continue in established pat, working 16 rows of Embossed Heart pat between markers, and [rep Plain Rows 1 and 2] 1 (2, 1, 2) times between each heart.

Work hearts in color sequence of D, C, B, A until 5 (5, 6, 6) hearts are complete. *At the same time* when front measures 6¾ (7¾, 7¾, 8¾) inches, begin sleeve shaping.

Begin left sleeve

Next row: Cable cast on 4 sts at beg of row, turn, k new sts, work to end of row.

Rep cast-on row at beg of next 3 RS rows. (37, 37, 40, 43 sts)

When the last heart is complete, work

Plain Rows 1 and 2.

Place all sts on holder.

Left Back

With larger needles and MC, cast on 21 (21, 24, 27) sts.

Plain Row 1: K2, pm, p15, pm, k4 (4, 7, 10).

Plain Row 2: P4 (4, 7, 10), k15, p2.

Work as for left front panel, reversing shaping by working cable cast on for sleeve at beg of WS rows and purling new sts.

Join Front and Back panels by using 3-needle bind-off method.

Sleeve Trim

With RS facing using smaller needles and MC, pick up and k 52 (52, 68, 68) sts along sleeve edge.

Knit 1 row.

Working in garter st, knit 2 rows A, 2 rows B, 2 rows C, 1 row D.

With D, bind off knitwise.

Garter Stitch Panel

With RS facing using smaller needles and MC, pick up and k 144 (156, 168, 180) sts evenly along long straight edge of combined heart panels.

Knit 1 row.

Knit 2 rows each of A, B and C. Knit 1 row D.

Next row (WS): K 60 (66, 72, 78) sts for back and place on holder, bind off next 36 sts for left side of neck, k remaining 48 (56, 60, 66) sts for front.

Right Front

Change to larger needles and MC.

Knit 1 row.

Next row (WS): Purl, dec 5 (9, 9, 11) sts evenly. (43, 47, 51, 55 sts)

Work Rows 1–24 of Jellybean pat.

Size 2 only: Rep Rows 1–16.

Sizes 4 and 6 only: Rep Rows 1–22.

Size 8 only: Rep rows 1–24.

Place all sts on holder, do not cut yarn.

Right Back

Sl back sts from holder to larger needle.

Join MC and knit 1 row.

Next row: Purl, dec 9 (11, 9, 11) sts evenly. (51, 55, 63, 67 sts)

Beg Jellybean pat and work same number of rows as for front.

Join front and back

Next row (RS): With MC, k 51 (55, 63, 67) sts of back, sl front sts from front holder to LH needle. Using yarn from front, cable cast on 26 sts for right side of neck, drop this ball of yarn and continue with yarn attached to back.

Knit cast-on sts, k 43 (47, 51, 55) front sts. (119, 127, 139, 147 sts)

Purl 1 row.

Continue in Jellybean pat as established until right shoulder measures 3½ (3½, 4, 4½) inches above cast-on sts, ending with a RS row in MC.

Right Sleeve

Next row (WS): Bind off 34 (38, 38, 42) sts, p 51 (51, 63, 63) sts for sleeve, bind off remaining 34 (38, 38, 42) sts.

Continue in established pat on sleeve for 8 rows.

Dec 1 st each end on next row, then [dec 1 st each end every 12th row] twice. (45, 45, 57, 57 sts)

Work even for 3 rows, ending with a RS row in MC.

Sleeve trim

Change to MC and smaller needles.

Knit 1 row, inc 7 (7, 11, 11) sts evenly. (52, 52, 68, 68 sts)

Work as for left sleeve trim.

Neck Trim—Right Edge

With RS facing using smaller needles and MC, pick up and k 36 sts along right side of neck opening.

Knit 1 row.

Complete as for sleeve trim.

Sew short ends of trim to back and front edges of neck.

Neck Trim—Back

With smaller needles and MC, pick up and k 23 (26, 26, 29) sts along edge of back neck between each side neck trim.

Complete as for side neck trim.

Neck Trim—Front

Work as for back neck.

Bottom Band

Sew 1 sleeve and side seam.

With RS facing using smaller needle and MC, pick up and k 146 (158, 170, 182) sts evenly along bottom edge.

Knit 1 row.

Complete trim as for sleeve.

Sew remaining sleeve and side seam. ✦

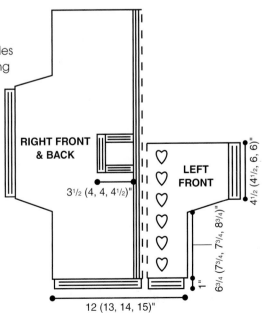

RIGHT FRONT & BACK

LEFT FRONT

3½ (4, 4, 4½)"

4½ (4½, 6, 6)"

6¾ (7¾, 7¾, 8¾)"

1"

12 (13, 14, 15)"

Sunflower Top

Design by Cindy Polfer

A bright sunflower adorns the front of this cool summer top.

Skill Level

Intermediate***

Size

Girl's 2 (4, 6, 8) Instructions are given for smallest size, with larger sizes in parentheses. When only 1 number is given, it applies to all sizes.

Finished Measurements

Chest: 24 (26, 28, 30) inches

Hemline circumference: 26 (28, 30, 32) inches

Length to underarm: 6¼ (6¾, 7¼, 8¾) inches

Armhole depth: 5¼ (5¾, 6¼, 6¾) inches

Materials

• Plymouth Wildflower D.K. 51 percent cotton/49 percent acrylic DK weight yarn (137 yds/ 50g per ball): 2 balls hot pink #59 (MC), 1 ball yellow #48 (C)

• Plymouth Wildflower Fancy D.K. 43 percent cotton/53 percent acrylic/4 percent nylon DK weight yarn (116 yds/50g per ball): 1 ball each hot pink #859 (A), black #847 (B)

• Size 4 (3.5mm) needles

• Size 5 (3.75mm) needles or size needed to obtain gauge

• Tapestry needle

• 2 (⁷⁄₁₆-inch) buttons

Gauge

23 sts and 33 rows = 4 inches/10cm in St st with larger size needles and MC

To save time, take time to check gauge.

Pattern Stitch

Border

Rows 1–3: With A, knit.

Row 4: With B, knit.

Row 5: With B, p1, *yo, p2tog, p1, rep from * across row.

Rows 6–9: With A, knit.

Pattern Notes

Front and back are made alike.

Row 2 and all even-numbered rows of Border pat are RS rows.

Sunflower appliqué is knit separately and sewn to front.

Eyelets in the pat st of strap form buttonhole closure. Straps are adjustable.

Back

With A and smaller needles, cast on 75 (81, 87, 93) sts.

Work Rows 1–9 of Border pat.

Change to MC and larger needles.

Beg with a k row, work in St st [dec 1 st each side every 10 (12, 12, 14) rows] 3 times. (69, 75, 81, 87 sts)

Work even until back measures 6¼ (6¾, 7¼, 8¾) inches, ending with a WS row.

Shape armhole

Bind off 7 sts at beg of next 2 rows. (55, 61, 67, 73 sts)

[Dec 1 st each end every row] 10 (12, 14, 16) times. (35, 37, 39, 41 sts)

Work even until back measures

8¼ (9¼, 10, 12) inches, ending with a RS row.

Top Border
Change to A and smaller needles.

Knit 4 rows.

Bind off firmly.

Front
Work as for back.

Shoulder Straps
Make 2

With A and smaller size needles, cast on 35 (35, 39, 39) sts.

Work Rows 1–9 of Border pat.

Bind off all sts knitwise.

Sunflower Appliqué
Petals
With larger needles and C, cast on 3 sts.

Row 1 (RS): Yo, k1, yo, k2tog. (4 sts)

Rows 2, 4, 6, 8 and 10: Knit.

Row 3: Yo, k2, yo, k2tog. (5 sts)

Row 5: Yo, k3, yo, k2tog. (6 sts)

Row 7: Yo, k4, yo, k2tog. (7 sts)

Row 9: Yo, k5, yo, k2tog. (8 sts)

Row 11: Yo, k2tog, [yo, k1] 4 times, yo, k2tog. (12 sts)

Row 12: Bind off 9 sts, k3. (3 sts)

[Rep Rows 1–12] 6 more times.

Bind off all sts. (7 petals)

Center
With RS facing, using B and smaller needles, pick up and k 1 st in each yo loop along straight edge. (43 sts)

Row 1: Knit.

Row 2: [K4, k2tog] 7 times, k1. (36 sts)

Row 3: K1, [yo, k2tog] 17 times, k1. (36 sts)

Row 4: [K3, k2tog] 7 times, k1. (29 sts)

Row 5: K1, [yo, k2tog] 14 times. (29 sts)

Row 6: [K2, k2tog] 7 times, k1. (22 sts)

Row 7: K1, [yo, k2tog] 10 times, k1. (22 sts)

Row 8: [K1, k2tog] 7 times, k1. (15 sts)

Row 11: [K1, k2tog] 7 times. (8 sts)

Cut yarn leaving a 12-inch end.

Thread tapestry needle and pull yarn through sts to form circle, removing sts from knitting needle.

Sew edges tog to form circular-shaped flower.

Block flower to shape.

Finishing
Sew flower to desired place on front of top, tacking center, outer edge of center and outer edges of petals to front.

Sew side seams.

Armhole Edging
With RS facing using A and smaller needles, pick up and k 52 (56, 60, 64) sts along entire armhole edge.

Knit 4 rows.

Bind off firmly.

Sew a short edge of each strap to back top border at each armhole edge aligning edges.

On front, sew buttons to front at top armhole edge.

Use eyelets of strap for buttonholes, adjusting strap to desired length. ✦

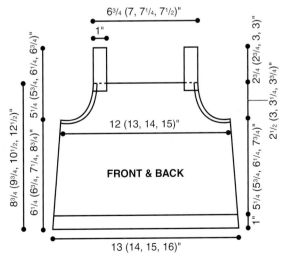

Sunny Fun Top

Design by Joan McGowan-Michael

An oversize sunflower grows on the front of this summery top.

Skill Level
Intermediate***

Size
Child's 2 (4, 6, 8) Instructions are given for smallest size, with larger sizes in parentheses. When only 1 number is given, it applies to all sizes.

Finished Measurements
Chest: 24 (26, 28, 30) inches

Length (shoulder to hem): 14 (15, 19, 20) inches

Materials
- Plymouth Wildflower D.K. 51 percent cotton/49 percent acrylic DK weight yarn (137 yds/50g per ball): 2 (3, 3, 4) balls pink #54
- Size 6 (4mm) needles or size needed to obtain gauge
- Cable needle
- Stitch markers
- 2 (½-inch) buttons
- Tapestry needle
- Sewing needle and matching thread

Gauge
20 sts and 28 rows = 4 inches/10cm in St st

To save time, take time to check gauge.

Special Abbreviations
M1 (Make 1): Make a backwards loop and place on RH needle.

Bobble: Knit into front, back and front of next st, turn, k3, turn, p3, turn, k3, turn, sl 1, k2tog, psso.

Dec 5 sts into 1: Drop working yarn to front of work. Sl 3 to RH needle, *pass 2nd st on RH needle over first (center) st, sl center st back to LH needle and pass 2nd st of LH needle over it *, sl center st back to RH needle again, rep from * to * once more, leaving center st on LH needle. Pick up dropped yarn and p remaining center st.

C3R (Cable 3 Right): Sl 1 to cn and hold in back, k2, p1 from cn.

C3L (Cable 3 Left): Sl 2 to cn and hold in front, p1, k2 from cn.

C4R (Cable 4 Right): Sl 2 to cn and hold in back, k2, p2 from cn.

C4L (Cable 4 Left): Sl 2 to cn and hold in front, p2, k2 from cn.

Pattern Notes
Garment will stretch slightly in length when worn.

Front panel is worked first. Sides and back are picked up along panel edges and worked outwards.

Front Panel
Cast on 26 sts.

Beg with a WS row and referring to chart, [work Rows 1–24] once (once, twice, twice). Work through Row 70.

Work in garter st for 4 rows.

Bind off.

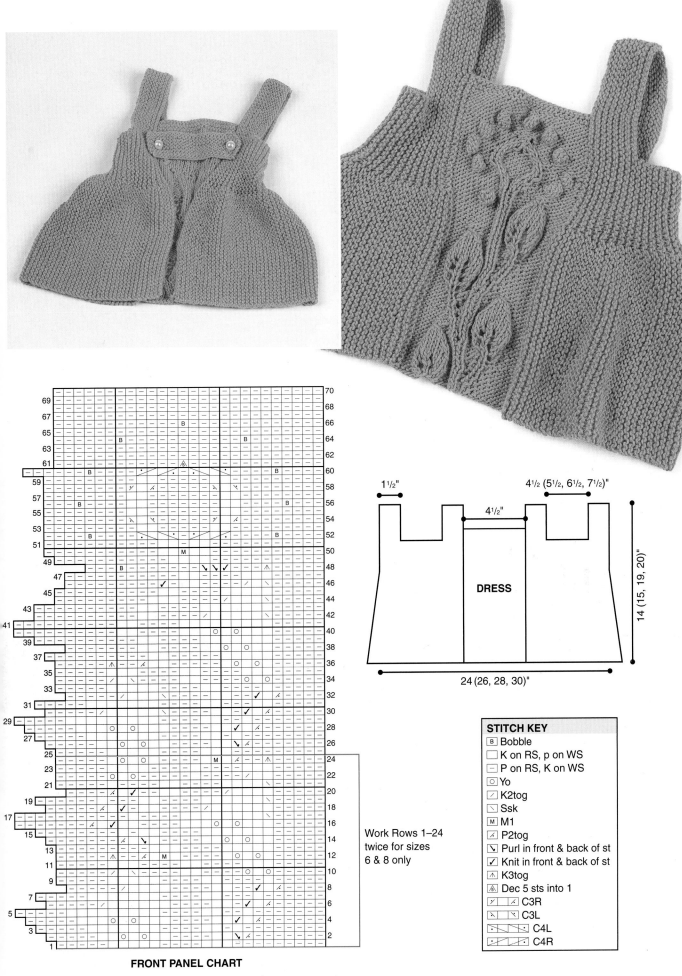

STITCH KEY

B	Bobble
☐	K on RS, p on WS
–	P on RS, K on WS
○	Yo
⟋	K2tog
⟍	Ssk
M	M1
⟋	P2tog
⟍	Purl in front & back of st
✓	Knit in front & back of st
⋀	K3tog
⏁	Dec 5 sts into 1
↗ ↖	C3R
↘ ↙	C3L
	C4L
	C4R

FRONT PANEL CHART

Work Rows 1–24 twice for sizes 6 & 8 only

DRESS

1½"   4½ (5½, 6½, 7½)"   4½"

14 (15, 19, 20)"

24 (26, 28, 30)"

Left Side & Back

Beg at bottom of panel with RS facing, pick up and k 52 (52, 70, 70) sts evenly along left edge, cast on 10 (14, 16, 18) sts for strap. (62, 66, 86, 88 sts)

Knit one row. Work in garter st from this point.

Next row (RS): K 32 (32, 50, 50) sts, pm, k to end of row.

Knit 1 row.

Short row: K 31 (31, 49, 49) sts, sl 1, bring yarn from back to front between next 2 sts, turn, knit to end of row.

Rep last 2 rows until 16 full rows have been worked.

Shape armhole

Bind off 16 (20, 22, 24) sts at shoulder.

Continue to work even until armhole measures 4½ (5½, 6½, 7½) inches, ending with a full row.

Cast on 16 (20, 22, 24) sts for back shoulder strap and work even for 16 rows. Bind off.

Right Side & Back

Work as for left side and back, reversing all shaping.

Buttonhole Tab

Cast on 25 sts.

Work in garter st for 8 rows.

Buttonhole row: K4, yo, k2tog, k14, k2tog, yo, k4.

Work in garter st for 8 more rows.

Bind off.

Finishing

Sew shoulder seams.

Sew buttons to back along edges, approximately ½ inch below bottom of armhole. Button tab to back just slightly above armhole. ◆

Summer Simplicity Tunic

Design by Laura Polley

This cute-as-a-button tunic top is the perfect easy project for a young or novice knitter!

Skill Level

Easy**

Size

Child's 2 (4, 6, 8) Instructions are given for smallest size, with larger sizes in parentheses. When only 1 number is given, it applies to all sizes.

Finished Measurements

Chest: 22 (24, 26, 28) inches

Length: 15 (17, 19, 20½) inches

Materials

- Plymouth Wildflower D.K. 51 percent cotton/49 percent acrylic DK weight yarn, (137 yds/50g per ball): 4 (4, 5, 5) balls lime green #58
- Size 5 (3.75mm) needles
- Size 6 (4mm) needles or size needed to obtain gauge
- Tapestry needle
- 30 (32, 34, 36) assorted coordinating buttons in various sizes, colors, shapes and styles

Gauge

22 sts and 31 rows = 4 inches/10cm in St st with larger needles

To save time, take time to check gauge.

Pattern Note

Tunic is worked in one piece, from lower edge of front to shoulder, then down back piece to lower edge.

102

Tunic

Beg at lower front edge with smaller needles, cast on 60 (66, 72, 78) sts.

Work even in garter st until front measures 4 (4½, 5, 5½) inches, ending with a WS row.

Record number of garter st rows as A. Change to larger needles.

Work in St st until front measures 9½ (10½, 11½, 12½) inches, ending with a WS row.

Record number of St st rows as B. Change to smaller needles.

Work in garter st for 1 (1½, 2, 2) inches more, end with a WS row.

Record number of garter-st rows as C.

Armhole shaping

Bind off 6 (7, 9, 11) sts at beg of next 2 rows. (48, 52, 54, 56 sts)

Next row (RS): K2, ssk, k to last 4 sts, k2tog, k2. (46, 50, 52, 54 sts)

Knit 1 row.

[Rep last 2 rows] 3 times more. (40, 44, 46, 48 sts)

Mark each end st for end of armhole.

Work even in garter st until front measures 12½ (14½, 16, 17½) inches, ending with a WS row.

Neck shaping

Next row (RS): K 10 (11, 11, 12) sts, join 2nd ball of yarn and bind off center 20 (22, 24, 24) sts for front neck, k remaining 10 (11, 11, 12) sts.

Working on both sides of neck with separate balls of yarn, work even in garter st until front measures 15 (17, 19, 20½) inches from beg, end with a WS row.

Do not cut yarns.

Mark ends of last row worked for shoulder.

Back

Working both sides at same time with separate balls of yarn as before, continue in garter st until back measures 2 (2, 2½, 2½) inches from shoulder markers, end with a WS row.

Shape neck

K10 (11, 11, 12) sts, with same ball of yarn, cast on 20 (22, 24, 24) sts, cut 2nd ball of yarn, k 10 (11, 11, 12) sts. (40, 44, 46, 48 sts)

Work even in garter st until back measures same as front from marked shoulder row to marked armhole row, end with a WS row.

Shape armhole

Next row (RS): K1, k into front and back of next st, k to last 3 sts, k into front and back of next st, k2. (42, 46, 48, 50 sts)

Knit 1 row.

[Rep last 2 rows] twice more, then rep first row. (48, 52, 54, 56 sts)

Cast on 6 (7, 9, 11) sts at beg of next 2 rows for underarms. (60, 66, 72, 78 sts)

Work even in garter st for 1 (1½, 2, 2) inches more, having same number of recorded C rows as for front and ending with a WS row.

Change to larger needles.

Work even in St st until back measures 11 (12½, 14, 15) inches from shoulder row, having same number of recorded B rows as for front.

Change to smaller needles.

Work even in garter st for 4 (4½, 5, 5½) inches, having same number of recorded A rows as for front.

Back should measure 15 (17, 19, 20½) inches from shoulder row.

Bind off loosely.

Finishing

Fold tunic in half at marked shoulder row.

Sew side seams, leaving 3½ (4, 4½, 5) inches free at lower edge for side slits.

Referring to photo for placement, sew 9 buttons evenly spaced around front neckline.

Sew 9 buttons around back neckline as for front.

Sew 1 button to each side seam just above side slit.

Sew remaining buttons evenly spaced along top of garter-st section between side seam buttons. ✦

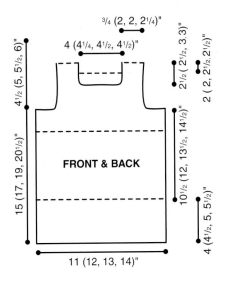

Meadow of Wildflowers

Design by Kennita Tully

The soft, pastel colors of spring wildflowers sprout on a child's pullover through the three-color basket tweed pattern.

Skill Level
Easy**

Size
Child's 2 (4, 6, 8) Instructions are given for smallest size, with larger sizes in parentheses. When only 1 number is given, it applies to all sizes.

Finished Measurements
Chest: 30 (31, 32, 34) inches

Length: 13½ (14½, 15½, 17½) inches

Materials
- Plymouth Wildflower D.K. 51 percent cotton/49 percent acrylic DK weight yarn (137 yds/50g per ball): 3 (4, 4, 5) balls sage #35 (A), 1 (2, 2, 2) balls plum #32 (B), khaki #31 (C)
- Size 4 (3.5mm) straight and 16-inch circular needle
- Size 6 (4.25mm) needles or size needed to obtain gauge
- Stitch markers

Gauge
24 sts and 44 rows = 4 inches/10cm in Basket Tweed pat with larger needles

To save time, take time to check gauge.

Pattern Stitch
Three-Color Basket Tweed
(Multiple of 4 sts + 1)

Row 1 (RS): With B, k1, *k3, sl 1 wyib; rep from * across, end last rep k4.

Row 2: With B, k1, *k3, sl 1 wyif; rep from * across, end last rep k4.

Row 3: With A, k2, *sl 1 wyib, k3; rep from * across, end last rep sl 1, k2.

Row 4: With A, p2, *sl 1 wyif, p3; rep from * across, end last rep sl 1, p2.

Rows 5 and 6: With C, rep Rows 1 and 2.

Rows 7 and 8: With A, rep Rows 3 and 4.

Rep Rows 1–8 for pat.

Pattern Notes
Edges of this design roll naturally.

Length measurements are taken with edges unrolled.

Back
With smaller needles and A, cast on 89 (93, 97, 101) sts.

Work in St st for 6 rows.

Change to larger needles and Basket Tweed pat.

Work even for 8½ (8½, 8½, 9½) inches, ending with a WS row.

Shape armhole

Bind off 10 sts at beg of next 2 rows. (69, 73, 77, 81 sts)

Work even until armhole measures approximately 5 (6, 7, 8) inches, ending with Row 4 or 8 of pat.

Bind off all sts.

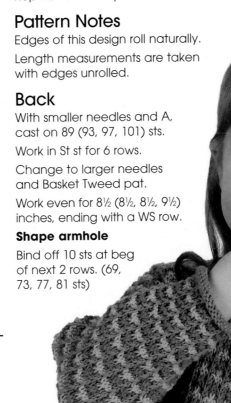

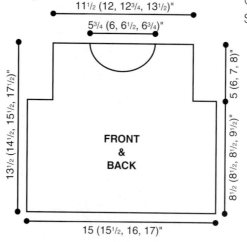

Mark 17 (18, 19, 20) sts at each end for shoulders.

Front

Work as for back until armhole measures 2 (3, 4, 5) inches, ending with a WS row.

Shape neck

Work across 29 (30, 31, 32) sts, attach 2nd ball of yarn and bind off center 11 (13, 15, 17) sts for front neck, work to end of row.

Working both sides simultaneously with separate balls of yarn, [bind off 2 sts at each neck edge] twice.

[Dec 1 st at each neck edge every other row] 4 times, then [every 4th row] 4 times. (17, 18, 19, 20 sts each side of neck)

Work even until armhole measures same as for back.

Bind off.

Sleeves

With smaller needles and A, cast on 33 (37, 41, 45) sts.

Work in St st for 6 rows.

Change to larger needles and Basket Weave pat.

Inc 1 st each end of 5th (5th, 3rd, 3rd) row.

[Inc 1 st each end every 6th (6th, 4th, 4th) row] 1 (4, 5, 1) times, then [every 8th (8th, 6th, 6th) rows 12 (13, 16, 24) times. (61, 73, 85, 97 sts)

Work even until sleeve measures 9¾ (12¼, 13¼, 13¾) inches.

Mark each end st for underarm.

Work even for approximately 1¾ inches more, ending with row 4 or 8 of pat.

Bind off all sts.

Sew shoulder seams.

Collar

With smaller circular needles and A, pick up and k 33 (35, 37, 39) sts across back neck and 70 (72, 74, 76) sts along front neck. (103, 107, 111, 115 sts)

Join, pm between first and last st.

Work in St st for 10 rows.

Bind off all sts loosely.

Finishing

Sew sleeves into armholes, matching underarm markers to first bound-off st of underarm.

Sew sleeve and side seams. ✦

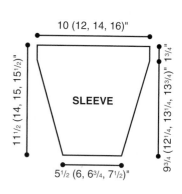

11½ (12, 12¾, 13½)"

5¾ (6, 6½, 6¾)"

13½ (14½, 15½, 17½)"

5 (6, 7, 8)"

FRONT & BACK

8½ (8½, 8½, 9½)"

15 (15½, 16, 17)"

10 (12, 14, 16)"

11½ (14, 15, 15½)"

1¾"

SLEEVE

9¾ (12¼, 13¼, 13¾)"

5½ (6, 6¾, 7½)"

Textured Fair Isle Pullover

Design by Celeste Pinheiro

Bright colors and subtle texture combine in an updated Fair Isle pullover for kids.

Skill Level

Intermediate***

Size

Child's 2 (4, 6, 8) Instructions are given for smallest size, with larger sizes in parentheses. When only 1 number is given, it applies to all sizes.

Finished Measurements

Chest: 26 (29, 32, 35) inches
Length: 14 (15, 16, 17) inches

Materials

- Plymouth Encore D.K. 75 percent acrylic/25 percent wool DK weight yarn (150 yds/50g per ball): 4 (5, 5, 6) balls pink #1385 (MC), 1 ball each orange #1383 (A), yellow #1382 (B), royal blue #133 (C)
- Size 4 (3.5mm) straight and double-pointed needles
- Size 5 (3.75mm) needles or size needed to obtain gauge
- Stitch markers

Gauge

22 sts and 29 rows = 4 inches/10cm in Fair Isle pat with larger needles

To save time, take time to check gauge.

Pattern Stitch

Eyelet Band

Rows 1 (RS) and 2: Knit.

Row 3: *K2 tog, yo, rep from * across.

Rows 4 and 5: Knit.

Pattern Notes

Edges roll naturally in this design.

Length measurements are taken with edges unrolled.

Back

With smaller needles and MC, cast on 72 (80, 88, 96) sts.

Work in St st for 9 rows.

Next row (RS):

Change to B and work 5 rows of Eyelet Band.

Change to larger needles and work 9 rows of Chart A.

Change to smaller needles and work 5 rows of Eyelet Band.

Change to larger needles and work 23 rows of Chart B.

Work even in texture pat of Chart C until back measures 13½ (14½, 15½, 16½) inches, ending with a WS row.

Back neck shaping

Next row (RS):

Work established pat across 23 (26, 28, 30) sts, join 2nd

CHART A

ball of yarn and bind off next 26 (28, 32, 36), sts for back neck, work to end of row.

Working on both sides of neck with separate balls of yarn, dec 1 st at each neck edge. (22, 25, 27, 29 sts for each shoulder)

Work even until back measures 14 (15, 16, 17) inches.

Bind off all sts.

Front

Work as for back until front measures 12 (13, 14, 15) inches, ending with a WS row.

Front neck shaping

Next row (RS): Work in established pat across 31 (35, 38, 42) sts, join 2nd ball of yarn and bind off next 10 (10, 12, 12) sts for front neck, work to end of row.

Working on both sides of neck with separate balls of yarn, bind off 4 sts at each neck edge, then [3 sts] 0 (1, 1, 2) times, and finally [2 sts] 2 (1, 1, 1) times.

[Dec 1 st at same edge] 1 (1, 2, 1) times. (22, 25, 27, 29 sts for each shoulder)

Work even until front measures same as for back.

Bind off all sts.

Sleeves

With smaller needles and MC, cast on 34 (34, 38, 38) sts.

Work Fair Isle and texture pats as for back, *at the same time* beg with Row 10, [inc 1 st each end every 6th row] 8 (10, 11, 14) times. (50, 54, 60, 66 sts)

Work even until sleeve measures 9 (10, 11, 12) inches.

Bind off.

Sew shoulder seams.

Collar

With smaller dpn and MC, pick up and k 74 (80, 85, 93) sts evenly around neck.

Join, pm between first and last st.

Work in St st until collar measures 2 inches.

Bind off loosely.

Finishing

Measure down 4½ (5, 5½, 6) inches on each side of each shoulder seam and mark.

Sew top of sleeve to body between markers.

Sew sleeve and side seams. ✦

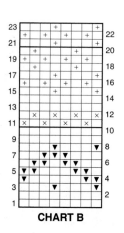

CHART B

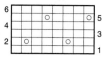

CHART C

COLOR & STITCH KEY
☐ Pink-K on RS, p on WS
⊙ Pink-P on RS, k on WS
▼ Royal blue
⊠ Yellow
⊞ Orange

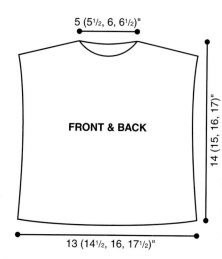

5 (5½, 6, 6½)"

FRONT & BACK

14 (15, 16, 17)"

13 (14½, 16, 17½)"

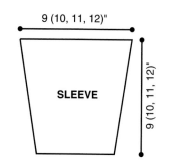

9 (10, 11, 12)"

SLEEVE

9 (10, 11, 12)"

Dots & Dashes Pullover

Design by E. J. Slayton

Bright, primary colors and an interesting texture pattern highlight this pullover. It is sure to become a classroom favorite.

Skill Level

Intermediate***

Size

Child's 2 (4, 6, 8) Instructions are given for smallest size, with larger sizes in parentheses. When only 1 number is given, it applies to all sizes.

Finished Measurements

Chest: 24 (26, 28, 30) inches

Length: 12 (14, 15½, 17) inches

Materials

- Plymouth Wildflower D.K. 51 percent cotton/49 percent acrylic DK weight yarn (137 yds/50g per ball): 3 (3, 4, 4) balls claret #63 (MC), 1 (1, 2, 2) balls royal blue #57 (A), 1 ball each dark teal #44 (B), apricot #79 (C)
- Size 3 (3.25mm) straight and 16-inch circular needles or size needed to obtain gauge
- Stitch holders
- Stitch markers
- Tapestry needle
- 2 (⅝-inch) buttons for size 2 (4)

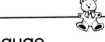

Gauge

25 sts and 42 rows = 4 inches/ 10cm in Dots & Dashes pat

To save time, take time to check gauge.

Pattern Stitch

Dots & Dashes [multiple of 10 sts + 5 (1, 7, 5)]

Row 1 (RS): With MC, knit.

Row 2: With MC, purl.

Rows 3 and 4: With A, k5 (3, 6, 5), *sl 2, k1, sl 2, k5, rep from * across, end last rep k5 (3, 6, 5).

Rows 5 and 6: With MC, rep Rows 1 and 2.

Rows 7 and 8: With B, k1, sl 1 (0, 0, 1), k1 (0, 1, 1), *sl 2, k5, sl 2, k1, rep from * across, end sl 1 (0, 2, 1), k1 (0, 1, 1).

Rows 9 and 10: With MC, rep Rows 1 and 2.

Rows 11 and 12: With A, rep Rows 3 and 4.

Rows 13 and 14: With MC, rep Rows 1 and 2.

Rows 15 and 16: With C, rep Rows 7 and 8.

Rep Rows 1–16 for pat.

Pattern Notes

Sl all sts purlwise with yarn on WS of fabric, being careful not to pull yarn too tightly behind sl sts.

Do not sl edge sts.

Work inc and dec 1 st in from edge.

Each chart row represents a RS row and its following WS row. The same sts are slipped or worked on each.

Back

With MC, cast on 66 (70, 78, 82) sts.

Row 1 (WS): P2, *k2, p2, rep from * across.

Row 2: K2, *p2, k2, rep from * across.

Rep Rows 1 and 2 until ribbing measures approximately 1½ (1½, 2, 2) inches, ending with a WS row.

Inc row (RS): K, inc 9 (11, 9, 13) sts evenly across. (75, 81, 87, 95 sts)

Next row: Purl.

Beg pat: With A, beg with Row 3.

Work even in pat until back measures approximately 7 (8½, 9½, 10½) inches, ending with Row 4, 8, 12 or 16.

Shape armholes

Working with MC, at beg of row,

[bind off 5 (5, 7, 8) sts] twice.

Maintaining pat, [dec 1 st at each edge every other row] 4 times. (57, 63, 65, 71 sts)

Work as established until armhole measures 5 (5½, 6, 6½) inches, ending with Row 2, 6, 10 or 14.

Mark center 31 (33, 35, 37) sts for back neck and place sts on holder.

Shoulder Tab
Sizes 2 & 4 only

Leave left shoulder sts on needle, mark each end of row with scrap yarn. With MC, work in St st until tab measures ¾ inch from marked row. K 3 rows, bind off knitwise on WS.

Front

Work as for back until armhole measures 2½ (3, 3, 3½) inches from underarm, ending with a WS row.

Shape neck

Work in established pat across 18 (20, 20, 22) sts, place center 21 (23, 25, 27) sts on holder for front neck, attach 2nd ball of yarn and work last 18 (20, 20, 22) sts.

Working both sides at once and maintaining pat, [dec 1 st at each neck edge every RS row] 5 times.

Work even on remaining 13 (15, 15, 17) sts until front matches back at shoulder, ending with a WS row. Place shoulder sts on holder.

Shoulder Tab
Size 2 & 4 only

Working on left shoulder sts, mark each end of row with scrap yarn and work shoulder tab with MC only.

Row 1 (RS): K5 (6), k2tog, yo, ssk, k to end.

Row 2: P to yo, [k1, p1] in yo, p to end.

Row 3: K, dec 2 sts evenly across.

Rows 4 and 5: Knit.

Bind off all sts knitwise on WS.

Sleeves

With MC, cast on 34 (34, 38, 42) sts and work in ribbing as for back.

Inc row (RS): K, inc 7 (11, 13, 13) sts evenly across. (41, 45, 51, 55 sts)

Next row: Purl.

Beg pat: Referring to chart, with A, work Rows 3 and 4.

Beg on Row 5, [inc 1 st at each edge every 4th row] 5 times, then [every 8th row] 6 (7, 7, 8) times, working new sts into pat. (63, 69, 75, 81 sts)

Continue to work even in pat until sleeve measures 9 (11, 13, 14½) inches or desired length to underarm, ending with Row 4, 8, 12 or 16.

Shape cap

Bind off 5 (5, 7, 8) sts at beg of next 2 rows.

Continuing to work in pat, [dec 1 st at each edge every other row] 4 times.

Bind off all sts knitwise on last WS row.

Finishing

Bind off right shoulder sts tog as follows: Hold needles containing shoulder sts parallel, RS tog; with 3rd needle, k first st on front and back needles tog, *k next st on both needles tog, bind off 1 st, rep from * until all sts are worked, fasten off.

Sizes 6 and 8 only: Rep for 2nd shoulder.

Neck Band
Sizes 2 & 4 only

Beg at left shoulder tab with MC, RS facing, pick up and k 4 sts across edge of tab, 14 sts along left neck edge, k 21 (23) front neck sts from holder dec 3 sts evenly across, pick up and k 14 sts along right neck edge, k 31 (33) back neck sts from holder dec 3 sts evenly across, pick up and k 4 sts along edge of tab. (82, 86 sts)

Row 1 (WS): K4, p2, *k2, p2, rep from * to last 4 sts, end k4.

Row 2: K2, k2tog, yo, ssk, *p2, k2, rep from * to last 4 sts, end k4.

Row 3: Rep Row 1, end by working [p1, k1] in yo, k4.

Rows 4 and 6: K6, *p2, k2, rep from * to last 4 sts, end k4.

Row 5: Rep Row 1.

Bind off all sts in pat on WS.

Sizes 6 & 8 only

Beg at left shoulder with MC and 16-inch circular needle, RS facing, pick up and k 15 (17) sts along left neck edge, k 25 (27) front neck sts from holder dec 3 sts evenly across, pick up and k 15 (17) sts along right neck edge, k 35 (37) back neck sts from holder dec 3 sts evenly across. (84, 92 sts)

Join and work in rnds of k2, p2 ribbing for 1 inch. Bind off all sts in pat.

Sizes 2 & 4 only

Pin or baste left shoulder tabs in place, matching markers.

Set sleeves into armholes.

Sew sleeve and body underarm seams.

Sizes 2 & 4 only

Sew buttons opposite buttonholes.

Sew armhole edge of back shoulder tab in place. ✦

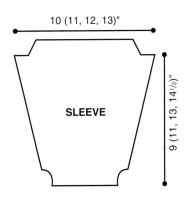

SLEEVE

10 (11, 12, 13)"

9 (11, 13, 14½)"

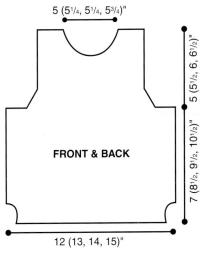

FRONT & BACK

5 (5¼, 5¼, 5¾)"

5 (5½, 6, 6½)"

7 (8½, 9½, 10½)"

12 (13, 14, 15)"

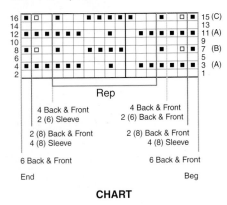

Rep

4 Back & Front
2 (6) Sleeve

4 Back & Front
2 (6) Back & Front

2 (8) Back & Front
4 (8) Sleeve

2 (8) Back & Front
4 (8) Sleeve

6 Back & Front

6 Back & Front

End

Beg

CHART

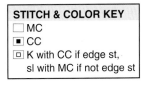

STITCH & COLOR KEY

☐ MC
■ CC
▣ K with CC if edge st, sl with MC if not edge st

Bam Bam Bath Set

Designs by Kennita Tully

Cuddle your child after bath time in a warm and thick robe with matching slippers.

Skill Level

Beginner*

Size

Child's small (medium, large)
Instructions are given for smallest size, with larger sizes in parentheses. When only 1 number is given, it applies to all sizes.

Finished Measurements

Chest (closed): 34 (36, 38) inches

Length: 25 (26, 27) inches

Materials

- Plymouth Bam 42 percent acrylic/40 percent nylon/18 percent wool bulky weight yarn (60 yds/50g per ball): Bathrobe: 13 (15, 17) balls; Slippers: 1 (1, 2) balls lagoon #3463
- Size 10 (6mm) needles or size needed to obtain gauge for slippers
- Size 13 (9mm) needles or size needed to obtain gauge for robe
- Stitch holders
- Stitch markers
- Tapestry needle

Gauge

10 sts and 14 rows = 4 inches/10cm in Seed st for bathrobe.

11½ sts and 22 rows = 4 inches/10cm in garter st for slippers. To save time, take time to check gauge.

112

Pattern Stitch

Seed Stitch (odd number of sts)

All rows: *K1, p1; rep from * across, end last rep k1.

Bathrobe

Back

With larger needles, cast on 41 (45, 49) sts.

Work even in Seed st for 18 inches.

Mark each end st for underarm.

Continue to work even in established pat for 7 (8, 9) inches more.

Bind off all sts.

Mark center 13 (15, 17) sts for back neck.

Right Front

With larger needles, cast on 25 (27, 29) sts.

Work even in Seed st until front measures same as for back, placing marker for underarm at right edge after 18 inches.

Shape back collar

Next row (WS): Bind off 14 (15, 16) sts at beg of row.

Continue to work even on remaining 11 (12, 13) sts until collar measures 3 (3¼, 3½) inches above bound-off row.

Bind off.

Left Front

Work as for right front, reversing shaping.

Sleeves

With larger needles, cast on 17 (21, 25) sts.

Working in Seed st, inc 1 st at each end on 3rd row, then [1 st each end every 4th row] 9 times more. (37, 41, 45 sts)

Work even until sleeve measures 13 inches.

Bind off.

Belt

Cast on 7 sts.

Work even in Seed st until belt measures 48 inches.

Bind off.

Finishing

Sew shoulders. Sew back collar extensions along short edge.

Sew collar to back neck.

Sew sleeves into armhole between underarm markers.

Sew side and sleeve seams.

Slippers

With smaller needles, leaving an 8-inch tail, cast on 17 (21, 23) sts.

Work even in garter st until slipper measures 1 (1¼, 1½) inches less than desired foot measurement.

Shape toe

Row 1: K2, *p1, k1; rep from * across, end last rep k2.

Row 2: P2, *k1, p1; rep from * across, end last rep p2.

[Rep Rows 1 and 2] 2 (2, 3) times.

Cut yarn leaving an 8-inch end for sewing.

Draw end through all sts, pull tightly to secure and sew ribbed section.

Fold cast-on edge in half to form back seam.

With tail of yarn from cast-on edge, sew edges tog for heel. ✦

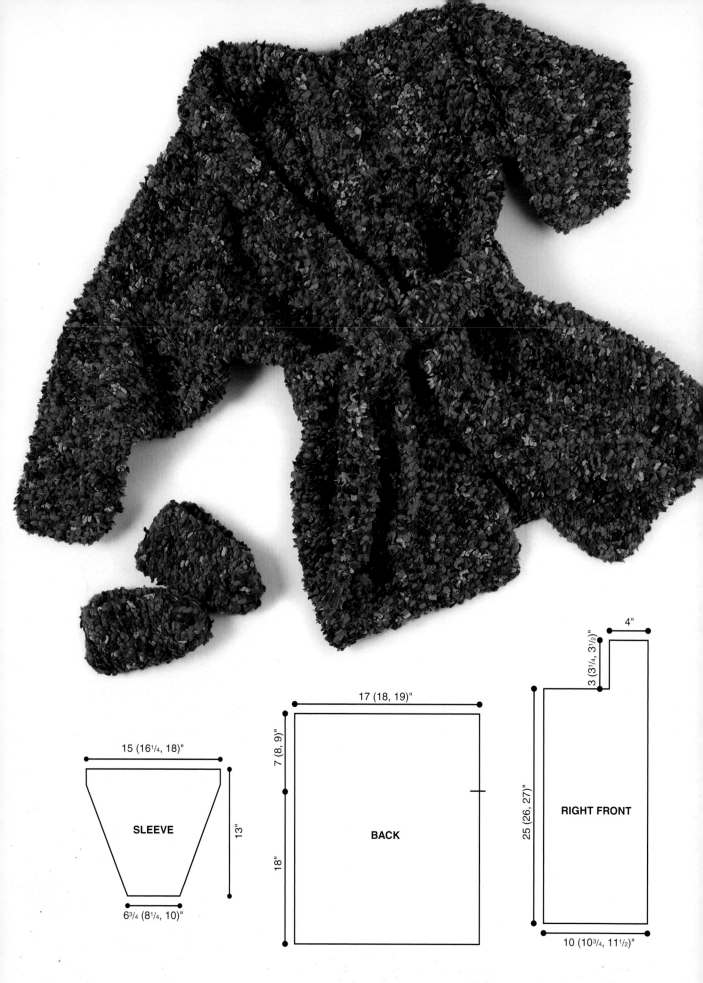

SLEEVE

15 (16¼, 18)"

13"

6¾ (8¼, 10)"

BACK

17 (18, 19)"

7 (8, 9)"

18"

RIGHT FRONT

4"

3 (3¼, 3½)"

25 (26, 27)"

10 (10¾, 11½)"

Happy Critters

Designs by E. J. Slayton

These safe and cuddly stuffed toys are based on old-time sock toys.
Use leftovers from a child's favorite sweater for each friend.

Skill Level
Intermediate***

Size
Approximately 9 (11) inches high

Materials
- Plymouth Encore D.K. weight 75 percent acrylic/25 percent wool DK weight yarn (150 yds/50g per ball): 1 ball
- Plymouth Encore Worsted 75 percent acrylic/25 percent wool worsted weight yarn (200 yds/ 100g per ball): 1 ball
- Size 3 (3.25mm)
- Size 5 (3.75mm) needles or size needed to obtain gauge
- Stitch markers
- Approximately 1–2 yds contrasting yarns or 6-strand embroidery floss for features
- Crochet hook
- Polyester fiberfill
- Tapestry needle

Gauge
13 sts and 16 rows = 2 inches/5cm with DK weight yarn and smaller needles

10 sts and 14 rows = 2 inches/5cm with worsted weight yarn and larger needles

Gauge is not critical for this project, but sts should be firm enough that fiberfill does not poke through.

Special Abbreviations
CDD (centered double decrease): Sl next 2 sts as if to k2tog, k1, p2sso.

M1 (Make 1): Inc by making a backward loop over RH needle. On next rnd, k in back of loop.

Pattern Notes
These toys are knitted as a tube with a sock toe at one end. All features are either knitted on or embroidered, so they are safe for any age.

Designs may be worked in either weight of yarn from same instructions. Sample projects were worked as follows:

Worsted weight: dog, medium blue #4045; frog, medium olive green #45

DK weight: cat, yellow gold #1382; pig, hot pink #1385

Using short sts that won't snag little fingers, work ears and features before stuffing so ends can be fastened off securely on inside. Purl side of ears will be toward front.

Most features on DK weight samples were embroidered with 6-strand floss. Check floss for color fastness before using.

features on worsted weight samples were worked with small amounts of yarn.

Body (All Animals)

Cast on 40 sts. Join without twisting, pm at beg of rnd and after st No. 20.

Rnd 1: Knit.

Rnd 2: [K1, M1, k to 1 st before marker, M1, k1] twice. (44 sts)

Rnds 3 and 4: Rep Rnds 1 and 2. (48 sts)

Rnds 5-64: Knit.

Shape top

Rnd 1: [K1, ssk, k to last 3 sts, k2tog, k1] twice.

Rnd 2: Knit.

Rnds 3-8: Rep Rnds 1 and 2.

Rnds 9-11: Rep Rnd 1. (16 sts)

Cut yarn, leaving a 12-inch end. Weave sts tog using Kitchener method.

Finishing

With crochet hook, pick up sts to work ears as needed for chosen critter.

Embroider features as shown in Figs. 1–4, making sure all ends are fastened off securely on inside.

Mark exact center of front and back at bottom edge and on Rnd 25. Stuff body lightly with fiberfill, then sew or weave bottom. Going through stuffing layer sew front and

back tog from Rnd 25 to bottom to form legs.

Fasten off securely.

Kitty

Referring to Fig. 1, embroider mouth, nose, eyes and whiskers as shown. Sample used 6 strands of floss for nose, mouth and eye outlines, and 3 strands for whiskers. Small amounts of green and pink yarn were used to fill eye and nose outlines.

Left Ear

With front facing, starting at 2nd dec of top shaping and working through both loops of last st of back, pick up and k [1 st in every other rnd] 6 times.

Row 1 (WS): K1, M1, [k2, M1] twice, k1. (9 sts)

Rows 2 and 4: K2, p5, k2.

Row 3: Knit.

Row 5: K1, ssk, k3, k2tog, k1. (7 sts)

Row 6: K2, p3, k2.

Row 7: K1, ssk, k1, k2tog, k1. (5 sts)

Row 8: Knit.

Row 9: K1, sl 1, k2tog, psso, k1. (3 sts)

Row 10: Sl 1, k2tog, psso. Fasten off.

Right Ear

Rep as for left ear, beg at same point of top shaping as left ear ended and picking up from top to bottom.

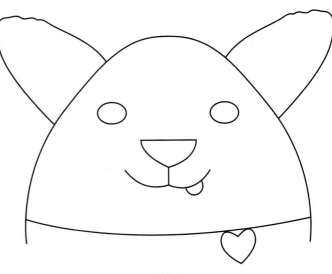

FIG. 1
KITTY

FIG. 2
DOGGY

Doggy

Collar

Referring to Fig. 2, knit Rnd 53 of body with CC, or work 1 rnd of duplicate st for collar after knitting is completed.

Embroider mouth, tongue, nose, eyes and heart tag as shown.

Sample used small amounts of black, pink and yellow gold yarn.

Left Ear

With front facing, starting at beg of top shaping and working through both loops of last st of back, pick up and k [1 st in every other rnd] 6 times.

Row 1 (WS): K1, M1, [k2, M1] twice, k1. (9 sts)

Row 2: K2, p5, k2.

Row 3: Knit.

Rows 4–6: Rep Rows 1 and 2, ending with Row 2.

Row 7: K1, ssk, k3, k2tog, k1. (7 sts)

Rows 8 and 10: K2, p3, k2.

Row 9: Knit.

Row 11: K1, ssk, k1, k2tog, k1. (5 sts)

Row 12: Knit.

Row 13: K1, cdd, k1. (3 sts)

Row 14: Sl 1, k2tog, psso. Fasten off.

Right Ear

Rep as for left ear, beg at same point of top shaping as left ear ended and picking up from top to bottom.

Froggy

Referring to Fig. 3, emboider eyes, brows, nostrils and mouth.

Sample used small amounts of black, blue and hot pink yarn.

Piggy

Referring to Fig. 4, embroider mouth, snout, brows and eyes as shown.

Sample used 6 strands of floss for all features.

Left Ear

Pick up and k 6 sts as for dog, placing ear approximately 1 st below end of top shaping.

Row 1 (WS): K1, M1, [p2, M1] twice, k1. (9 sts)

Rows 2, 4 and 6: Knit.

Row 3: K2, p5, M1, k2. (10 sts)

FIG. 3
FROGGY

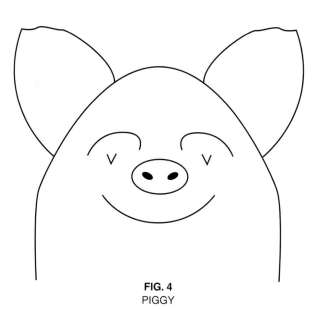

FIG. 4
PIGGY

Bobbles the Lamb

Design by Kennita Tully

*Bobbles is a cuddly lamb that your child
will be happy to snuggle.*

Skill Level
Intermediate***

Size
Approximately 9 inches tall x 12
inches long

Materials
- Plymouth Sinsation 80 percent
  rayon/20 percent wool bulky
  chenille yarn (40 yds/50g per
  ball): 4 balls white #3300.
- Plymouth Wildflower D.K. 51
  percent cotton/49 percent
  acrylic DK weight yarn (137 yds/
  50g per ball): small amount bright
  blue #55, canary yellow #48
- Size 9 (6mm) needles
- Stitch holders
- Tapestry needle
- Polyester fiberfill
- ½ yd (⅞-inch) ribbon

Gauge
9 sts and 18 rows = 4 inches/10cm in
garter st

Row 5: K2, p6, M1, k2. (11 sts)

Row 7: K2, p7, k2.

Row 8: K1, ssk, k to end. (10 sts)

Row 9: K2, p6, k2.

Row 10: Rep Row 8. (9 sts)

Row 11: K3, Cdd, k3. (7 sts)

Row 12: K2, p3, k2.

Row 13: K2, cdd, k2. (5 sts)

Row 14: K5.

Row 15: K1, Cdd, k1. (3 sts)

Row 16: Sl 1, k2tog, psso. Fasten off.

Right Ear
Rep as for left ear, beg at same
point of top shaping as left ear
ended and picking up from top
to bottom. ✦

Gauge is not critical for this project, but sts should be knit firmly to prevent fiberfill from poking through.

Pattern Note
Lamb is knit in garter st throughout.

Top Piece
Left Front Leg
Cast on 6 sts, work even in garter st for 4 inches, ending with a WS row.

Next row (RS): K in front and back of first st, k to end of row.

Knit 1 row.

Rep last 2 rows. (8 sts)

Next row (RS): Knit in front and back of first st, knit to end of row.

Row 2: K to last st, knit in front and back of last st.

Rep last 2 rows. (12 sts)

Cut yarn and place sts on holder.

Left Back Leg
Cast on 6 sts, work even in garter st for 3 inches, ending with a WS row.

Shape leg

Next row: K to end of row, k in front and back of last st.

Knit 1 row.

Rep last 2 rows. (8 sts)

Next row (RS): K2tog, k to last st, k in front and back of last st.

Knit 1 row.

[Rep last 2 rows] 3 times.

Joining row: K across sts of back leg, sl sts of front leg from holder to LH needle and k across. (20 sts)

Body
Knit 17 rows.

Shape back
Next row (RS): K2tog, k to end of row.

Knit 1 row.

Rep last 2 rows. (18 sts)

Knit 1 row. Mark this row as center of back.

Head Opening
Bind off 6 sts at beg of next row.

Cast on 6 sts at end of following row.

Next row (RS): K in front and back of first st, k to end of row.

Knit 1 row.

Rep last 2 rows. (20 sts)

Knit 18 rows.

Shape right back leg
Next row (RS): K in front and back of first st, k5, k2tog. (8 sts)

Place remaining 12 sts on holder.

Work on these 8 sts only.

Next row (RS): K in front and back of first st, knit to last two sts, k2tog.

Knit 1 row.

Rep last 2 rows] twice.

Next row: K to last two sts, k2tog.

Knit 1 row.

Rep last 2 two rows. (6 sts)

Work even for 3 inches.

Bind off.

Shape right front leg

Sl sts from holder to LH needle. Join yarn at inside of legs.

Next row (RS): K2tog, k to end of row.

Row 2: K to last 2 sts, k2tog.

[Rep last 2 rows] twice. (8 sts)

Next row: K2tog, k to end of row.

Knit row.

Rep last 2 rows. (6 sts)

Work even for 4 inches. Bind off.

Underside
Right Front Leg

Cast on 6 sts, work even in garter st for 4 inches, ending with a WS row.

Next row (RS): K in front and back of first st, k to end of row.

Knit 1 row.

Rep last 2 rows. (8 sts)

Next row (RS): Knit in front and back of first st, knit to end of row.

Row 2: K to last st, knit in front and back of last st.

Rep last 2 rows. (12 sts)

Cut yarn and place sts on holder.

Right Back Leg

Cast on 6 sts, work even in garter st for 3 inches, ending with a WS row.

Shape leg

Next row: K to end of row, k in front and back of last st.

Knit 1 row.

Rep last 2 rows. (8 sts)

Next row (RS): K2tog, k to last st, k in front and back of last st.

Knit 1 row.

[Rep last two rows] 3 times.

Joining row: K across sts of back leg, sl sts of front leg from holder to LH needle and k across. (20 sts)

Knit 35 rows.

Shape left back leg

Next row (RS): K in front and back of first st, k5, k2tog. (8 sts)

Place remaining 12 sts on holder.

Work on these 8 sts only.

Next row (RS): K in front and back of first st, knit to last two sts, k2tog.

Knit 1 row.

[Rep last 2 rows] twice.

Next row: K to last two sts, k2tog.

Knit 1 row.

Rep last 2 rows. (6 sts)

Work even for 3 inches.

Bind off.

Shape left front leg

Sl sts from holder to LH needle. Join yarn at inside of legs.

Next row (RS): K2tog, k to end of row.

Row 2: K to last 2 sts, k2tog.

[Rep last 2 rows] twice. (8 sts)

Next row: K2tog, k to end of row.

Knit 1 row.

Rep last 2 rows. (6 sts)

Work even for 4 inches. Bind off.

Head
Left Half

Pick up and k 1 st in each bound-off st above left front leg.

Knit 1 row.

Next row (RS): K in front and back of first st, knit to end of row, turn and cable cast on 2 sts.

Knit 1 row.

Rep last 2 rows until there are 18 sts on needle.

Next row (RS): Knit in front and back of first st, k7, k in front and back next st, k8, k in front and back of last st. (21 sts)

Row 2: Knit.

Row 3: K to last 2 sts, k2tog. (20 sts)

Row 4: Knit.

[Rep Rows 3 and 4] 3 times. (17 sts)

Row 11: K2tog, k to last 2 sts, k2tog.

Row 12: Knit.

[Rep Rows 11–12] twice. (11 sts)

Row 17: K2tog, k to last 2 sts, k2tog.

Rep Row 17 until 3 sts remain. This is top of head.

Beg right half

Reverse shaping by knitting in front and back of first and last st every row until there are 11 sts on needle, then every other row until there are 17 sts. Knit 1 row.

Next row: K to last 2 sts, k in front and back of last st.

Knit 1 row.

Rep last 2 rows until there are 21 sts.

Next row (RS): K2tog, k7, k2tog, k8, k2tog. (18 sts)

Knit 1 row.

Next row (RS): K2tog, k to end of row.

Row 2: Bind off 2 sts, k to end of row.

Rep last 2 rows until 6 sts remain.

Bind off.

Tail

Cast on 6 sts and work even in garter st for 3 inches.

Bind off.

Fold tail in half and sew side edges tog.

Ears

Cast on 5 sts.

[Inc 1 st each end every other row] 3 times. (11 sts)

Knit 1 row.

Bind off.

Finishing

Pin head to body and sew in place.

Sew underside to top body piece, leaving holes for stuffing at tail and back of head.

Stuff head and body with fiberfill. Sew head and tail seams.

Sew on tail and ears.

Referring to photo, embroider eyes in blue satin st and mouth in yellow straight st.

Place ribbon around neck and tie in a bow. ✦

Bonnie Bunny

Design by Shari Haux

Here is a fluffy, easy-to-knit bunny that will add a touch of whimsy to the decor of any child's room.

Skill Level
Easy**

Size
Approximately 17 inches tall

Materials
- Plymouth Sinsation 80 percent rayon/20 percent wool bulky chenille yarn (40 yds/50g per ball): 4 balls white #3300 (MC)
- Plymouth Fantasy Naturale 100 percent mercerized cotton worsted weight yarn (140 yds/100g per skein): 1 skein green #5228 (CC), small amount black #8990
- Size 7 (4.5mm) double-pointed needles
- Size 10½ (6.5mm) double-pointed and 16-inch circular needles or size needed to obtain gauge
- 4 (12-inch) white chenille stems
- 2 (15mm) movable eyes
- Fabric glue
- Small plastic bag of marbles, rice, or small stones for bottom weight
- Polyester fiberfill
- Polyester batting
- White embroidery floss for sewing
- Stitch marker
- Tapestry needle

Gauge
10 sts and 22 rows = 4 inches/10cm in St st with larger needles

Gauge is not critical in this project, but sts should be worked tightly so stuffing does not show through.

Bunny

Body & Head
With circular needle and MC, cast on 50 sts. Join without twisting, pm between first and last st.

Knit 2 rnds, purl 2 rnds.

Work even in St st until body measures 14 inches.

Shape top of head

Dec rnd: K2tog around. (25 sts)

Rep dec rnd until 3 sts remain, changing to dpn when necessary.

Cut yarn, leaving an 8-inch end.

Draw yarn through remaining sts and pull tightly. Run yarn end to inside and weave in.

Ears

With larger dpns and MC, cast on 60 sts leaving a 6-inch end.

Knit 1 row. Cut yarn, leaving a 6-inch end.

Sl all sts from needle to chenille stem. Tie yarn ends tog.

Scrunch yarn onto stem, fold in half and twist ends tog, leaving 1 inch at bottom of each stem.

Referring to photo, insert ears into top of head having a st or 2 between each end.

On inside, twist ends tog again.

Pull yarn ends to inside and weave in place.

Scarf

With smaller dpn and CC, cast on 15 sts. Join without twisting, pm between first and last st.

Work even in St st until scarf measures 29 inches.

Bind off.

Finishing

Referring to photo, embroider nose and mouth with black.

To create head, stuff head area fully with polyester fiberfill.

Tie area just below head very tightly with CC.

Glue eyes in place.

Sl 2 chenille stems through nose area for whiskers. If you like curled ends, curl ends around pencil.

Stuff bunny's body very tightly with fiberfill.

Just before body is completely filled, add plastic bag weight wrapped in batting and continue filling until well stuffed.

Weave white embroidery floss through cast-on sts and fasten off.

Shape body by pounding on table to stand.

Make pompom tail by wrapping yarn around 4 fingers and tying off with embroidery floss, sew through back area and tie off.

Tie scarf around neck. ◆

WINTER CUDDLERS

Purple Power Jacket & Purse

Designs by Kennita Tully

This stylish jacket with its matching purse is very easy to work.
Trendy yarns and colorway make a real fashion statement.

Skill Level
Beginner*

Size
Girl's 2 (4, 6, 8) Instructions are given for smallest size, with larger sizes in parentheses. When only 1 number is given, it applies to all sizes.

Finished Measurements
Chest (buttoned): 28 (30, 33, 36) inches

Length: 13 (14, 15, 16) inches

Materials
• Plymouth Rimini Rainbow 60 percent acrylic/40 percent wool bulky weight yarn (38 yds/50g per ball): Jacket: 7 (8, 9, 10) balls, Purse: 2 balls charcoal #16 (MC)
• Plymouth Flash 100 percent nylon eyelash yarn (190 yds/50g per ball): 1 ball lilac #965 (CC)
• Size 7 (4.5mm) needles
• Size 11 (8mm) needles
• Size 13 (9mm) straight and 24-inch circular needles or size needed to obtain gauge
• Small amount matching smooth yarn for sewing
• Stitch markers
• Tapestry needle
• Size H/8 crochet hook
• 1 (1⅛-inch) button

Gauge
8 sts and 14 rows = 4 inches/10cm in garter st with larger needles

To save time, take time to check gauge.

Jacket

Back
With size 13 needles and MC, cast on 28 (30, 34, 36) sts.

Work even in garter st for 7 (7½, 8, 8, 12) inches.

Mark each end of last row for armholes.

Work even for 6 (6½, 7, 7½) inches more.

Bind off all sts.

Mark center 12 sts for back of neck.

Right Front
With MC, cast on 14 (15, 17, 18) sts.

Work as for back until front measures 10 (11, 12, 13) inches.

Shape neck
[Dec 1 st every other row] 6 times. (8, 9, 11, 12 sts)

Bind off all sts.

RIGHT FRONT

4 (4½, 5½, 6)"

7 (7½, 8¼, 9)"

SLEEVE

12 (13, 14, 15)"

10 (12½, 13, 13½)"

6 (6, 7, 8)"

BACK

13 (14, 15, 16)"

14 (15, 16½, 18)"

Left Front

Work as for right front, reversing shaping.

Sleeves

With size 13 needles and MC, cast on 12 (12, 14, 16) sts.

Work in garter st, inc 1 st each end on 3rd (5th, 5th, 5th) row.

[Inc 1 st each end every 4 (6, 6, 6) rows] 1 (6, 5, 4) times, then [every 6 (0, 8, 8) rows] 4 (0, 1, 2) times. (24, 26, 28, 30 sts)

Work even until sleeve measures 10 (12½, 13, 13½) inches

Bind off all sts loosely.

Collar

With CC and size 7 needles, cast on 74 sts.

Work in garter st for 2 inches.

Bind off.

Finishing

Sew shoulder seams.

Sew collar to jacket.

Sew sleeves to body between markers.

Sew sleeve and side seams.

Button Loop

Join MC at beg of neck shaping of right front.

With crochet hook, ch 10. Fasten off.

Attach end of loop to jacket front, just below beg of loop.

Sew on button.

Purse

Bottom & Sides

With size 11 needles and MC, cast on 8 sts.

Work in garter st for 4 inches. Do not bind off.

Change to size 13 circular needle.

Pick up and k 8 sts along each of remaining 3 sides of square. (32 sts)

Join, pm between first and last st.

Work even in garter st for 8 inches.

Eyelet row: *Yo, k2tog, k2; rep from * around.

Work even for 1 inch more.

Bind off loosely.

Trim

With CC and size 7 needles, cast on 80 sts.

Work in garter st for 1 inch.

Bind off all sts loosely.

Sew trim to top of bag.

Cord

With MC, make a twisted cord approximately 46 inches long.

Thread cord through eyelet row.

Tie ends tog in overhand knot. ✦

Reversible Cuddle Coat

Design by Barbara Venishnick

Two layers in different patterns shape a coat that is not only reversible, but extra warm.

Skill Level

Intermediate***

Size

Child's 2 (4, 6, 8) Instructions are given for smallest size, with larger sizes in parentheses. When only 1 number is given, it applies to all sizes.

Finished Measurements

Chest: 30 (32, 34, 36) inches

Total length (without hood): 17 (18, 19, 20) inches

Materials

- Plymouth Encore Worsted 75 percent acrylic/25 percent wool worsted weight yarn (200 yds/ 100g per skein): 6 (6, 7, 7) skeins purple #1606 (A),1 (2, 2, 2) skeins cornflower #4045 (B), orange #1383 (C), yellow #1382 (D), 1 skein each black #217, white #146
- Size 3 (3.25mm) double-pointed needles (2 only)
- Size 5 (3.75mm) straight and 40-inch circular needles
- Size 7 (4.5mm) needles or size needed to obtain gauge
- 4 (⅞₈-inch) buttons

Gauge

18 sts and 24 rows = 4 inches/10cm in Woven Basket pat with larger needles

To save time, take time to check gauge.

Pattern Stitches

A. Woven Basket (multiple of 4 sts + 2)

Row 1 (RS): Knit.

Row 2: *P2, k2, rep from * across, end last rep p2.

Row 3: *K2, p2, rep from * across, end last rep k2.

Row 4: Purl.

Row 5: Rep Row 2.

Row 6: Rep Row 3.

Rep Rows 1–6 for pat.

B. Color Stripe Sequence

Cast on all pieces with A.

Work in St st of 1 row each D, B, C, D, A, C, B, A.

Do not cut yarn at end of row; carry those not in use up side of work.

C. Diagonal Stripes

For sizes 2 & 6 only

Row 1 (RS): *K2 E, k2 F, rep from * across.

Row 2: *P1 F, p2 E, p1 F, rep from * across.

Row 3: *K2 F, k2 E, rep from * across.

Row 4: *P1 E, p2 F, p1 E, rep from * across.

Row 5: Rep Row 1.

Row 6: Rep Row 2.

Rep Rows 1–6 for pat.

For sizes 4 & 8 only

Row 1 (RS): *K2 E, k2 F, rep from * across, end last rep k2 E.

Row 2: *P1 F, p2 E, p1 F, rep from * across, end last rep p1 F.

Row 3: *K2 F, k2 E, rep from * across, end last rep k2 F.

Row 4: *P1 E, p2 F, p1 E, rep from * across, end last rep p1 E.

Row 5: Rep Row 1.

Row 6: Rep Row 2.

Rep Rows 1–6 for pat.

Pattern Notes

Coat is worked in two layers that are the same except for the pat st. If extra warmth is desired, a

RIGHT FRONT
8½ (9, 9½, 10)"

SLEEVE
14 (15, 16, 17)"
15 (16, 17, 18)"
3"
9 (10, 11, 12)"

BACK
11 (12, 13, 14)"
1"
7 (7½, 8, 8½)"
9 (9½, 10, 10½)"
17 (18, 19, 20)"
15 (16, 17, 18)"

HOOD
8½ (9, 9½, 10)"
9"
8½ (9, 9½, 10)"

windproof lining may be placed between layers.

When working in Woven Basket pat, always keep first and last st of row in st st for selvage edge.

Selvage sts are included in st count.

Woven Basket Layer

Back

With size 7 needles and A, cast on 68 (72, 76, 80) sts.

Work even in Woven Basket pat until back measures 9 (9½, 10, 10½) inches, ending with a WS row.

Shape armholes

[Dec 1 st each end every other row] 9 times. (50, 54, 58, 62 sts)

Work even in established pat until armhole measures 7 (7½, 8, 8½) inches, ending with a WS row.

Shape shoulders

Bind off 5 (5, 5, 6) sts at beg of next 4 rows, then 4 (5, 6, 5) sts at beg of next 2 rows.

Work across remaining 22 (24, 26, 28) sts and place on holder for back neck.

Right Front

With size 7 needles and A, cast on 40 (42, 44, 46) sts.

Work even in Woven Basket pat, until front measures same as back to underarm.

Shape armhole

[Dec 1 st at armhole edge every other row] 9 times. (31, 33, 35, 37 sts)

Work even in established pat until armhole measures 5 (5½, 6, 6½) inches, ending with a WS row.

Shape front neck

Bind off 12 (13, 14, 15) sts at beg of next row.

[Dec 1 st at neck edge every other row] 5 times.

Work even on remaining 14 (15, 16, 17) sts until armhole measures same as for back.

Shape shoulder

[Bind off at armhole edge 5 (5, 5, 6) sts] twice, then [4 (5, 6, 5) sts] once.

Left Front

Work as for right front, reversing shaping.

Sleeves

With size 7 needles and A, cast on 42 (44, 46, 48) sts.

Work even in Woven Basket pat for 18 rows.

[Inc 1 st each end every 6th row] 10 (11, 12, 13) times. (62, 66, 70, 74 sts)

Work even until sleeve measures 12 (13, 14, 15) inches, ending with a WS row.

Shape cap

[Dec 1 st each end every other row] 9 times.

Bind off remaining 44 (48, 52, 56) sts.

Sew shoulder seams.

Sew in sleeves matching dec edges of armhole and sleeve cap.

Do not sew underarm seams.

Hood

Sl 22 (24, 26, 28) back neck sts from holder to larger needles.

Work even in established pat for 8½ (9, 9½, 10) inches, ending with a WS row.

Cable cast on 38 (40, 42, 44) sts at beg of next 2 rows. (98, 104, 110, 116 sts)

Working new sts into pat, work even until hood measures 9 inches above cast-on edge, ending with a WS row.

Shape front edge

Bind off 10 (10, 10, 11) sts at beg of next 6 rows, then 8 (10, 11, 11) sts at beg of following 2 rows.

Bind off the remaining 22 (24, 26, 28) sts.

Stripe Layer

Work as for woven basket layer, substituting Color Stripe sequence for Woven Basket pat.

Assemble & Join Layers

Sew cast-on edges of hood to each side of back hood section.

Sew bottom edges of hood to each side of front neck opening.

Rep for remaining layer.

Place stripe layer into woven basket layer, having WS tog.

Sleeves

With woven basket layer facing, using size 3 needles and A, pick up and k 1 st in each cast-on st, going through both sleeve layers. (42, 44, 46, 48 sts)

Turn and knit 1 row.

Work Diagonal Stripe pat for 6 rows.

Bind off all sts knitwise with A.

Fold trim over joining edge to stripe layer side.

With A, sew trim to stripe layer, placing sts underneath bound-off

edge to create a knit-ch edge along stripe layer.

Sew all underarm and side seams, keeping each layer separate. You will have 2 long seams for each layer.

Body and Hood Trim

Having WS tog, pin both layers tog along hood and body edge, matching neck seam, lower, and front edges carefully.

Hold work upside down with woven basket side facing.

With long circular needle and A, beg at lower right seam, pick up and k 1 st in each cast-on st through both layers along lower edge of right front, 67 (70, 75, 78) sts along right front edge 1 st in each bound-off st along front edge of hood, 67 (70, 75, 78) sts along left front edge, 1 st in each cast-on st along lower edge of left front and back. (380, 400, 424, 444 sts)

Pm between first and last st.

With A, purl 1 rnd.

Next rnd: *K2 E, k2 F, rep from * around.

Work in Diagonal Stripe pat as established for 5 more rnds, moving stripe colors 1 st to the left on each rnd.

With A, bind off all sts.

Fold trim in half and sew in place as for sleeve trim.

Button Loops
Make 4

With dpn and E, cast on 4 sts.

*K4 F, slide sts to other end of needle, k4 E, slide sts to other end of needle.

Rep from * until I-cord is 3 inches long.

Bind off.

Sew 1 end of I-cord to front edge just under front neck and hood seam.

Sew remaining end 1 inch below first end.

Measure down 1½ inches from first button loop and rep for 2nd loop.

Rep for 2nd side.

Sew 2 buttons to each side of coat.

Fold lower 3 inches of sleeve back to form cuff. ✦

SNOW FUN

Fiesta Jacket & Mittens

Designs by Janet Rehfeldt

The brightly colored chunky yarn, snuggly zipped front and protective hood of this jacket will keep active kids cozy during winter weather. The addition of mittens means warm hands when playing in the snow.

Skill Level
Easy**

Size
Jacket: Child's 2 (4, 6, 8) Mittens: 2–4 (4–6, 6–8) Instructions are given for smallest size, with larger sizes in parentheses. When only 1 number is given, it applies to all sizes.

Finished Measurements

Jacket
Chest: 30 (32, 34, 36) inches
Length: 15 (16, 17, 18) inches

Mittens
Hand Circumference: 5½ (6, 6½) inches

Materials
- Plymouth Rimini Rainbow 60 percent acrylic/40 percent wool novelty bouclé yarn (38 yds/50g per ball): 9 (11, 13, 15) balls fiesta #19 (MC)
- Plymouth Encore Worsted 75 percent acrylic/25 percent wool worsted weight yarn (200 yds/ 100g per skein): 2 skeins olive #45 (CC)
- Size 8 (5mm) double-pointed needles
- Size 10 (6mm) double-pointed and 36-inch circular needles
- Size 15 (10mm) 36-inch circular needle or size to obtain gauge
- Stitch holders
- Stitch markers
- Tapestry needle
- 2 (¾-inch) buttons
- 12 (14, 14, 16-inch) separating zipper
- Matching sewing thread and sewing needle
- Matching smooth yarn for seaming
- Decorative zipper pull (optional)

Gauge

8 sts and 12 rows = 4 inches/10cm in Reverse St st with MC on largest needles

To save time, take time to check gauge.

Special Abbreviation

M1 (Make 1): With RH needle, lift bar between sts from back to front and place onto LH needle, p this st.

Pattern Notes

Two strands of CC are held tog for all ribbed borders or cuffs.

The nature of the yarn and st structure make this a very stretchy fabric.

To match the same color patterning when working front pieces or sleeves, begin and end with the same color sequence in the yarn. You may find it easier if you knit two fronts at the same time.

The sleeves are knit from the top down.

Lighter weight yarn to match MC is used for seaming.

Jacket

Back

With larger circular needle and MC, cast on 28 (30, 32, 34) sts. Work in Reverse St st until back measures 7

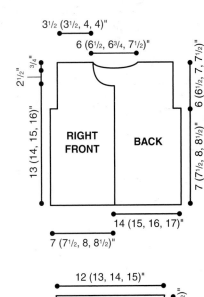

(7½, 8, 8½) inches from beg, ending with a WS row.

Shape armhole

Bind off 1 st at beg of next 2 rows. (26, 28, 30, 32 sts)

Work even until armhole measures 5½ (6, 6½, 7) inches, ending with a RS row.

Shape neck

Next row (WS): Knit 8 (8, 9, 9) sts, sl next 10 (12, 12, 14) sts to holder for front neck, join 2nd ball of yarn, k remaining 8 (8, 9, 9) sts.

Dec 1 st at each neck edge.

Loosely bind off remaining 7 (7, 8, 8) sts for each shoulder.

Left Front

With larger circular needle and MC, cast on 14 (15, 16, 17) sts. Work in Reverse St st until front measures 7 (7½, 8, 8½) inches from beg, ending with a WS row.

Shape armhole

Next row (RS): Bind off 1 st at beg of next row. (13, 14, 15, 16 sts)

Work even until armhole measures 3½ (4, 4½, 5) inches, ending with a RS row.

Shape neck

Next row (WS): Bind off 3 (3, 4, 4) sts, k to end of row. (10, 11, 11, 12 sts)

[Dec 1 st at neck edge every row] 3 (4, 3, 4) times. (7, 7, 8, 8 sts)

Work even until armhole measures same as for back.

Bind off loosely.

Right Front

Work as for left front, reversing shaping.

Sew shoulder seams.

Sleeves

With RS facing using larger circular needle and MC, pick up and k 24 (26, 28, 30) sts evenly around armhole opening.

Work 3 rows in Reverse St st.

Dec 1 st each end on next row, then [every following 5th row] 2 (1, 3, 2) times. (18, 22, 20, 24 sts)

[Dec 1 st each end every 4th row] 2 (4, 2, 4) times. (14, 14, 16, 16 sts)

Work even until sleeve measures 9½ (10½, 11½, 12½) inches.

Bind off loosely.

Cuffs

With RS facing using medium needles and 2 strands of CC, pick up and k 28 (28, 32, 32) sts along bottom edge of sleeve.

Work in k2, p2 ribbing for 2 inches.

Bind off in pat.

Hood

Row 1 (RS): With larger size circular needles and MC, pick up and k 10 (11, 12, 13) sts along right front neckline to shoulder seam, 3 sts along back neckline, k 10 (12, 12, 14) back neck sts from holder, pick up and k 3 sts along back neckline to shoulder

seam, 10 (11, 12, 13) sts along left front neckline. (36, 40, 42, 46 sts)

Row 2: K 17 (19, 20, 22) sts, pm, k2, pm, k 17 (19, 20, 22) sts.

Rows 3 and 4: Working in Reverse St st, dec 1 st at each neck edge. (34, 38, 40, 44 sts)

Row 5: P2tog, work to marker, [p in front and back of next st] twice, work 2 last 2 sts, p2tog.

Rows 6 and 7: Rep Rows 3 and 4. (30, 34, 36, 40 sts)

Rows 8 and 9: Work even.

Row 10: Work to first marker, inc 1 st, k2, inc 1 st, work to end of row. (32, 36, 38, 42 sts)

Rows 11–15: Work even.

Row 16: Work to first marker, inc 1 st, k4, inc 1 st, work to end of row. (34, 38, 40, 44 sts)

Rows 17–21: Work even.

Row 22: Work to first marker, inc 1 st, k6, inc 1 st, work to end of row. (36, 40, 42, 46 sts)

Rows 23–28: Work even until hood measures 9¼ (9¼, 9½, 9½) inches from picked-up row, ending with a WS row.

Top shaping

Next row (RS): P 15 (17, 18, 20) sts, join 2nd ball of yarn and bind off next 6 sts, p 15 (17, 18, 20) sts.

Working on both sides of hood with separate balls of yarn, bind off at center of hood [5 sts] twice, then [4 sts] twice. (6, 7, 8, 9, 11 sts on each side)

Bind off all sts.

Pockets

Mark each front and back piece for pocket placement as follows:

Measure up ½ inch from bottom edge and mark. Measure up 5 inches from first marker and place 2nd marker.

Right Front Pocket

With RS facing using medium needles and MC, pick and k 9 sts between markers.

Next row: Inc 1 st in each st across. (18 sts)

Change to CC and work 18 rows in st making sure k side is facing RS of work.

Cut yarn, leaving an end for sewing.

Rep for remaining 3 marked pocket areas.

Sew open sts from back pocket to open sts of front pocket using Kitchener method.

Sew sleeve and side seams.

Bottom Band

With RS facing using medium circular needles and CC, pick up and k 102 (110, 114, 118) along bottom edge of jacket.

Work in k2, p2 ribbing for 2 inches.

Bind off loosely in rib.

Front & Hood Bands

With RS facing using medium circular needles and CC, pick up and k 46 (48, 52, 56) sts along right front, 78 (78, 82, 86) sts around hood and 46 (48, 52, 56) sts along left front edges. (179, 174, 186, 202 sts)

Work in k2, p2 ribbing for 1 inch.

Bind off loosely in rib.

Button Tabs

Work tabs on right front for girls and left front for boys.

Top Tab

With RS facing using medium needles and CC, pick up and k 5 sts from neckline downward.

Purl 1 row, knit 1 row.

Buttonhole row: P3, yo, p2tog, p1.

Row 4: K3, k2tog.

Row 6: P2, p2tog.

Loosely bind off remaining 3 sts.

Bottom Tab

Rep for lower button tab beg with first st at bottom of band.

Finishing

Sew zipper to front bands.

Sew buttons to top and bottom of front bands.

Sew top edges of pockets tog.

Sew bottom edges of pocket loosely to top of bottom bands.

Attach zipper pull if desired.

Mittens

With medium dpn and MC, cast on 13 (15, 17) sts.

Arrange st onto 3 dpn as follows: 4 (4, 5) sts on first needle, 5 (5, 5) sts on 2nd needle, 6 (6, 5) sts on 3rd needle. Join without twisting, pm between first and last st.

Purl 1 rnd.

Begin gusset

Rnd 1: P 6 (7, 8) sts, pm, M1, p1, M1, p to end of rnd. (3 gusset sts between markers)

Rnd 2: Purl.

Rnd 3: P to first marker, sl marker, M1, p to next marker, M1, sl marker, p to end of rnd.

Rnd 4: Purl.

Rnd 5: Rep Rnd 3. (7 gusset sts between markers)

Rnd 6: P to first marker, removing markers sl gusset sts to holder, cast on 1 st over gap left by gusset, p to end of rnd. (13, 15, 17 sts)

Work even until mitten measures 3 (3½, 4) inches from beg or to top of little finger.

Shape top

Rnd 1: Dec 1 (3, 2) sts evenly. (12, 12, 15 sts)

Rnd 2: Purl.

Rnd 3: *P2 (2, 3), p2tog, rep from * around. (9, 9, 12 sts)

Rnd 4: Purl.

Rep Rnds 3 and 4, working 1 less st between decs until 3 (3, 6) sts remain.

Cut yarn leaving an 8-inch end, draw yarn through remaining sts and pull tightly.

Thumb

Place gusset sts onto 3 dpn.

Pick up and purl 1 st in gusset gap. (8 sts)

Work even until thumb measures ¾ (1, 1¼) inches or to middle of thumbnail.

Shape top

Rnd 1: [P2tog, p2] twice. (6 sts)

Rnd 2: Purl.

Rnd 3: [P2tog, p1] twice. (4 sts)

Cut yarn leaving an 8-inch end, draw yarn through remaining sts and pull tightly.

Cuff

With smaller dpn and CC, pick up and k 24 (28, 32) sts evenly along cast-on edge of mitten. Divide sts evenly onto 3 needles.

Work even in k2, p2 ribbing until cuff measures 1½ inches.

Bind off loosely in rib. ◆

Jazzy Jewels Set

Designs by Cindy Polfer

Combine three very different yarns for a warm and cozy jacket, hat, and mitten set for that special youngster.

Skill Level
Easy**

Size
Jacket: Child's 2 (4, 6, 8)

Hat & Mittens: Child's 2–4 (6–8)
Instructions are given for smallest size, with larger sizes in parentheses. When only 1 number is given, it applies to all sizes.

Finished Measurements
Jacket
Chest: 29 (31, 33, 35) inches

Side to underarm: 9 (9½, 9¾, 11½) inches

Armhole depth: 6 (6¾, 7¼, 7½) inches

Total length: 15 (16, 17, 19) inches

Sleeve: 9½ (10½, 11½, 12½) inches

Hat
Circumference: 20 (21½) inches

Mittens
Length: 7 (7¾) inches

Hand circumference: 6¾ (7½) inches

Materials
- Plymouth Rimini Rainbow 40 percent wool/60 percent acrylic novelty bouclé yarn (38 yds/50g per ball): 11 (12, 13, 15) balls green #2 (MC)
- Plymouth Flash 100 percent nylon eyelash yarn (190 yds/50g per ball): 1 ball red #985 (A)
- Plymouth Encore Chunky 75 percent acrylic/25 percent wool chunky weight yarn (143 yds/100g per skein): 1 skein blue #133 (B)
- Size 7 (4.5mm) needles
- 10 (6mm) needles or size needed to obtain gauge
- Tapestry needle
- Stitch holders
- Stitch markers
- 4 (5, 5, 5) ¾-inch shank-type buttons
- 4 (5, 5, 5) small flat buttons

Gauge
10 sts and 19 rows = 4 inches/10cm in Body pat with larger needles and 1 strand each of MC and A held tog

To save time, take time to check gauge.

Pattern Stitches
A. 1/1 Rib
Row 1 (WS): K1, *p1, k1; rep from * across row.

Row 2: P1, *k1, p1; rep from * across row.

Rep Rows 1–2 for pat.

B. Body Pattern
Rows 1 and 3 (RS): With MC, knit.

Rows 2 and 4: With MC, purl.

Row 5: With 1 strand each MC and A held tog, purl.

Row 6: With 1 strand each MC and A held tog, knit.

Rep Rows 1–6 for pat.

Pattern Notes

Color A may be carried up the side of work when not in use on Rows 1–4 of Body pat.

Keep all incs or decs in pat st when shaping garments.

Incs are worked by knitting into front and back of stitch.

Jacket

Back

With B and smaller needles, cast on 73 (77, 81, 87) sts.

Work 1/1 Rib for 2 inches ending with a WS row.

Change to MC and larger needles.

Set up pat: K2tog across row, ending with k1. (37, 39, 41, 44 sts)

Beg with Row 2 of Body pat, work even until back measures 9 (9¼, 9¾, 11½) inches.

Mark each end st of last row for underarm.

Continue to work even in pat until back measures 14½ (15 ½, 16½, 17½) inches, ending with a WS row.

Shape back neck

Work across 12 (13, 14, 15) sts, place next 13 (13, 13, 14) sts onto holder for back neck, join 2nd ball of yarn and work across remaining 12 (13, 14, 15) sts.

Working on both sides of neck with separate balls of yarn, [dec 1 st at each neck edge] once.

Work even for 1 row.

Place shoulder sts on holders.

Right Front

With B and smaller needles, cast on 35 (37, 39, 41) sts.

Work 1/1 Rib for 2 inches, ending with a WS row.

Change to MC and larger needles.

Set up pat: K2tog across row, ending with k1. (18, 19, 20, 21 sts)

Beg with Row 2 of Body pat, work even until front measures same as back to underarm.

With RS facing, mark left edge for underarm.

Work even until front measures 12½ (13½, 14½, 15½) inches, ending with a WS row.

Shape front neck

Bind off 3 sts at beg of next row.

[Dec 1 st at neck edge every other row] 3 times. (12, 13, 14, 15 sts)

Work even until armhole measures same length as back.

Place sts on holder.

Left Front

Work as for right front, reversing shaping.

Join shoulders, using 3-needle bind-off method.

Neck Band

With RS facing, using B and smaller needles, pick up and k 24 sts along right neck edge, k back neck sts inc 1 st in each of next 6 sts, k2 (1, 1, 1), inc 1 st in each of next 5 (6, 6, 7) sts, pick up and k 24 sts along left neck edge. (71, 73, 73, 75 sts)

Work in 1/1 Rib for 5 rows.

Bind off in pat.

Sleeves

With RS facing, using MC and larger needles, pick up and k 30 (34, 36, 38) sts along edge between armhole markers.

Beg with Row 2 of Body pat, [dec 1 st each end every 10th (8th, 8th, 8th) row] 3 (4, 5, 5) times. (24, 26, 26, 28 sts)

Work even until sleeve measures 7½ (8½, 9½, 10½) inches, ending with a WS row.

Begin cuff

Change to B and smaller needles.

Knit 1 row, inc 3 sts evenly. (27, 29, 29, 31 sts)

Work in 1/1 Rib for 11 rows.

Bind off in pat.

Button Band

With B and smaller needles, cast on 9 sts.

Work even in 1/1 Rib until band measures same as front edge to neckline, marking Row 2 as RS of band.

Place sts on holder.

Sew band to left front edge for a girl, or right front edge for a boy. Since band is not bound off you can adjust by adding or removing rows as needed. Bind off at proper length of band.

Buttonhole Band

Mark button band for 4 (5, 5, 5) buttons, having bottom button 1 inch from lower edge and top button ¾ inch from upper edge, spacing remainder evenly in between.

Work buttonhole band as for button band, making buttonhole row at markers as follows:

Buttonhole row: [P1, k1] twice, yo, k2tog, p1, k1, p1.

Work row following buttonhole row in established Rib pat.

Finishing

Sew buttonhole band to remaining front edge.

Sew on buttons, using small flat buttons as anchor on inside of band.

Sew side and sleeve seams.

Hat

With B and smaller needles, cast on 103 (105) sts.

Work 1/1 Rib for ¾ inch, ending with a WS row.

Change to MC and larger size needles.

Set up pat: K2tog across row, ending with k1. (52, 53 sts)

Beg with Row 2 of Body pat, work even until hat measures 6½ (7) inches, ending with a WS row.

Shape top

Row 1: K0 (1), [k2tog, k2] 13 times. (40, 41 sts)

Row 2: Purl.

Row 3: K1 (2), [k2tog, k1] 13 times. (27, 28 sts)

Row 4: Purl.

Row 5: P1 (0), [p2tog] across. (14 sts)

Row 6: [K2tog] across. (7 sts)

Cut yarn leaving an 18-inch end.

With tapestry needle, draw end through sts on needle and fasten snugly.

Sew back seam.

Make a 2-inch pompom and sew to top of hat.

continued on page 190

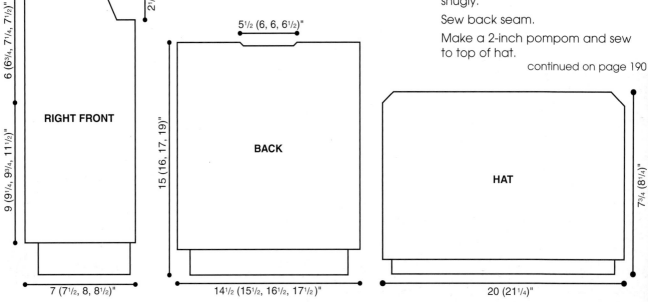

SLEEVE

12 (13½, 14½, 15)"

9½ (10½, 11½, 12½)"

9½ (10½, 10½, 11¼)"

RIGHT FRONT

2½"

6 (6¾, 7¼, 7½)"

9 (9¼, 9¾, 11½)"

7 (7½, 8, 8½)"

BACK

5½ (6, 6, 6½)"

15 (16, 17, 19)"

14½ (15½, 16½, 17½)"

HAT

20 (21¼)"

7¾ (8¼)"

Grape Confetti Hat & Scarf Set

Designs by Laura Polley

Novelty yarn and big needles make this set ultra-quick and lots of fun!

Skill Level

Easy**

Size

Child's 2 (4, 6, 8) Instructions are given for smallest size, with larger sizes in parentheses. When only 1 number is given, it applies to all sizes.

Finished Measurements

Hat

Circumference: 19 (20, 21, 22) inches

Total length: 7½ (7½, 8½, 9) inches

Scarf

Width: 6½ (6½, 7½, 7½) inches

Length (without fringe): 38½ (42, 45½, 49) inches

Materials

• Plymouth Rimini Rainbow 40 percent wool/60 percent acrylic novelty yarn (38 yds/50g per ball): Hat: 1 (2, 2, 2) balls purple rainbow #05, Scarf: 3 (3, 3, 4) balls purple rainbow #05

• Size 13 (9mm) double-pointed and straight needles, or size needed to obtain gauge
• Tapestry needle
• Size G/6 crochet hook

Gauge

9½ sts and 18 rnds = 5 inches in St st

8 sts and 18 rows = 4 inches/10cm in ribbing

To save time, take time to check gauge.

Hat

With dpn, very loosely cast on 36 (38, 40, 42) sts.

Divide sts evenly among 3 dpns. Join without twisting, pm between first and last st.

Work in k1, p1 rib for 6 rnds.

Work even in St st until hat measures 3 (3, 3½, 4) inches, dec 0 (2, 0, 2) sts evenly on last rnd. (36, 36, 40, 40 sts)

Shape crown

Rnd 1: *K7 (7, 8, 8), k2tog, rep from * around. (32, 32, 36, 36 sts)

Rnd 2: Knit.

Rnd 3: *K6 (6, 7, 7), k2tog, rep from * around. (28, 28, 32, 32 sts)

Rnd 4: Knit.

Continue to dec every other row as before, having 1 less st between decs each time, until 4 (4, 8, 8) sts remaining, end with a dec row.

Sizes 6 & 8 only

Next rnd: K2tog around. (4 sts)

Cut yarn, leaving a 6-inch end.

Draw end through remaining sts twice and pull tightly to secure.

continued on page 189

Fishing Penguin Pullover

Design by Nazanin S. Fard

Your child will love to wear this pullover, with its fun-loving penguin. Dinner already dangles from his wing, as his wiggly eyes search for more fish.

Skill Level

Intermediate***

Size

Child's 2 (4, 6, 8) Instructions are given for smallest size, with larger sizes in parentheses. When only 1 number is given, it applies to all sizes.

Finished Measurements

Chest: 23 (25, 27, 30) inches

Sleeve length: 8½ (10, 12½, 15½) inches

Armhole depth: 4½ (6, 7, 8) inches

Total length: 12½ (14½, 17½, 21) inches

Materials

- Plymouth Encore Colorspun Worsted 75 percent acrylic/25 percent wool worsted weight yarn (200 yds/100g per skein): 1 (2, 3, 4) skeins ice #7064 (MC)
- Plymouth Encore Worsted 75 percent acrylic/25 percent wool worsted weight yarn (200 yds/ 100g per skein): 1 skein each baby blue #793, charcoal #520, white #208, gold #1014
- Size 8 (5mm) straight and 16-inch circular needles
- Size 9 (5.5mm) needles or size needed to obtain gauge
- 2 (⅜-inch) wiggle eyes, JHB International #20191
- 1 fish button, JHB International, #25012

Gauge

18 sts and 24 rows = 4 inches/10cm in St st with larger needles

To save time, take time to check gauge.

Pattern Note

To avoid choking hazard, you may wish to omit wiggle eyes and fish if sweater is for a small child. Embroider eyes with duplicate st in position shown on chart.

Back

With smaller needles cast on 48 (55, 62, 68) sts.

Work k1, p1 ribbing for 1½ inches, inc 4 (5, 6, 8) sts evenly on last row. (52, 60, 68, 76 sts)

Change to larger needles and St st.

Work even until back measures 8 (8½, 10½, 13) inches. Mark each end st for underarm.

Continue to work even until back measures 12½ (14½, 17½, 21) inches.

Place sts on 3 holders, having 26 (28, 28, 30) sts on one holder for back neck and 13 (16, 20, 23) sts for each shoulder on remaining holders.

Front

Work as for back until front measures 2 (2, 3, 3) inches, ending with a WS row.

Set up pat: K9 (13, 17, 21), pm, work

end every 6th (6th, 8th 12th) row] 8 (8, 8, 6) times. (34, 48, 52, 60 sts)

Work even until sleeve measures 6½ (8, 10½, 13) inches, dec 4 (10, 8, 10) sts evenly on last WS row. (30, 38, 44, 50 sts)

Change to smaller needles.

Work even in k1, p1 ribbing for 2 (2, 2, 2½) inches.

Bind off loosely in ribbing.

Finishing

Duplicate st or sew wiggle eyes to penguin's face.

Cut a 3-inch piece of MC. Attach fish button to one end and sew other end to penguin's flipper.

Sew sleeve and side seams. ✦

Row 1 of chart, pm, k to end of row.

Keeping sts between markers in color pat and remaining sts in MC, work even until front measures 10 (12, 14½, 18) inches, marking underarm as for back.

Shape neck

Next row (RS): K 19 (23, 27, 30) sts, sl next 14 (14, 14, 16) sts to holder for front neck, join 2nd ball of yarn and k to end of row.

Working on both sides of neck with separate balls of yarn, [dec 1 st at each neck edge every other row] 6 (7, 7, 7) times. (13, 16, 20, 23 sts for each shoulder)

Work even until front measures same as back above underarm markers.

Join front and back shoulders using 3-needle bind-off method.

Neck Band

With RS facing using smaller circular needle and MC, k across 26 (28, 28, 30) sts of back neck, pick up and k 8 (12, 20, 22) sts along left side of neck, k across 14 (14, 14, 16) sts of front neck, pick up and k 8 (12, 20, 22) sts along right edge of neck. (56, 66, 82, 88 sts)

Pm between first and last st.

Work even in k1, p1 ribbing for 1½ (1½, 2, 2) inches. Do not bind off.

Fold band in half to the inside and loosely sew live sts to first row of band.

Sleeve

With MC and larger needles, pick up and k 50 (64, 68, 72) sts along arm edge between under-arm markers.

Working in St st, [dec 1 st each

COLOR KEY
☐ MC
■ Charcoal
☐ White
▨ Gold
▨ Baby blue

FISHING PENGUIN CHART

Swimming Turtles Cardigan

Design by Nazanin S. Fard

A pair of turtles swims lazily across the fronts of this cardigan. More terrapins join them in the form of buttons.

Skill Level

Intermediate***

Size

Child's 2 (4, 6, 8) Instructions are given for smallest size, with larger sizes in parentheses. When only 1 number is given, it applies to all sizes.

Finished Measurements

Chest: 30 (31½, 33, 35) inches

Sleeve length: 10 (11, 12½, 14) inches

Armhole depth: 6 (6½, 7, 7½) inches

Total length: 14½ (15½, 17½, 19½) inches

Materials

- Plymouth Wildflower D.K. 51 percent mercerized cotton/49 percent acrylic DK weight yarn (136 yds/50g per ball): 4 (5, 6, 6) balls off-white #40 (MC), 1 ball each khaki #31, green #49, lime #58
- Size 5 (3.75mm) needles
- Size 6 (4.25mm) needles or size needed to obtain gauge
- 4 (⅜-inch) wiggle eyes, JHB International #20191
- 5 (5, 6, 6) ⅞-inch turtle buttons, JHB International #94626
- Stitch holders

Gauge

20 sts and 28 rows = 4 inches/10cm in St st with larger needles

To save time, take time to check gauge.

Pattern Notes

To avoid choking hazard, you may wish to omit wiggle eyes if sweater is for a small child. Instead embroider eyes with duplicate st in position shown on chart.

Reverse direction of turtle for left front, so it faces center of sweater.

Back

With smaller needles and MC, cast on 68 (72, 74, 80) sts.

Work even in k1, p1 ribbing for 2 inches, inc 8 sts evenly on last WS row. (76, 80, 82, 88 sts)

Change to larger needles and St st.

Work even until back measures 8½ (9, 10½, 12) inches. Mark each end st for underarm.

Continue to work even for 6 (6½, 7, 7½) inches more.

Place sts on 3 holders, having center 28 (28, 30, 30) sts on one holder for back neck and 24 (26, 26, 29) sts for shoulders on each of remaining holders.

Right Front

With smaller needles and MC, cast on 34 (36, 37, 40) sts.

Work even in k1, p1 ribbing for 2 inches, inc 4 sts evenly on last WS row. (38, 40, 41, 44 sts)

Change to larger needles.

Work even in St st for 1 (2, 2, 3) inches, ending with a WS row.

Set up pat: K 3 (3, 4, 4) sts MC, pm, work Row 1 of chart over next 33 sts, pm, k to end of row.

Keeping sts between markers in turtle pat and remaining in MC, work even until front measures 12 (13, 14½, 16½) inches, ending with a WS row and placing underarm marker at 8½ (9, 10½, 12) inches.

Shape neck

Bind off 7 (7, 8, 8) sts at beg of next RS row.

[Dec 1 st at neck edge every other row] 7 times. (24, 26, 26, 29 sts)

Work even until armhole measures same as for back.

Join front and back shoulders, using 3-needle bind-off method.

Left Front

Work as right front, reversing shaping and beginning turtle chart 1 inch before placing underarm marker.

Sleeve

With larger needles and MC, pick up and k 60 (66, 70, 76) sts between underarm markers at arm edge.

Working in St st, [dec 1 st each end every 5th row] 2 (2, 8, 10) times, then [every 4th row] 10 (12, 7, 7) times. (36, 38, 40, 42 sts)

Work even until sleeve measures 8 (9, 10½, 12) inches, dec 4 sts evenly on last WS row. (32, 34, 36, 38 sts)

Change to smaller needles and work even in k1, p1 ribbing for 2 inches.

Bind off loosely in ribbing.

Neck Band

With RS facing, join MC at right front neck. With smaller needles, pick up

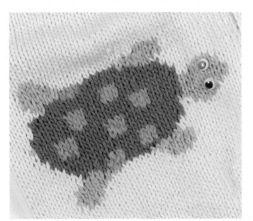

and k 24 (26, 29, 29) sts along right side of neck, k 28 (28, 30, 30) sts of back neck, pick up and k 24 (26, 29, 29) sts along left side of neck. (76, 80, 88, 88 sts)

Work even in k1, p1 ribbing for 1 inch.

Bind off loosely in ribbing.

Button Band

With RS facing, using MC and smaller needles, pick up and k 50 (55, 62, 70) sts along right front edge.

Work even in k1, p1 ribbing for 8 rows.

Bind off loosely in ribbing.

Buttonhole Band

Work 3 rows of ribbing as for button band.

Mark front edge for 5 (5, 6, 6) buttonholes, having top and bottom

markers 1½ inches from ends and remainder spaced evenly.

Buttonhole row: [Work to marker, bind off 2 sts, turn work and cable cast on 2 sts, turn] 5 (5, 6, 6) times, work to end of row.

Work 4 more rows in established ribbing.

Bind off loosely in ribbing.

Finishing

Duplicate st or sew wiggle eyes to turtles' heads.

Sew sleeve and side seams.

Sew on buttons. ◆

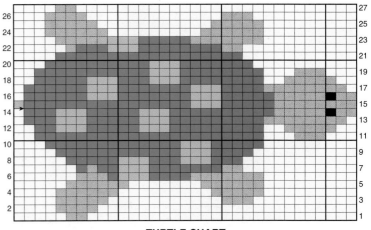

TURTLE CHART

Froggy Goes to School

Design by Shari Haux

A wide-eyed frog will gladly tote books and papers home from school.

Skill Level
Easy**

Size
Approximately 15 x 17 inches

Materials
- Plymouth Fantasy Naturale 100 percent mercerized cotton worsted weight yarn (140 yds/100g per skein): 3 skeins yellow #1242, 2 skeins black #8990, 1 skein bright green #5228
- Size 5 (3.75mm) needles
- Size 7 (4.5mm) double-pointed and straight needles or size needed to obtain gauge
- Tapestry needle
- 2 (30mm) wiggle eyes
- Aleene's OK to Wash-it Permanent Fabric Bond glue

Gauge
18 sts and 26 rows = 4 inches/10cm in St st with larger needles

To save time, take time to check gauge.

Pattern Notes
Wind separate bobbins of yellow and green for each section at top of frog's head.

To avoid holes when changing colors, always bring new color up over old.

Backpack
With yellow and smaller needles, cast on 80 sts, leaving a long tail for sewing later.

Work in garter st for 16 rows. Change to larger needles.

Work in St st for 22 rows.

Referring to chart, work in color pat for 68 rows.

Change to yellow and work in garter st for 14 rows.

Change to St st and work even for 90 rows.

Change to smaller needles and work in garter st for 16 rows.

Bind off loosely leaving a long yarn tail for sewing.

Straps
Make 2

With smaller dpn and black, cast on 24 sts.

Divide sts evenly on 3 needles.

Knit every rnd until strap measures 29 inches.

Bind off, leaving a long tail for sewing.

Finishing

With black, embroider mouth and nose in running st as shown on chart.

Fold top garter st edge in half to inside and pin in place to form casing.

Sew casing, leaving ends open.

Rep for 2nd side.

With RS tog, fold bag in half along center garter-st section.

Sew sides, beg just below casing to bottom edge.

Pin straps to back of pack as shown in Fig. 1. Sew in place.

Glue on eyes and allow to dry.

Drawstring

Cut 9 strands of yarn, each 50 inches long.

Braid, using 3 strands for each group.

Knot 1 end loosely and run braid through casings.

Untie knot and reknot all ends tog.

Trim ends evenly. ✦

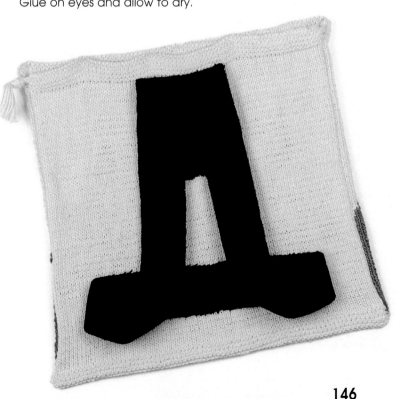

146

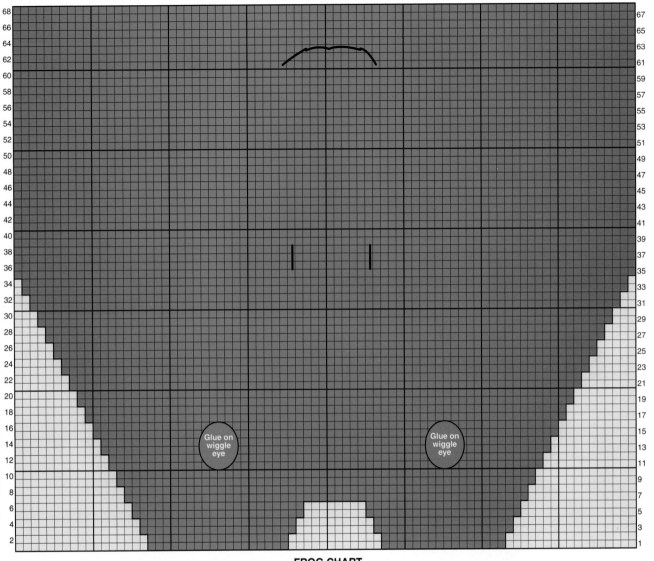

FROG CHART

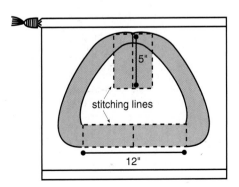

5"

stitching lines

12"

Fig. 1
Strap Placement

David & His Sheep

Design by Kathy Sasser

David tends his sheep in a rainbow colored pasture.

Skill Level
Intermediate***

Size
Child's 2 (4, 6, 8) Instructions are given for smallest size, with larger sizes in parentheses. When only 1 number is given, it applies to all sizes.

Finished Measurements
Chest: 23 (25, 27, 29) inches

Sleeve: 7½ (10, 11, 12½) inches

Total length: 13 (14½, 15½, 17½) inches

Materials
- Plymouth Encore Worsted 75 percent acrylic/25 percent wool worsted weight yarn (200 yds/ 100g per skein): 2 (2, 2, 3) skeins yellow #1382, 1 skein each violet #1384, blue #133, green #054, orange 1383, red #1386, white #146, black #217, pink #597
- Size 5 (3.75mm) straight and 16-inch circular needle
- Size 7 (4.5mm) needle or size needed to obtain gauge
- Tapestry needle
- Stitch holders

Gauge
20 sts and 26 rows = 4 inches/10cm in St st with larger needles

To save time, take time to check gauge.

Pattern Notes
Large areas of color can be worked in intarsia, while smaller areas are more successfully worked in duplicate st.

For added fun, place French knots in David's beard.

Back
With smaller needles and yellow, cast on 54 (58, 62, 68) sts.

Work in k1, p1 rib for 1½ (2, 2, 2) inches, inc 6 (6, 8, 6) sts evenly across last WS row. (60, 64, 70, 74 sts)

Change to larger needles and St st.

Referring to Chart A for desired size, work even for 75 (81, 88, 101) rows, pm for each underarm at Rows 42 (46, 50, 60) as indicated on chart.

Sl all sts to holder.

Front
Work as for back substituting Chart B for Chart A, placing underarm markers as before, and working neck shaping as indicated.

Place shoulder sts on holders.

Sleeves
With smaller needle and yellow, cast on 30

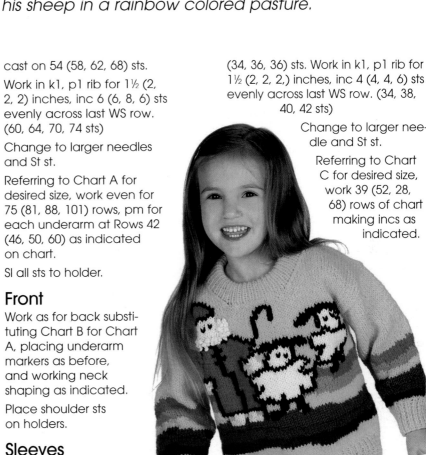

(34, 36, 36) sts. Work in k1, p1 rib for 1½ (2, 2, 2,) inches, inc 4 (4, 4, 6) sts evenly across last WS row. (34, 38, 40, 42 sts)

Change to larger needle and St st.

Referring to Chart C for desired size, work 39 (52, 28, 68) rows of chart making incs as indicated.

Bind off loosely.

With RS facing, bind off shoulder sts tog, leaving 28 (28, 30, 30) back center sts on holder.

Neck Band

Beg at left shoulder with RS facing using smaller circular needle and yellow, pick up and k 16 (16, 21, 21) sts along left side of neck, k across center 14 (14, 16, 16) sts, pick up and k 16 (16, 21, 21) sts along right side of neck, k across 28 (28, 30, 30) back neck sts. (74, 74, 88, 88 sts)

Join, pm between first and last st.

Work in k1, p1 rib for 2 (2, 2, 2½) inches.

Bind off loosely in rib.

Fold neck ribbing in half and sew loosely in place.

Finishing

Sew sleeves into armhole between markers.

Sew side and sleeve seams.

Weave in all loose ends. ◆

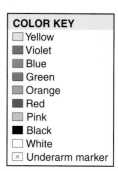

COLOR KEY
- ☐ Yellow
- ■ Violet
- ■ Blue
- ■ Green
- ■ Orange
- ■ Red
- ■ Pink
- ■ Black
- ☐ White
- ☒ Underarm marker

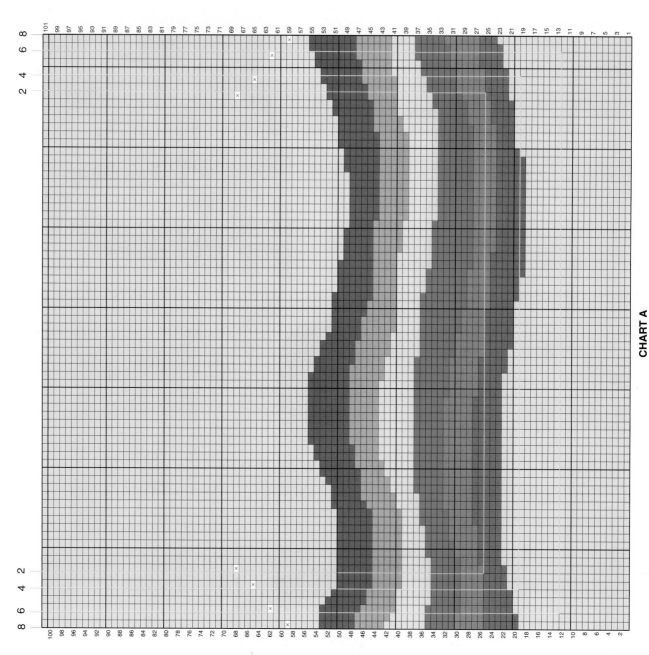

CHART A
BACK

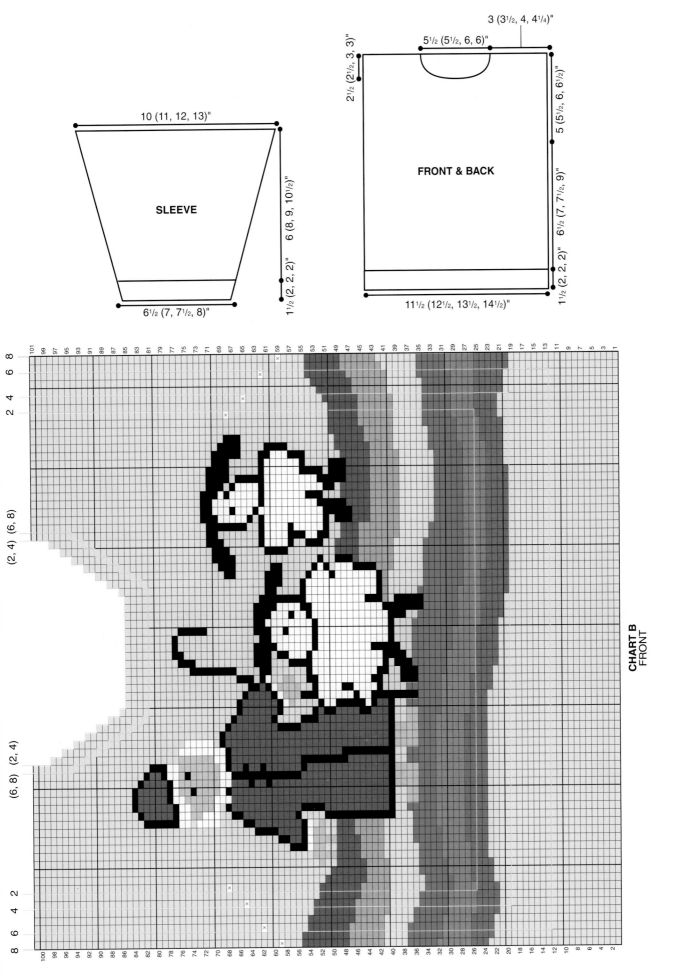

SLEEVE

10 (11, 12, 13)"

6 (8, 9, 10½)"

1½ (2, 2, 2)"

6½ (7, 7½, 8)"

FRONT & BACK

3 (3½, 4, 4¼)"

5½ (5½, 6, 6)"

2½ (2½, 3, 3)"

5 (5½, 6, 6½)"

6½ (7, 7½, 9)"

1½ (2, 2, 2)"

11½ (12½, 13½, 14½)"

CHART B
FRONT

151

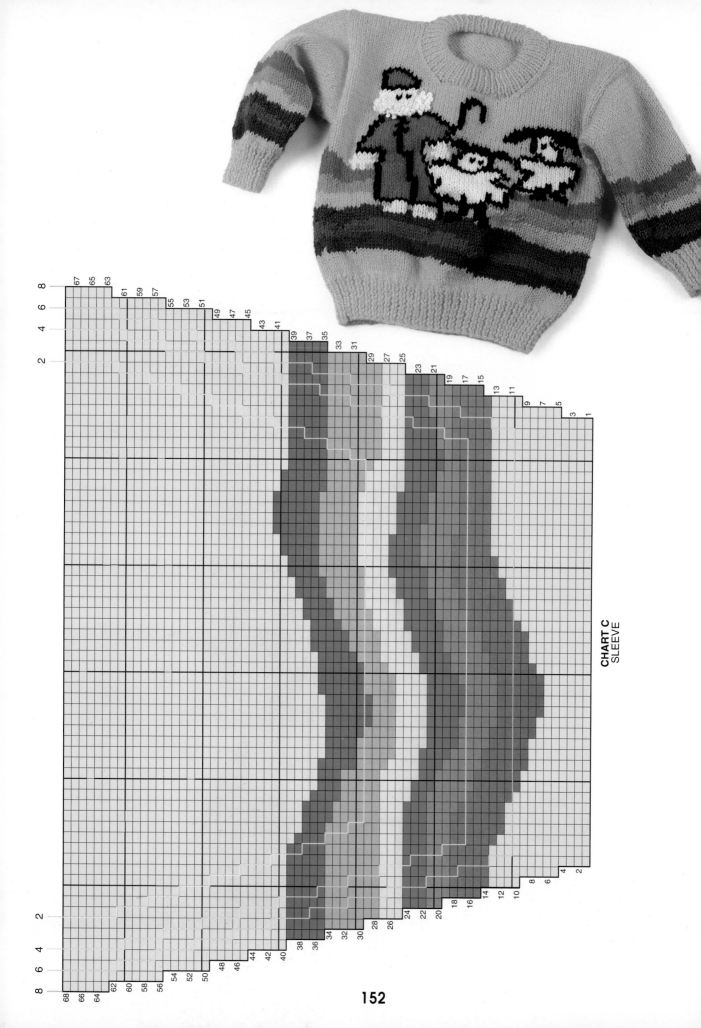

CHART C
SLEEVE

Jonah & His Whale

Design by Kathy Sasser

Jonah has landed safely on the shore after being inside the whale.

Skill Level

Intermediate***

Size

Child's 2 (4, 6, 8) Instructions are given for smallest size, with larger sizes in parentheses. When only 1 number is given, it applies to all sizes.

Finished Measurements

Chest: 23 (25, 27, 29) inches

Sleeve: 7½ (10, 11, 12½) inches

Total length: 13 (14½, 15½, 17½) inches

Materials

- Plymouth Encore Worsted 75 percent acrylic/25 percent wool worsted weight yarn (200 yds/100g per skein): 1 (1, 1, 2) skeins blue #133, 1 (1, 2, 2) skeins light blue #4045, 1 skein each red #1386, green #054, light charcoal #194, black #217, white #146, pink #597
- Size 5 (3.75mm) straight and 16-inch circular needle
- Size 7 (4.5mm) needle or size needed to obtain gauge
- Tapestry needle
- Stitch holders

Gauge

20 sts and 26 rows = 4 inches/10cm in St st with larger needles

To save time, take time to check gauge.

Pattern Notes

Large areas of color can be worked in intarsia, while smaller areas are more successfully worked in duplicate st.

For added fun, add French knots to Jonah's beard.

Back

With smaller needles and blue, cast on 54 (58, 62, 68) sts.

Work in k1, p1 rib for 1½ (2, 2, 2) inches, inc 6 (6, 8, 6) sts evenly across last WS row. (60, 64, 70, 74 sts)

Change to larger needles and St st.

Referring to Chart A for desired size, work even for 75 (81, 88, 101) rows, pm for each underarm at Rows 42 (46, 50, 60) as indicated on chart.

Sl all sts to holder.

Front

Work as for back substituting Chart B for

Chart A, placing underarm markers as before, and working neck shaping as indicated.

Place shoulder sts on holders.

Sleeves

With smaller needle and blue, cast on 30 (34, 36, 36) sts. Work in k1, p1 rib for 1½ (2, 2, 2) inches, inc 4 (4, 4, 6) sts evenly across last WS row. (34, 38, 40, 42 sts)

Change to larger needle and St st.

Referring to Chart C for desired size, work 39 (52, 28, 68) rows of chart making incs as indicated.

Bind off loosely.

With RS facing, bind off shoulder sts tog, leaving 28 (28, 30, 30) back center sts on holder.

Neck Band

Beg at left shoulder with RS facing using smaller circular needle and light blue, pick up and k 16 (16, 21, 21) sts along left side of neck, k across center 14 (14, 16, 16) sts, pick up and k 16 (16, 21, 21) sts along right side of neck, k across 28 (28, 30, 30) back neck sts. (74, 74, 88, 88 sts)

Join, pm between first and last st.

Work in k1, p1 rib for 2 (2, 2, 2½) inches.

Bind off loosely in rib.

Fold neck ribbing in half and sew loosely in place.

Finishing

Sew sleeves into armhole between markers.

Sew side and sleeve seams.

Weave in all loose ends. ◆

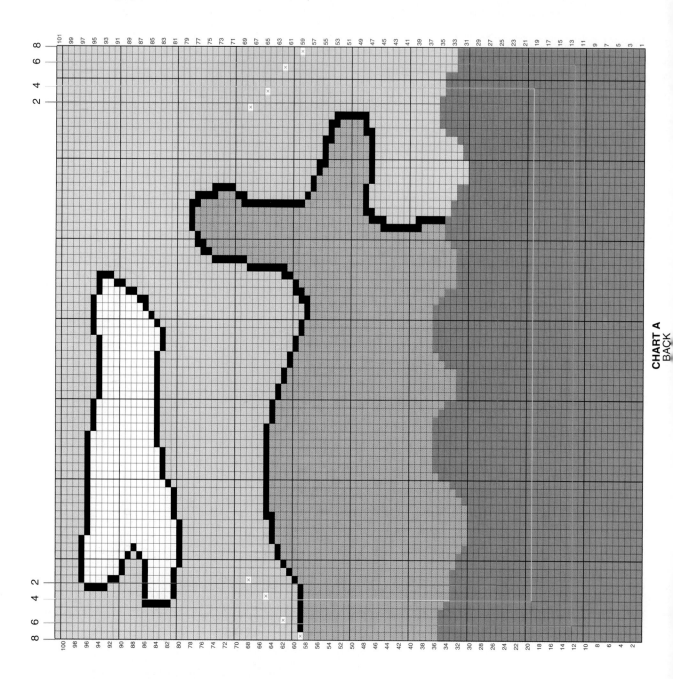

CHART A
BACK

154

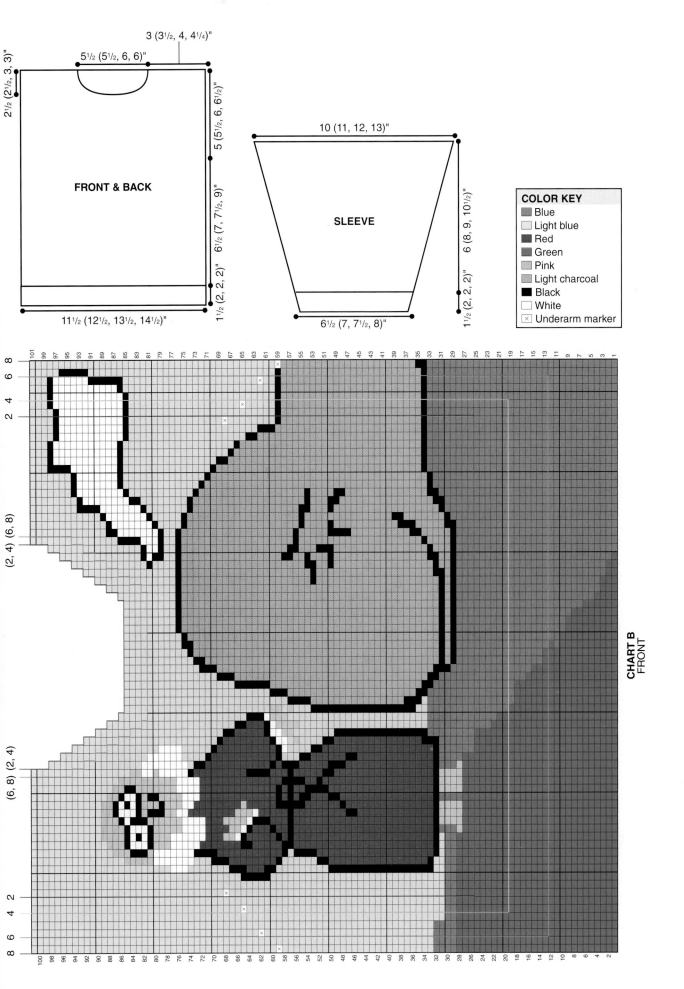

3 (3½, 4, 4¼)"

5½ (5½, 6, 6)"

2½ (2½, 3, 3)"

FRONT & BACK

5 (5½, 6, 6½)"

6½ (7, 7½, 9)"

1½ (2, 2)"

11½ (12½, 13½, 14½)"

10 (11, 12, 13)"

SLEEVE

6 (8, 9, 10½)"

1½ (2, 2)"

6½ (7, 7½, 8)"

COLOR KEY
- Blue
- Light blue
- Red
- Green
- Pink
- Light charcoal
- Black
- White
- ⊠ Underarm marker

CHART B
FRONT

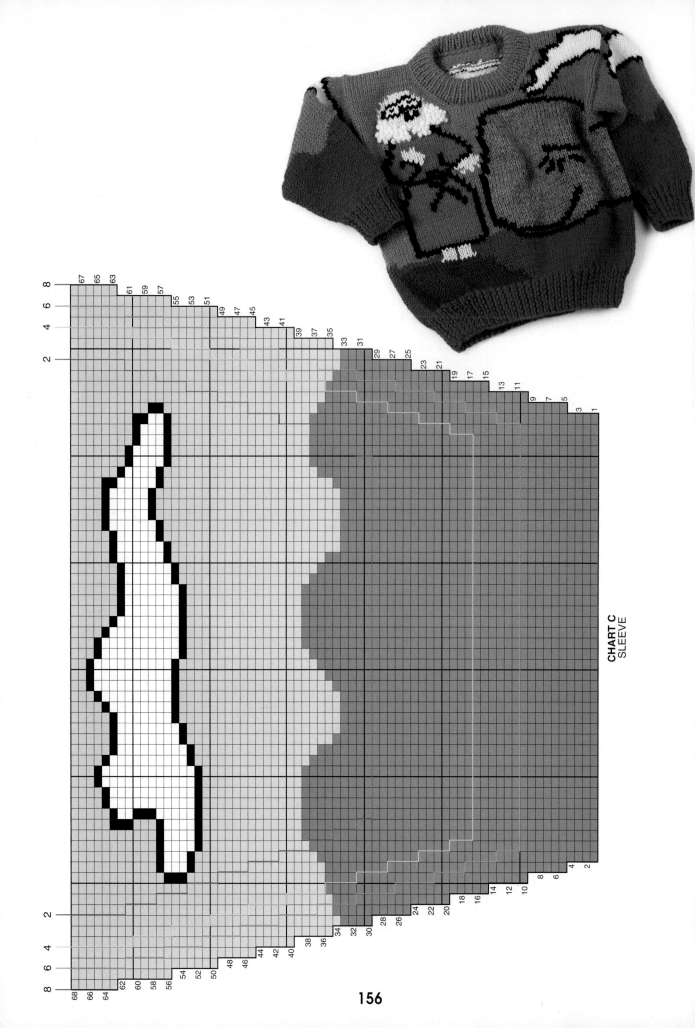

CHART C
SLEEVE

40 Days & 40 Nights

Design by Kathy Sasser

Noah's ark battles the storm with the promise of a rainbow at the end.

Skill Level

Intermediate***

Size

Child's 2 (4, 6, 8) Instructions are given for smallest size, with larger sizes in parentheses. When only 1 number is given, it applies to all sizes.

Finished Measurements

Chest: 23 (25, 27, 29) inches

Sleeve: 7½ (10, 11, 12½) inches

Total length: 13 (14½, 15½, 17½) inches

Materials

- Plymouth Encore Worsted 75 percent acrylic/25 percent wool worsted weight yarn (200 yds/ 100g per skein): 2 (2, 2, 3) skeins light blue #4045, 1 skein each blue #133, white #146, yellow #1382, red #1386, gray #678, orange #1383, black #217
- Size 5 (3.75mm) straight and 16-inch circular needle
- Size 7 (4.5mm) needle or size needed to obtain gauge
- Tapestry needle
- Stitch holders

Gauge

20 sts and 26 rows = 4 inches/10cm in St st with larger needles

To save time, take time to check gauge.

Pattern Note

Large areas of color can be worked in intarsia, while smaller areas are more successfully worked in duplicate st.

Back

With smaller needles and blue, cast on 54 (58, 62, 68) sts.

Work in k1, p1 rib for 1½ (2, 2, 2) inches, inc 6 (6, 8, 6) sts evenly across last WS row. (60, 64, 70, 74 sts)

Change to larger needles and St st.

Referring to Chart A for desired size, work even for 75 (81, 88, 101) rows, pm for each underarm at Rows 42 (46, 50, 60) as indicated on chart.

Sl all sts to holder.

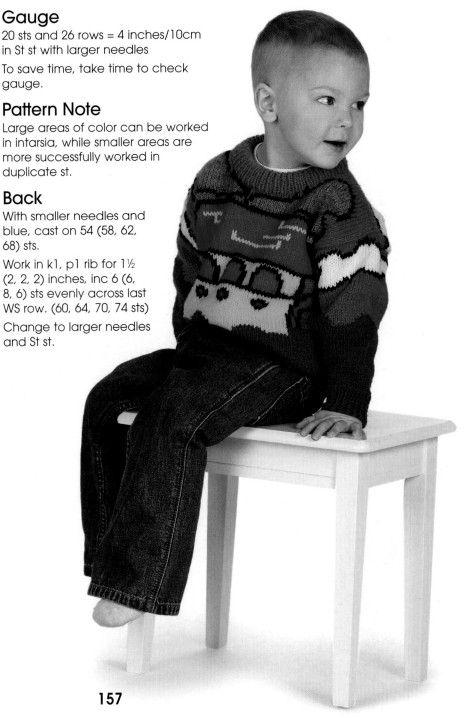

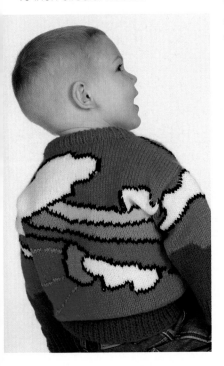

Front

Work as for back substituting Chart B for Chart A, placing underarm markers as before, and working neck shaping as indicated.

Place shoulder sts on holders.

Sleeves

With smaller needles and blue, cast on 30 (34, 36, 36) sts. Work in k1, p1 rib for 1½ (2, 2, 2) inches, inc 4 (4, 4, 6) sts evenly across last WS row. (34, 38, 40, 42 sts)

Change to larger needles and St st.

Referring to Chart C for desired size,

work 39 (52, 28, 68) rows of chart making incs as indicated.

Bind off loosely.

With RS facing, bind off shoulder sts tog, leaving 28 (28, 30, 30) back center sts on holder.

Neck Band

Beg at left shoulder with RS facing using smaller circular needle and light blue, pick up and k 16 (16, 21, 21) sts along left side of neck, k across center 14 (14, 16, 16) sts, pick up and k 16 (16, 21, 21) sts along right side of neck, k across 28 (28, 30,

30) back neck sts. (74, 74, 88, 88 sts)

Join, pm between first and last st.

Work in k1, p1 rib for 2 (2, 2, 2½) inches.

Bind off loosely in rib.

Fold neck ribbing in half and sew loosely in place.

Finishing

Sew sleeves into armhole between markers.

Sew side and sleeve seams.

Weave in all loose ends. ◆

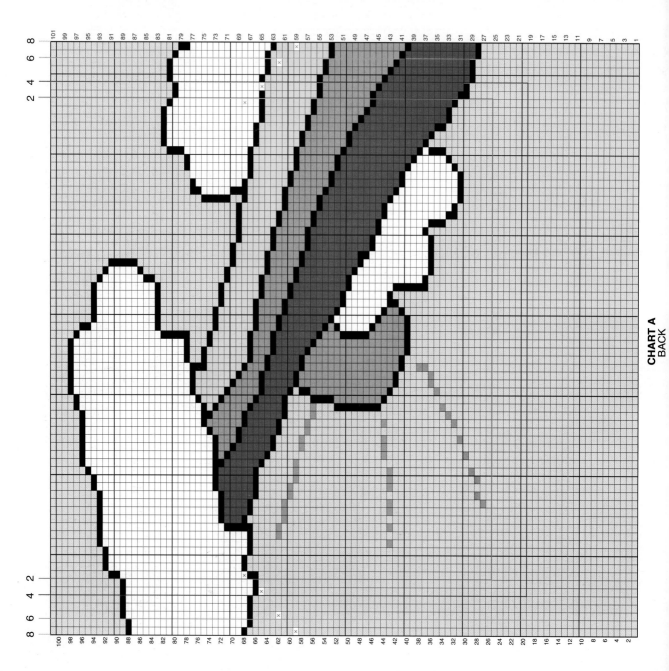

CHART A
BACK

158

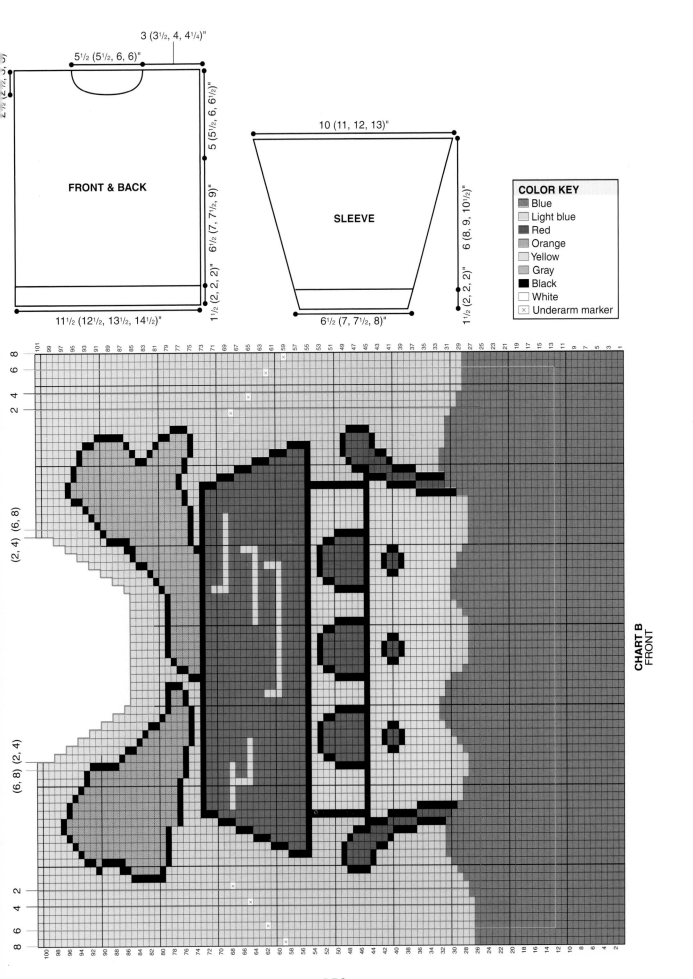

3 (3½, 4, 4¼)"

5½ (5½, 6, 6)"

2½ (2½, 3, 3)"

FRONT & BACK

5 (5½, 6, 6½)"

6½ (7, 7½, 9)"

1½ (2, 2, 2)"

11½ (12½, 13½, 14½)"

10 (11, 12, 13)"

SLEEVE

6 (8, 9, 10½)"

1½ (2, 2)"

6½ (7, 7½, 8)"

COLOR KEY
- Blue
- Light blue
- Red
- Orange
- Yellow
- Gray
- Black
- White
- ☒ Underarm marker

CHART B
FRONT

159

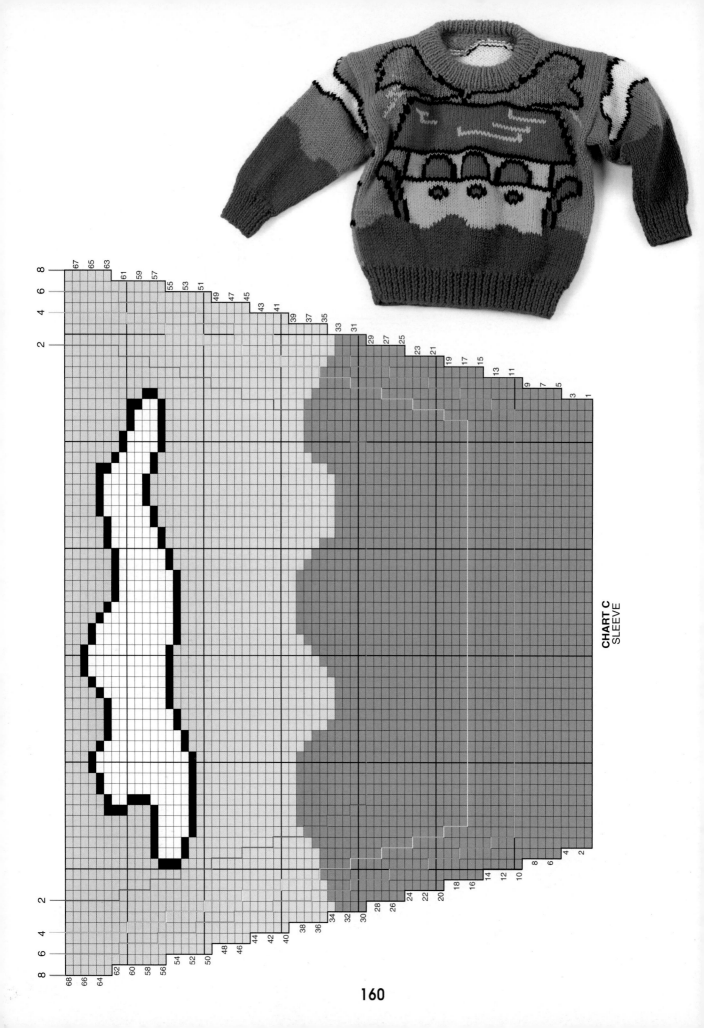

CHART C
SLEEVE

DENIM
HEARTS & STARS

Little Miss Denim Set

Designs by Lois S. Young

Brother and sister will be well-dressed in denim ensembles accented with either stars or hearts.

Cardigan

Skill Level
Intermediate***

Size
Child's 2 (4, 6, 8) Instructions are given for smallest size, with larger sizes in parentheses. When only 1 number is given, it applies to all sizes.

Finished Measurements
Chest: 23½ (25, 26½, 28) inches

Length: 13½ (14½, 16, 17½) inches

Materials
- Plymouth Wildflower D.K. 51 percent cotton/49 percent acrylic DK weight yarn (137 yds/50g per ball): 3 (3, 4, 5) balls denim #10 (MC), small amounts red #46 (A), off-white #40 (B)
- Size 4 (3.5mm) needles
- Size 5 (3.75mm) needles or size needed to obtain gauge
- Stitch holder
- 6 (6, 7, 7) ⅝-inch buttons, JHB International #49786
- Sewing needle and matching thread
- Tapestry needle

Gauge
20 sts and 28 rows = 4 inches/10cm in St st

To save time, take time to check gauge.

Pattern Stitch
Seed Stitch

Row 1: *K1, p1, rep from *, end k1 if odd number of sts in row.

Row 2: K the p sts and p the k sts. Rep Rows 1–2 for pat.

Pattern Note
All pieces in this set can be worked with either heart or star motif.

One ball each of A and B is enough to make entire set.

If making cardigan for a boy, put buttonholes on left band instead of right.

Back
With smaller needles, cast on 64 (68, 72, 76) sts.

Work in Seed st for 10 rows. Change to larger needles and St st.

Work even until back measures 8 (9, 10, 11) inches, ending with a WS row.

Shape underarms
Bind off 4 (4, 5, 5) sts at beg of next 2 rows. (56, 60, 62, 66 sts)

[Dec 1 st each end every other row] 4 times. (48, 52, 54, 58 sts)

Work even until armhole measures 5 (5, 5½, 6) inches.

Shape shoulders
Bind off 5 (6, 6, 7) sts at beg of next 2 rows, then 5 (6, 6, 6) sts at beg of following 2 rows.

Put remaining 28 (28, 30, 32) sts on holder for back of neck.

Right Front
With MC and smaller needles, cast on 32 (34, 36, 38) sts.

Work as for back to armhole, working armhole decs on left edge only. (24, 26, 27, 29 sts)

Work even until armhole measures 3½ (3½, 4, 4½) inches, ending with a WS row.

Shape neckline
Bind off 10 (10, 10, 11) sts at beg of next row.

of chart have been completed.

Work in St st for 4 rows, then Seed st for 4 rows.

Bind off in pat.

Sew shoulder seams.

Neck Band

With RS facing using smaller needles and MC, pick up and k 10 (10, 10, 11) sts of right neck front, 9 (9, 11, 13) sts along side neck, k 28 (28, 30, 32) sts of neck back, pick up and k 9 (9, 11, 13) sts along side neck and 10 (10, 10, 11) sts along front neck. (66, 66, 72, 80 sts)

Work in Seed st for 7 rows.

Bind off in pat.

Button Band

With RS facing using smaller needles and MC, pick up and k 58 (65, 75, 85) sts along front edge.

Work Seed st for 6 rows.

Bind off in pat.

Buttonhole Band

Mark front edge for 6 (6, 7, 7) buttons.

Pick up and k as for button band. Work in Seed st for 2 rows.

Buttonhole row: [Work in pat to marker, k2tog, yo] 6 (6, 7, 7) times, work to end of row.

Work in pat for 3 more rows.

Bind off in pat.

Finishing

Sew sleeves into armholes, matching decs and having top 1 inch of sleeve at bound-off underarm sts.

Sew sleeve and side seams.

Sew pockets to front, ¾ (1, 1¼, 1½) inches from front edge and ⅝ (¾, ⅞, 1) inch above bottom border.

Sew on buttons.

Jumper

Skill Level

Intermediate ***

Size

Girl's 2 (4, 6, 8) Instructions are given for smallest size, with larger sizes in parentheses. When only 1 number is given, it applies to all sizes.

[Dec 1 st at neck edge every other row] 4 (4, 5, 5) times. (10, 12, 12, 13 sts)

Work even until armhole measures same as for back.

Shape shoulders

At armhole edge, [bind off 5 (6, 6, 7) sts] twice (twice, twice, once), then 0 (0, 0, 6) sts once.

Left Front

Work as for right front, reversing shaping.

Sleeves

With smaller needles, cast on 32 (34, 36, 36) sts.

Work Seed st for 10 rows, inc 2 sts evenly on last row. (34, 36, 38, 38 sts)

Change to larger needles and St st.

[Inc 1 st each end every 6th row] 10 (10, 11, 12) times. (54, 58, 60, 62 sts)

Work even until sleeve measures 10 (11½, 12¾, 14) inches, ending with a WS row.

Shape cap

[Dec 1 st each end every other row] 4 times.

Bind off remaining 46 (50, 52, 54) sts.

Pockets

With MC and larger needles, cast on 21 sts.

Work in St st for 6 rows.

Set up pat (RS): K6 MC, pm, work Row 1 of Chart A or B over next 9 sts, pm, k6 MC.

Work in established pat until 8 rows

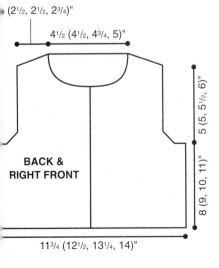

BACK & RIGHT FRONT

(2½, 2½, 2¾)"

4½ (4½, 4¾, 5)"

5 (5, 5½, 6)"

8 (9, 10, 11)"

11¾ (12½, 13¼, 14)"

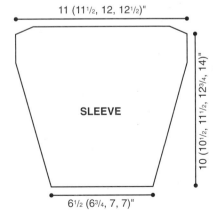

SLEEVE

11 (11½, 12, 12½)"

10 (10½, 11½, 12¾, 14)"

6½ (6¾, 7, 7)"

Gauge

20 sts and 28 rows = 4 inches/ 10cm in St st

To save time, take time to check gauge.

Special Abbreviation

Sssk: Sl 3 sts individually as if to k, return sts in reversed position to LH needle, k3tog through back of sts.

Pattern Notes

When working bib and strap, sl first st of each row purlwise if the last st of the preceding row was k; sl it knitwise if the last st was p.

If desired, white sts of heart motif may be worked as duplicate st after jumper is complete.

Skirt

With circular needle and MC, cast on 188 (188, 196, 204) sts. Join without twisting, pm between first and last st. This will be center back.

Work in Seed st for 8 rnds.

Change to St st and work even until skirt measures 4 (4, 5, 5) inches.

Set up shaping: K23 (23, 24, 25), pm, [k47 (47, 49, 51), pm] 3 times, k24 (24, 25, 26).

Dec rnd: [K to 3 sts before marker, k2tog, k1, k1, ssk] 4 times, k to end of rnd. *Note: Do not work decs at end of rnd marker.*

Rep dec rnd 8 more times, working 11 (11, 13, 13) rnds even between first and 2nd dec rnds, 7 rnds even between 2nd and 3rd dec rnds, and 4 (4, 5, 5) rnds even between remaining rnds. (116, 116, 124, 132 sts)

Knit 5 rnds even.

Next rnd: Dec 1 (0, 1, 1) st at each dec marker. (112, 116, 120, 128 sts)

Remove all markers except one at beg of rnd.

Divide for front & back

Next rnd: K30 (32, 33, 37), pm for left side seam, k53 (53, 55, 55) for front, pm for side seam, k29 (31, 32, 36), remove original marker.

Begin waistband & bib

Set up pat: Seed st over 5 sts, k to 5 sts before marker, Seed st over next 5 sts, work in k1, p1 rib across remaining back sts.

Work even in established pats for 1 inch.

Sl front sts to holder.

Work in rows across back ribbing only for 1 inch more.

Bind off in pat.

Bib

Sl sts from holder to needle. Join yarn with RS facing.

Next row: Seed st over 5 sts, k2tog, k to last 7 sts, ssk, Seed st over 5 sts.

Work even for 3 rows.

Dec row: Seed st over 5 sts, k3tog, k to last 8 sts, sssk, Seed st over 5 sts.

Work even for 3 rows.

[Rep last 4 rows] twice. (39, 39, 41, 41 sts)

Work even for ¾ (1, 1¼, 1½) inches

Finished Measurements

Skirt length: 9 (10, 11, 12) inches

Total length: 16½ (18, 19½, 21) inches

Materials

- Plymouth Wildflower D.K. 51 percent cotton/49 percent acrylic DK weight yarn (137 yds/50g per ball): 4 (4, 5, 5) balls denim #10 (MC), small amounts red #46 (A), off-white #40 (B)
- Size 5 (3.75mm) straight and 24-inch circular needle or size needed to obtain gauge
- Stitch markers
- 2 (⅝-inch) buttons, JHB International #49786
- ⅓ yd (⅝-inch) elastic
- Sewing needle and matching thread
- Tapestry needle

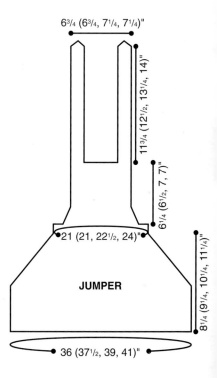

6¾ (6¾, 7¼, 7¼)"

11¾ (12½, 13¼, 14)"

6¼ (6½, 7, 7)"

21 (21, 22½, 24)"

8¼ (9¼, 10¼, 11¼)"

JUMPER

36 (37½, 39, 41)"

above last dec row, ending with a WS row.

Begin motif

Next row (RS): Work across 13 (13, 14, 14) sts, pm, work Row 1 of Chart C or D over next 13 sts, pm, work to end of row.

Work 13 rows of chart in established pat, then work in MC only in Seed and St st for 1¾ inches more.

Work 7 rows Seed st.

Strap

Next row: Work Seed st over 8 sts and sl to hold, bind off 23 (23, 25, 25) sts in pat, Seed st over 8 sts.

Work even until strap measures 11¾ (12½, 13⅓, 14) inches when stretched.

Buttonhole row: Work 3 sts, k2tog, yo, work 3 sts.

Work 2 rows even.

Shape end: Dec 1 st at beg of next 6 rows. (2 sts)

Next row: K2tog, fasten off final st.

Complete 2nd strap as for first.

Finishing

Fold waistband in half to inside. Sew bound-off edge to first row of ribbing.

Cut elastic ½ inch shorter than waistband or to desired length.

Insert elastic in casing. Sew ends of elastic to front of skirt; sew short ends of waistband to front of skirt.

Sew buttons to back waist-band directly above dec lines for skirt.

Purse

Skill Level
Easy**

Finished Size
Approximately 5 x 5½ inches

Materials
• Plymouth Wildflower D.K. 51 percent cotton/49 percent acrylic DK weight yarn (137 yds/50g per ball): 1 ball denim #10 (MC), small amounts red #46 (A), off-white #40 (B)
• Size 5 (3.75mm) straight and 2 double-pointed needles or size needed to obtain gauge
• Tapestry needle

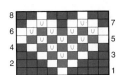

Gauge
20 sts and 28 rows = 4 inches/10cm in St st

To save time, take time to check gauge.

Purse

With MC, cast on 33 sts.

Work in Seed st for 5 rows. Change to St st.

Next row (RS): K 5 sts, pm, work Row 1 of Chart A or B over next 9 sts, pm, k 5 sts, pm, work Row 1 of chart A or B over next 9 sts, pm, k 5 sts.

Work even in established pats through Row 8 of chart.

Work even in MC only until purse measures 11¾ inches.

Work 3 rows Seed st.

Bind off.

Strap

With MC and 2 dpn, cast on 4 sts. K4, *slide sts to other end of needle, k4, rep from * until strap measures 24 inches when stretched.

Finishing

Fold purse with WS tog, so hearts form a 2½ inch flap.

Sew side seams.

Sew strap to top edge of purse at fold of flap. ✦

COLOR & STITCH KEY
- ■ Denim (MC)
- ▨ Red
- □ Off-white
- U With red, p on RS, k on WS

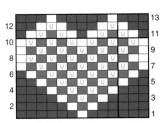

CHART A

CHART C

Little Master Denim Set

Designs by Lois S. Young

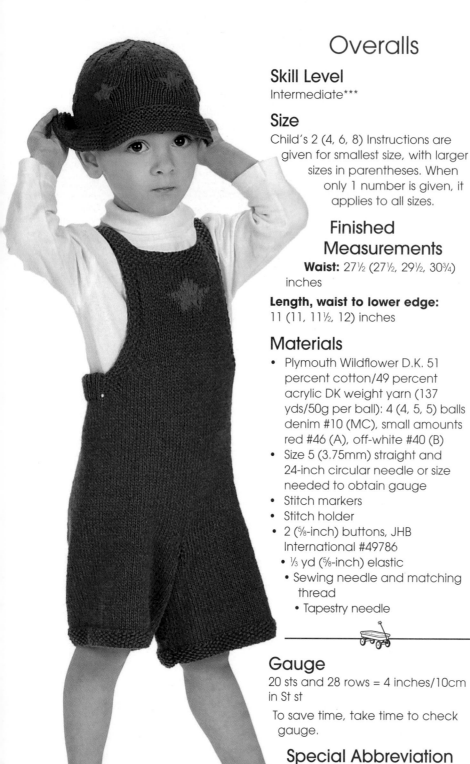

Overalls

Skill Level
Intermediate***

Size
Child's 2 (4, 6, 8) Instructions are given for smallest size, with larger sizes in parentheses. When only 1 number is given, it applies to all sizes.

Finished Measurements
Waist: 27½ (27½, 29½, 30¾) inches

Length, waist to lower edge: 11 (11, 11½, 12) inches

Materials
- Plymouth Wildflower D.K. 51 percent cotton/49 percent acrylic DK weight yarn (137 yds/50g per ball): 4 (4, 5, 5) balls denim #10 (MC), small amounts red #46 (A), off-white #40 (B)
- Size 5 (3.75mm) straight and 24-inch circular needle or size needed to obtain gauge
- Stitch markers
- Stitch holder
- 2 (⅝-inch) buttons, JHB International #49786
- ⅓ yd (⅝-inch) elastic
- Sewing needle and matching thread
- Tapestry needle

Gauge
20 sts and 28 rows = 4 inches/10cm in St st

To save time, take time to check gauge.

Special Abbreviation
Sssk: Sl 3 sts individually as if to k, return sts to LH needle in reversed position, k3tog through back of sts.

Pattern Stitch
Seed Stitch

Row 1: *K1, p1, rep from *, end k1 if odd number of sts in row.

Row 2: K the p sts and p the k sts.

Rep Rows 1–2 for pat.

Pattern Notes
All pieces in this set can be worked with either heart or star motif.

One ball each of color A and color B is enough to make entire set.

When working bib and strap, sl first st of each row purlwise if the last st of the preceding row was k; sl it knitwise if the last st was p.

Right Leg
With MC, cast on 42 (42, 44, 47) sts for front of leg, pm, cast on 50 (50, 53, 56) sts for back of leg. (92, 92, 97, 103 sts)

Work in Seed st for 9 rows.

Change to St st and work even for 0 (0, 4, 8) rows.

[Inc 1 st at front edge every 8th row] twice, *at the same time* [inc 1 st at back edge every 6th row] 3 times. (97, 97, 102, 108 sts)

Work even for ½ (½, ¾, 1) inch above last inc, ending with a WS row.

Shape crotch

At front edge, [bind off 3 sts] twice, [2 sts] once, then [dec 1 st every other row] 3 times, *at the same time* at back edge [bind off 6 sts] once, [4 sts] once, [2 sts] twice, then [dec 1 st every other row] twice, end with a WS row. (70, 70, 75, 81 sts)

Cut yarn and sl sts to holder.

Left leg
Work as for right leg, reversing shaping. Do not cut yarn or remove marker.

oin for body

Change to circular needle. Sl sts of ght leg to LH needle, followed by ts of left leg.

New beg of rnd will be at side marker of left leg.

to last st of left leg, k2tog and mark resulting st as center front, k to ast st of right leg, k2tog and mark esulting st as center back, k to end of rnd. (138, 138, 148, 160 sts)

Dec rnd: [K to 2 sts before marked t, k2tog, k marked st, ssk] twice, k o end of rnd.

Knit 3 rnds, rep dec rnd. Remove enter front and back markers. (130, 30, 140, 154 sts)

Work even until body measures 11 (11, 1½, 12) inches from cast-on edge.

Divide for front & back

Next rnd: Remove beg of rnd marker, k5, replace marker for new beg of rnd, k51 (53, 57, 61) for front, pm or side, k79 (77, 83, 85) for back.

Set up pat: Seed st over 5 sts, k to 5 sts before marker, Seed st over next 5 sts, work in k1, p1 rib across all back sts.

Work even in established pats for 1 inch.

Sl front sts to holder.

Work in rows across back ribbing for 1 inch more.

Bind off in pat.

Bib

Sl sts from holder to needle. Join yarn with RS facing.

Dec row: Seed st over 5 sts, k3tog, k to last 8 sts, sssk, Seed st over 5 sts.

Work even for 3 rows.

[Rep last 4 rows] twice. (39, 41, 45, 49 sts)

Next row: Seed st over 5 sts, k2tog, k to last 7 sts, ssk, Seed st over 5 sts.

Work even for 3 rows.

Rep last 4 rows. (35, 37, 41, 45 sts)

Work even for ½ (¾, 1¼,1½) inches above last dec row, ending with a WS row.

Begin motif

Next row (RS): Work across 11 (12,14,16) sts, pm, work Row 1 of Chart C or D over next 13 sts, pm, work to end of row.

When 13 rows of chart in established pat, then work in MC only in Seed and St st for ¾ inches more.

Work 7 rows Seed st.

Straps

Next row:
Seed st over 8 sts and sl these sts to holder, bind off 19 (21, 25, 29) sts in pat, Seed st over 8 sts.

Work even until strap measures 7 (9, 12, 15) inches when stretched.

Buttonhole row: Work 3 sts, k2tog, yo, work 3 sts.

Work 2 rows even.

Shape end: Dec 1 st at beg of next 6 rows. (2 sts)

Next row: K2tog, fasten off final st.

Complete 2nd strap as for first.

Finishing

Fold waistband in half to inside. Sew bound-off edge to first row of ribbing.

Cut elastic ½ inch shorter than waistband or to desired length.

Insert elastic in casing. Sew ends of elastic to front of overall; sew short ends of waistband to front of overall.

Continued on page 191

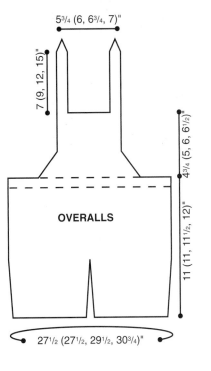

COLOR & STITCH KEY
- ■ Denim (MC)
- ■ Red
- □ Off-white
- Ⓥ With red, p on RS, k on WS

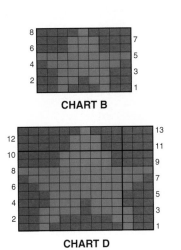

CHART B

CHART D

5¾ (6, 6¾, 7)"

7 (9, 12, 15)"

4¾ (5, 6, 6½)"

OVERALLS

11 (11, 11½, 12)"

27½ (27½, 29½, 30¾)"

TEAM COLORS

Diamonds V-Neck Pullover

Design by Joyce Englund

Team colors accent this sporty pullover in a parade of alternating diamonds.

Skill Level

Intermediate***

Size

Child's 2 (4, 6, 8) Instructions are given for smallest size, with larger sizes in parentheses. When only 1 number is given, it applies to all sizes.

Finished Measurement

Chest: 27 (29, 30, 32) inches

Materials

- Plymouth Encore Worsted 75 percent acrylic/25 percent wool worsted weight yarn (200 yds/ 100g per skein): 3 skeins sand #240 (MC), 1 skein each royal #133 (A) and dark red #9601 (B)
- Size 5 (5, 6, 6) needles
- Size 7 (7, 8, 8) needles or size needed to obtain gauge
- Bobbins
- Stitch holders
- Stitch markers

Gauge

20 sts and 27 rows = 4 inches/10cm in St st with size 7 needles

18 sts and 24 rows = 4 inches/10cm in St st with size 8 needles

To save time, take time to check gauge.

Pattern Notes

Size 5 and 7 needles are used for sizes 2 and 4; sizes 6 and 8 needles are used for size 6 and 8.

Cuffs are worked long enough to be turned back. If shorter cuffs are desired, adjust pat accordingly.

This sweater is designed to be rather roomy to allow for growth. If length adjustments are needed, make them before armhole decs to guarantee fit of sleeve.

Wind separate bobbins for each diamond; carry MC across back of each diamond.

To avoid holes when changing colors, always bring new color up over old.

Back

With smaller needles and MC, cast on 61 (67, 61, 67) sts.

Work in k1, p1 ribbing for 1½ (1¾, 2, 2) inches, inc 6 (5, 6, 5) sts on last WS row. (67, 72, 67, 72 sts)

Change to larger needles.

Row 1 (RS): Knit.

Row 2: Purl.

Row 3: K5 (4, 5, 4) MC, k1 A, k7 (8, 7, 8) MC, k1 B, k7 (8, 7, 8) MC, k1 A, k7 (8, 7, 8) MC, [k1 B, k7 (8, 7, 8) MC] twice, k1 A, k7 (8, 7, 8) MC, k1 B, k7 (8, 7, 8) MC, k1 A, k5 (4, 5, 4) MC.

Row 4: P4 (3, 4, 3) MC, p3 A, p5 (6, 5, 6) MC, p3 B, p5 (6, 5, 6) MC, p3 A, p6 (7, 6, 7) MC, [p3 B, p5 (6, 5, 6) MC] twice, p3 A, p5 (6, 5, 6) MC, p3 B, p5 (6, 5, 6) MC, p3 A, p4 (3, 4, 3) MC.

Row 5: K3 (2, 3, 2) MC, k5 A, k3 (4, 3, 4) MC, k5 B, k3 (4, 3, 4) MC, k5 A, k3 (4, 3, 4) MC, [k5 B, k3 (4, 3, 4) MC] twice, k5 A, k3 (4, 3, 4) MC, k5 B, k3 (4, 3, 4) MC, k5 A, k3 (2, 3, 2) MC.

Row 6: P2 (1, 2, 1) MC, p7 A, p1 (2, 1, 2) MC, p7 B, k4 (5, 4, 5) MC, p7 A, p1 (2, 1, 2) MC, [p7 B, p1 (2, 1, 2) MC] twice, p7 A, p1 (2, 1, 2) MC,

p7 B, p1 (2, 1, 2) MC, p7 A, p2 (1, 2, 1) MC.

Row 7: Rep Row 5.

Row 8: Rep Row 4.

Row 9: Rep Row 3.

Continue in St st with MC only until back measures 8½ (9, 10½, 12) inches, ending with a WS row.

Shape armholes

Bind off 5 (6, 7, 8) sts at beg of next 2 rows. (57, 60, 53, 56 sts)

Work even until armhole measures 6½ (7, 7½, 8) inches.

Place all sts on holder.

Left Front

Work as for back through Row 9 of Diamond pat.

Purl 1 row, knit 1 row, purl 1 row.

Continue working center diamonds only, alternating colors as shown in photo and having 3 rows MC between each diamond.

When front measures 8½ (9, 10½, 12) inches, bind off underarm sts as for back.

Begin neck shaping

Next row (RS): Work across 28 (30, 26, 28) sts, place center st of sizes 2 and 6 only on holder, place remaining sts of all sizes on 2nd holder.

Working on left side of neck only, p8 in established color pat, pm, p to end of row.

Dec row (RS): K to 2 sts before marker, k2tog, work in established color pat to end of row.

[Rep dec row every following 6th row] 7 (7, 6, 7) times more. (20, 22, 19, 20 sts)

Work even until armhole measures same as for back.

End with complete diamond motif. If necessary, work in MC only to complete front.

Right Front

Work as for left front, reversing shaping.

Sl shoulder sts from holders to separate needles.

Bind off front and back shoulders tog by using 3-needle method.

Sleeves

With smaller needle and MC, cast on 27 (29, 31, 33) sts.

Work in k1, p1 ribbing for 4 inches, inc 6 sts evenly on last WS row. (33, 35, 37, 39 sts)

Change to larger needle.

Row 1: Knit.

Row 2: Purl.

Row 3: K16 (17, 18, 19) MC, k1 A, k16 (17, 18, 19) MC.

Row 4: P15 (16, 17, 18) MC, p3 A, p15 (16, 17, 18) sts MC.

Continue working diamonds as on body, having 3 rows St st between diamonds and alternating colors, *at the same time* [inc 1 st each end every 4th row] 16 (14, 15, 15) times. (65, 63, 67, 69 sts)

Work even until sleeve measures 10

(12, 14, 15) inches, or desired length. Bind off.

Neck Band

With smaller needle and MC, beg at left shoulder, pick up and k 5 sts for every 6 rows along left side of neck.

Sizes 2 and 6 only: K center st from holder.

Sizes 4 and 8 only: With LH needle, pick up bar between sts at center front, k-tbl to avoid hole.

All sizes: Mark center st. Pick up and k 5 sts for every 6 rows along left side of neck, k across sts of back neck. You must have an odd number of sts.

Pm between first and last st.

Next rnd: Work in k1, p1 ribbing to 1 st before center st, sl 2 tog knitwise, k next st, p2sso, re-mark new center st, work in ribbing to end of rnd.

Rep this rnd until neck band measures 1 (1¼, 1½, 1½) inches.

Bind off in rib, dec at center front as before.

Finishing

Sew in sleeves, centering diamond pat with shoulder seam.

Sew side and sleeve seams, joining bound-off underarm sts of body to upper rows of sleeves. ◆

Team Spirit Pullover

Design by Celeste Pinheiro

For a first project, knit this pullover in your sports fan's favorite team colors.

Skill Level
Beginner*

Size
Child's 2 (4, 6, 8) Instructions are given for smallest size, with larger sizes in parentheses. When only 1 number is given, it applies to all sizes.

Finished Measurements
Chest: 26 (28, 30, 32) inches
Total length: 15 (16, 17, 18) inches

Materials
• Plymouth Encore Worsted 75 percent acrylic/25 percent wool (200 yds/100g per skein): 1 (1, 1, 2) skeins dark red #9601 (A), 1 skein each medium charcoal #389 (B), light charcoal #194 (C), dark charcoal #520 (D)
• Size 6 (4mm) straight and double-pointed needles
• Size 8 (5mm) straight and double-pointed needles or size needed to obtain gauge
• Stitch markers
• Tapestry needle

Gauge
16 sts and 23 rows = 4 inches/10cm in St st with larger needles

To save time, take time to check gauge.

Pattern Notes
Lower edges of body and sleeves roll automatically.

All measurements are taken with edges unrolled.

Back
With smaller needles and B, cast on 52 (56, 60, 64) sts.

Work in St st for 7 rows changing to larger needles on last WS row.

Work even until back measures 7 (7½, 8, 8½) inches from beg, ending with a RS row.

Change to A and knit 1 row.

Continue in St st until back measures 14½ (15½, 16½, 17½) inches from beg, ending with a WS row.

Back neck shaping
Next row (RS): K17 (18, 19, 20), join 2nd ball of yarn and bind off next 18 (20, 22, 24) sts for back neck, k to end of row.

Working on both sides of neck with separate balls of yarn, dec 1 st at each neck edge. (16, 17, 18, 19 sts on each side of neck)

Work even until back measures 15 (15, 17, 18) inches.

Bind off.

Front
Work as for back until front measures 13 (14, 15, 16) inches, ending with a WS row.

Front neck shaping
K22 (24, 26, 27), join 2nd ball of yarn and bind off next 8 (8, 8, 10) sts, knit to end of row.

Working on both sides of neck with separate balls of yarn, bind off 3 sts at each neck edge, then 2 sts at each neck edge.

[Dec 1 st at each neck edge

every row] 1 (2, 3, 3) times. (16, 17, 18, 19 sts at each side of neck)

Work even until front measures same as for back.

Bind off.

Neck Band
Sew shoulder seams.

With smaller dpn and B, pick up and k 52 (56, 60, 64) sts evenly around neck edge.

Join, pm between first and last st.

Purl 1 rnd.

Knit 7 rnds, change to larger dpn and knit 7 more rounds.

Bind off loosely.

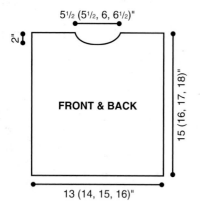

5½ (5½, 6, 6½)"

2"

FRONT & BACK

15 (16, 17, 18)"

13 (14, 15, 16)"

Sleeves

With smaller needles and C, cast on 32 sts.

Work in St st for 7 rows changing to larger needles on last WS row.

Inc 1 st at each end of needle on

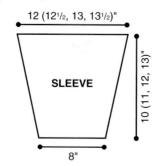

12 (12½, 13, 13½)"

SLEEVE

10 (11, 12, 13)"

8"

Row 12, then [every following 6th row] 7 (8, 9, 10) times. (48, 50, 52, 54 sts)

At the same time when sleeve measures 4 (5, 6, 7) inches, change to D after a RS row.

Next row (WS): Knit.

Continue in St st, inc as before until sleeve measures 10 (11, 12, 13) inches.

Bind off.

Finishing

Measure down 6 (6¼, 6½, 6¾) inches on either side of shoulder seam and mark for armhole.

Sew sleeves between markers.

Sew sleeve and underarm seams. ✦

Star Player Pullover

Design by Jean Schafer-Albers

Your player will achieve all-star status wearing this team pullover.

Skill Level

Intermediate***

Size

Child's 2 (4, 6, 8) Instructions are given for smallest size, with larger sizes in parentheses. When only 1 number is given, it applies to all sizes.

Finished Measurements

Chest: 27 (29½, 30½, 32½) inches

Length: 10½ (11½, 12½, 14½) inches

Materials

- Plymouth Encore Worsted 75 percent acrylic/25 percent wool worsted weight yarn (200 yds/ 100g per skein): 2 (2, 2, 3) skeins royal #133 (MC), 1 skein each red #1386 (A), gold #1014 (B), Aran #256 (C)
- Size 6 (4mm) straight and 16-inch circular needles
- Size 8 (5mm) needles or size needed to obtain gauge
- Stitch markers
- Stitch holders

- Tapestry needle

Gauge

18 sts and 24 rows = 4 inches/10cm in St st with larger needles

To save time, take time to check gauge.

Special Abbreviation

M1: (Make 1): Inc by inserting left needle from front to back into horizontal strand between last st worked and first st on the LH needle. Knit this strand through the back loop to twist it.

Pattern Notes

For ease in working motifs, place markers at beg and end of each star motif.

When working pat, catch unused strand in back of work every few sts.

Motifs may also be worked in intarsia method, using a separate bobbin or butterfly of yarn for each star.

All incs are worked by M1 method.

Back

With smaller needles and A, cast on 54 (60, 62, 64) sts.

Work in k1, p1 ribbing for 1 row. Cut A, join B.

Next row: Knit.

Work in k1, p1 ribbing for 1 row. Cut B, join MC.

COLOR KEY
☐ MC
☒ CC

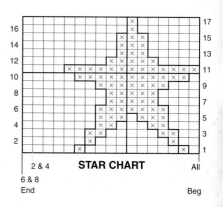

STAR CHART

2 & 4
6 & 8
End

All
Beg

Next row: Knit.

Work in k1, p1 ribbing until band measures 2 inches, inc 7 (7, 7, 9) sts evenly across last RS row. (61, 67, 69, 73 sts)

Change to larger needles.

Work 5 rows in St st.

Set up pat

Next row (RS): K8 (11, 11, 13) MC, pm, referring to chart and pm between each rep, work first star in C, 2nd star in B, 3rd star in A, pm, k5 (8, 7, 9) MC.

Work even through Row 17 of chart, then in MC only until back measures 10½ (11½, 12½, 14½) inches, ending with a WS row.

Shape shoulders

K 20 (23, 23, 25) sts and place on holder for right shoulder, bind off next 21 (21, 23, 23) sts for back neck, k 20 (23, 23, 25) sts and place on 2nd holder for left shoulder.

Front

Work as for back until front measures 8½ (9½, 9¾, 11¾) inches, ending with a WS row.

Shape neckline

K24 (27, 28, 30), join 2nd ball of yarn and bind off next 13 sts, k to end of row.

Working both sides of neck with separate balls of yarn, [dec 1 st at each neck edge every other row] 4 (4, 5, 5) times. (20, 23, 23, 25 sts)

Work even until front measures same as back, place shoulder sts on holders.

Sleeves

With smaller needles and A, cast on 30 (32, 32, 34) sts.

Work k1, p1 ribbing for 1 row. Cut A, join C.

Next row: Knit.

Work in k1, p1 ribbing for 1 row. Cut C, join MC.

Next row: Knit.

Work in k1, p1 ribbing until band measures 1½ inches, inc 3 sts evenly on last WS row.

Change to larger needles and St st.

Beg Star pat on

Row 5, making sure to center motif. Star is worked in A for right sleeve and B for left sleeve.

At the same time, [inc 1 st each end every 4th row] 7 (0, 1, 0) times, then [every 6th row] 2 (6, 9, 4) times, and finally [every 8th row] 0 (2, 0, 5) times. (51, 51, 55, 55 sts)

Continued on page 190

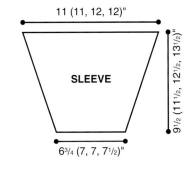

11 (11, 12, 12)"

SLEEVE

9½ (11½, 12½, 13½)"

6¾ (7, 7, 7½)"

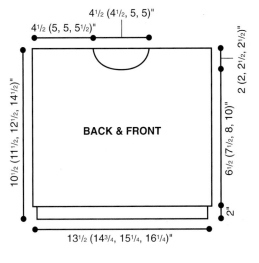

4½ (4½, 5, 5)"

4½ (5, 5, 5½)"

10½ (11½, 12½, 14½)"

BACK & FRONT

2 (2, 2½, 2½)"

6½ (7½, 8, 10)"

2"

13½ (14¾, 15¼, 16¼)"

Sunny Dots Set

Designs by Lois S. Young

Bright color and wrapped stitches make this set one that any little girl will want to wear over and over again.

Skill Level
Intermediate***

Size
Girl's 2 (4, 6, 8) Instructions are given for smallest size, with larger sizes in parentheses. When only 1 number is given, it applies to all sizes.

Finished Measurements
Chest: 23 (24, 26, 28) inches

Length: 13½ (14¾, 16¼, 17¾) inches

Materials
- Plymouth Encore D.K. 75 percent acrylic/25 percent wool DK weight yarn (150 yds/50g per ball): 3 (4, 4, 5) balls gold #1014 (MC), 1 ball soft white #146 (CC)
- Size 4 (3.5mm) 24-inch circular needle
- Size 5 (3.75mm) 24-inch circular needle or size needed to obtain gauge
- Stitch holders
- 10 (11, 12, 14) ⅜-inch white shank buttons
- Tapestry needle

Gauge
23 sts and 31 rows = 4 inches/10cm in St st with larger needles

To save time, take time to check gauge.

Special Abbreviation
WR1 (wrap 1): Insert tip of right needle between first and 2nd sts on LH needle, pull up a loop of CC and place on LH needle, with CC k st just made and sl off needle, with MC work ssk over next 2 sts on LH needle.

Pattern Stitch
Floral Wrap
Rows 1 and 5 (RS): *K3 MC, WR1, k2 MC, rep from * across, end last rep k1.

Rows 2, 4 and 6: With MC, purl.

Row 3: *K2 MC, WR1, k1 MC, WR1, k1 MC, rep from * across, end last rep k1.

Cardigan
Body
With smaller needle and MC, cast on 127 (133, 145, 157) sts.

Working in garter st, knit 1 row MC, 2 rows CC, 4 rows MC, 2 rows CC, 2 rows MC.

Work in St st for 4 rows.

Set up front border pat (RS): K3 MC, WR1, with MC work to last 4 sts, WR1, k3 MC.

Row 2: Purl 1 row MC.

Row 3: K2 MC, WR1, k1 MC, WR1, with MC work to last 5 sts, WR1, k1 MC, WR1, k2.

Row 4: Purl 1 row MC.

Row 5: Rep Row 1.

Work in St st for 5 rows with MC only.

Work in established pat until body measures 8½ (9½, 10½, 11½) inches, ending with a WS row.

Divide for fronts & back
Work across 27 (28, 31, 33) sts for right front and sl to holder, bind off 9 (10, 11, 12) sts for right underarm, work across 55 (57, 61, 67) sts for back and sl to 2nd holder, bind off 9 (10, 11, 12) sts for

left underarm, work 27 (28, 31, 33) sts for left front.

Left Front
Working on left front only, [dec 1 st at armhole edge every RS row] 2 (2, 3, 3) times. (25, 26, 28, 30 sts)

Work even until armhole measures approximately 2½ (2½, 3, 3½) inches,

ending with a RS row after a complete floral wrap motif.

Shape neckline

Work across 8 sts and sl to holder for neck, work across remaining 17 (18, 20, 22) sts.

[Dec 1 st at neck edge every WS row] 3 (3, 4, 4) times. (14, 15, 16, 18 sts)

Work even until armhole measures 5 (5¼, 5¾, 6¼) inches, ending with a WS row.

Bind off all sts for shoulder.

Right Front

With WS facing, join MC at armhole. Work right front as for left, making armhole dec on WS rows and neck dec on RS rows.

Back

With WS facing, join MC at left armhole.

[Dec 1 st each end every RS row] 2 (2, 3, 3) times. (51, 53, 55, 61 sts)

Work even until armhole measures same as for fronts.

Shape shoulders

Next row (RS): Bind off 14 (15, 16, 18) sts for shoulder, k 23 (23, 23, 25) sts for back neck and sl to holder, bind off remaining 14 (15, 16, 18) sts.

Sew shoulder seams.

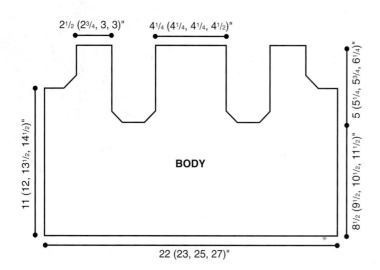

2½ (2¾, 3, 3)"   4¼ (4¼, 4¼, 4½)"

5 (5¼, 5¾, 6¼)"

BODY

11 (12, 13½, 14½)"

8½ (9½, 10½, 11½)"

22 (23, 25, 27)"

Sleeves

With smaller needles, cast on 35 (39, 43, 43) sts.

Work border as for body.

Change to larger needles, and work 4 rows in St st, inc 1 st at each end of first RS row.

Work Rows 1–6 of Floral Wrap pat, working an extra k3 (k4, k2, k2) at beg and end of row when starting pat.

Inc 1 st each end every 4th row] 4 times, and then [every 6th row] 4 (4, 4, 6) times. (51, 55, 59, 63 sts)

Work even until sleeve measures 9¾ (11¼, 12¾, 14) inches, ending with a WS row.

Shape cap

Bind off 1 st at beg of next 4 (4, 6, 6) rows, bind off remaining 47 (51, 53, 57) sts.

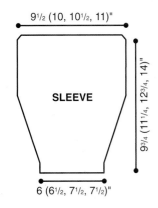

9½ (10, 10½, 11)"

9¾ (11¼, 12¾, 14)"

SLEEVE

6 (6½, 7½, 7½)"

Neck Band

With RS facing using smaller needle and MC, k 8 sts of right neck front, pick up and k 14 (15, 15, 15) sts along right neck, k 23 (23, 23, 25) sts of back neck, pick up and k 14 (15, 15, 15) sts along left neck, k 8 sts of left neck front. (67, 69, 69, 71 sts)

Working in garter st, knit 11 rows in color sequence as for bottom band.

Bind off.

Button Band

With RS facing using smaller needle and MC, pick up and k 3 sts for every 4 rows, and 1 st for every ridge of garter st along left front.

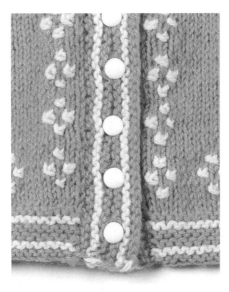

Work as for neck band. When binding off border, work last 2 sts as k2tog to prevent point.

Buttonhole Band

Mark right front edge for 10 (11, 12, 14) buttonholes, having 1 marker at center of each flower and remainder centered with top and bottom borders.

Work as for button band, making [k2tog, yo] buttonhole at each marker on center MC row.

Finishing

Sew sleeve into armhole, matching ¾ (¾, 1, 1) inch just before cap shaping to bound-off underarm sts of body.

Sew sleeve seams.

Sew on buttons.

Purse

Skill Level
Easy **

Finished Measurements
Approximately 6¼ x 5 inches

Materials
- Plymouth Encore D.K. 75 percent acrylic/25 percent wool DK weight yarn (150 yds/50g per ball): 1 ball gold #1014 (MC), 1 ball soft white #146 (CC)
- Size 4 (3.5mm) needle
- Size 5 (3.75mm) needle or size needed to obtain gauge
- 3 snaps
- Tapestry needle

Purse

With smaller needles and MC, cast on 43 sts.

Work border as for cardigan body.

Change to larger needles and work 4 rows St st.

Work Rows 1–6 of Floral Wrap pat.

Work even in St st until purse measures 13¾ inches, ending with a RS row.

Knit 2 rows.

Bind off knitwise on WS.

Strap

With smaller needles and MC, cast on 132 sts.

Work 11 rows of border pat.

Bind off.

Finishing

Fold up top 5 inches of plain part of purse and sew side seams.

Sew strap to purse along top of seam.

Sew 3 snaps under flap of purse. ✦

Strawberry Parfait Set

Designs by Barbara Venishnick

Stripes, colorwork and a stylish closure are the key features of a chic cardigan and purse set for a young miss.

Skill Level
Intermediate***

Size
Girl's 4 (6, 8, 10) Instructions are given for smallest size, with larger sizes in parentheses. When only 1 number is given, it applies to all sizes.

Finished Measurements
Chest: 27 (31, 35, 38) inches
Length: 14 (15, 16, 17) inches

Materials
- Plymouth Encore Worsted 75 percent acrylic/25 percent wool worsted weight yarn (200 yds/ 100g per skein): 2 (2, 2, 3) skeins off-white #146 (A), 1 (1, 2, 2) skeins light rose #9408 (B), 1 skein each kiwi #1552 (C), burgundy #1607 (D)
- Size 6 (4mm) double-pointed needles
- Size 7 (4.5mm) needles or size needed to obtain gauge
- Size F/5 crochet hook

Gauge
19 st and 25 rows = 4 inches/10cm in St st with larger needles

To save time, take time to check gauge.

Pattern Notes
Cardigan is worked in one piece to armhole, then divided for fronts and back.

Purse is worked from top edge downward.

Stripe pat is worked in St st of 10 rows A, then 10 rows B.

Cardigan

Body
With A and larger needles, cast on

121 (137, 153, 169) sts.

Work in St st for 4 rows, forming hem.

Referring to chart and beg with a RS row, work 20 rows of Triangle pat.

Change to Stripe pat and continue to work even until body measures 8 (8½, 9, 9½) inches above first row of Triangle pat, ending with a WS row.

Divide for fronts and back

Next row (RS): K 30 (34, 38, 42) sts and place on holder for right front, k 61 (69, 77, 85) back sts, place remaining 30 (34, 38, 42) sts on 2nd holder for left front.

Shape armhole

Working in established pat on back sts only, bind off 4 sts at beg of next 2 rows, then 3 sts at beg of following 2 rows, and finally 2 sts at beg of next 2 rows.

Dec 1 st each end of next row. (41, 49, 57, 65 sts)

Work even until armhole measures 5 (5½, 6, 6½) inches above first bound-off row, ending with a WS row.

Shape shoulders

Bind off 3 (5, 5, 6) sts at beg of next 2 rows, then 3 (4, 5, 6) sts at beg of next 4 rows. (23, 23, 27, 29 sts)

Bind off all sts for back neck.

Right Front

Sl sts from first holder to needles.

With WS facing, join yarn at armhole.

Shape armhole

Continuing in established Stripe pat, bind off at arm edge [4 sts] once, then [3 sts] once, and finally [2 sts] once. Dec 1 st at same edge on

following RS row. (20, 24, 28, 32 sts)

Work even until armhole measures 3 (3½, 4, 4½) inches above first bound-off row.

Shape neck

Next row (RS): K 6 (6, 8, 9) sts and place on holder for front neck, k to end of row.

[Dec 1 st at neck edge every other row] 5 times. (9, 13, 15, 18 sts)

At the same time when armhole measures same as for back beg shoulder shaping.

Shape shoulders

Bind off at arm edge, [3 (5, 5, 6) sts] once, then [3 (4, 5, 6) sts] twice.

Sew shoulder seams.

Left Front

Sl sts from 2nd holder to needle. With RS facing, join yarn at armhole.

Work left front as for right, reversing shaping.

Sleeves

With A and larger needles, cast on 30 (32, 34, 36) sts.

Work in St st for 5 rows.

Knit 1 row on WS for turning ridge.

Continue in Stripe pat, [inc 1 st each end every 6th row] 9 (10, 11, 12) times. (48, 52, 56, 60 sts)

Work even until sleeve measures 9 (10, 11, 12) inches above turning ridge.

Shape cap

Bind off 4 sts at beg of next 2 rows, then 3 sts at beg of following 2 rows, and finally 2 sts at beg of next 2 rows.

[Dec 1 st each end every other row] 6 times. (18, 22, 26, 30 sts)

Bind off 2 sts at beg of next 2 rows, then 3 sts at beg of following 2 rows. (8, 12, 16, 20 sts)

Neck Facing

With RS facing and A, knit 6 (6, 8, 9) sts of right front neck, pick up and k 14 sts along right edge of neck, knit 23 (23, 27, 29) sts of back neck, pick up and k 14 sts along left edge of neck, knit 6 (6, 8, 9) sts of left front neck. (63, 63, 71, 75 sts)

Knit 1 row.

Work in St st for 4 rows, [dec 1 st each end every other row] twice. (59, 59, 67, 71 sts)

Bind off loosely.

Right Front Facing

With RS facing and A, pick up and k 52 (57, 62, 67) sts along right front edge beg at row 1 of Triangle pat and ending at neck edge.

Knit 1 row.

Next row: Bind off 4 sts, k to end of row.

Work in St st for 4 more rows, [dec 1 st at neck edge every other row] twice. (46, 51, 56, 61 sts)

Bind off.

Left Front Facing

Work as for right front facing, reversing shaping.

Finishing

Sew sleeves into armhole.

Sew sleeve and side seams.

Fold facings to inside and sew in place.

Button

With B and crochet hook, ch 4, join to form a ring.

Rnd 1: Ch 1, work 12 sc in ring, join with sl st. Cut B.

Rnd 2: With D, work 1 sc in first sc of

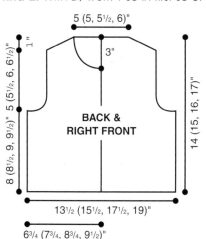

previous rnd, *insert hook in center of ring and work a sc through ring, sc in each of next 2 sc of previous rnd; rep from * around, join with sl st. (18 sts)

Rnd 3: Ch 1, turn, *working in back loops of previous rnd, pull up a loop in each of next 2 sc, yarn over needle and pull through all 3 loops on hook, rep from * 8 times. (9 sts)

Rnd 4: Do not turn, sc in first st, rep from * of rnd 3. (5 sts)

Fasten off, leaving a long end. Draw end through sts of final rnd to close opening.

Sew button to left front, 1½ inches below neck opening.

Frog Closures

With C and crochet hook, make a chain measuring 16 inches. Turn, and work 1 sc in the back bump of each ch st.

Make a 2nd chain measuring 13 inches.

Pin shorter chain to left front, folding

center of chain tightly around base of button. Referring to Fig. 1, shape frog as shown. Sew in place.

Pin longer chain to right front as shown in Fig. 2, having 3 inches at center folded to form a loop. Sew in place.

Thread 1 strand each of B and D into tapestry needle. With both strands tog, work a French knot at outer point of each frog, wrapping strands around needle 5 times.

Purse

With dpn and D, cast on 64 sts.

Join without twisting, pm between first and last st.

Change to B and purl 1 rnd.

Change to A, and knit 8 rnds.

Eyelet rnd: *K2tog, yo; rep from * around.

Knit 1 rnd.

Change to B and knit 10 rnds.

Change to A and knit 10 rnds.

Referring to chart, work 20 rnds of Triangle pat, beg with Rnd 20 and working backward through Rnd 1.
Note: *Read chart from right to left for all rows and use 8-st rep only, omitting first extra st needed for body.*

Shape bottom

Change to A.

Rnd 1 and all odd-numbered rnds: Knit.

Rnd 2: *K2tog, k6; rep from * around (56 sts)

Rnd 4: *K2tog, k5; rep from * around (48 sts)

Continue in this fashion, dec 8 st every other rnd until 8 sts remain.

Next rnd: K2tog around. (4 sts)

Cut yarn and draw through remaining sts, pulling tightly to close bottom of purse.

Draw Strings
Make 2

With C and crochet hook, make a 28-inch ch.

Working on inside of purse, thread one drawstring through eyelets, leaving equal lengths hanging on inside where ends meet.

Rep procedure with 2nd drawstring, starting and ending at opposite sides of purse.

Sew ends of each drawstring tog.

Pull ends to close bag. ✦

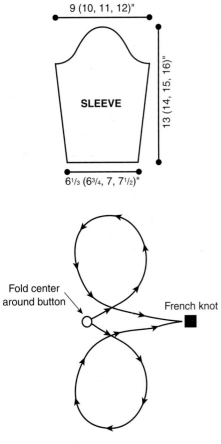

9 (10, 11, 12)"

SLEEVE

13 (14, 15, 16)"

6⅓ (6¾, 7, 7½)"

Fold center around button

French knot

FIG. 1

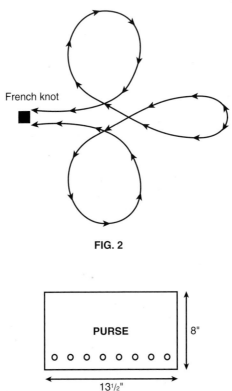

French knot

FIG. 2

PURSE

8"

13½"

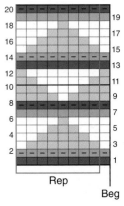

20 19
18 17
16 15
14 13
12 11
10 9
8 7
6 5
4 3
2 1

Rep

Beg

TRIANGLE PATTERN CHART

COLOR & STITCH KEY	
☐	Off-White (A)
▨	Light rose (B)
▨	Kiwi (C)
■	Burgundy (D)
–	K on WS in color indicated

WILDLIFE

Leaping Lizard Pullover

Design by Celeste Pinheiro

A dashing lizard suns himself on the front of this sweater. An easy zigzag pattern fills the background.

Skill Level

Advanced****

Size

Boy's 2 (4, 6, 8) Instructions are given for smallest size, with larger sizes in parentheses. When only 1 number is given, it applies to all sizes.

Finished Measurements

Chest: 26 (28, 30, 32) inches

Length: 15 (16, 17, 18) inches

Materials

* Plymouth Encore Worsted 75 percent acrylic/25 percent wool worsted weight yarn (200 yds/100g per skein): 2 skeins dark brown #1444 (A), 1 skein each denim #436 (B), beige #240 (C), fir #670 (D), lime #1552 (E)
* Size 6 (4.25mm) straight and double-pointed needles
* Size 8 (5mm) needles or size needed to obtain gauge
* 2 small dark buttons

Gauge

16 sts and 24 rows = 4 inches/10cm in St st using larger needles

To save time, take time to check gauge.

Pattern Stitches

A. Corrugated Rib

Row 1 (RS): *K2 A, p2 C, rep from * across row.

Row 2: *K2 C, p2 A, rep from * across row.

Rep Rows 1–2 for pat.

B. Sleeve Stripe

Work in St st and stripe sequence of 4 rows E, then 4 rows D.

Back

With smaller needles and B, cast on 52 (56, 60, 64) sts.

Knit 2 rows.

Work in Corrugated Rib pat for 8 rows, ending with a WS row.

Change to larger needles.

Referring to Chart A, work even until back measures 14½ (15½, 16½, 17½) inches, ending with a WS row.

Back neck shaping

Next row (RS): K 17 (18, 19, 20) sts, join 2nd ball of yarn and bind off next 18 (20, 22, 24) sts, k to end of row.

Working on both sides of neck with separate balls of yarn, [dec 1 each side of neck] once. (16, 17, 18, 19 sts remain for each shoulder)

Work even until back measures 15 (16, 17, 18) inches.

Bind off.

Front

Referring to Chart B, work as for back until front measures 13 (14, 15, 16) inches, ending with a WS row.

Front neck shaping

Next row (RS): Work in established pat across 22 (24, 26, 27) sts, join 2nd ball of yarn and bind off next 8 (8, 8, 10) sts for front neck, work to end of row.

Working on both sides of neck with separate balls of yarn, bind off at each neck edge [3 sts] once, then [2 sts] once.

[Dec 1 st at each neck edge every row] 1 (2, 3, 3) times. (16, 17, 18, 19 sts remain for each shoulder)

Bind off.

Sleeve

With smaller needles and B, cast on 32 sts.

Work Corrugated Rib as for back. Change to larger needles and Stripe pat.

Beg with 12th row, [inc 1 st each end every 6th row] 8 (9, 10, 11) times. (48, 50, 52, 54 sts)

Work even until sleeve measures 10 (11, 12, 13) inches.

Bind off.

Sew shoulder seams.

Neck Band

With smaller dpn and A, pick up

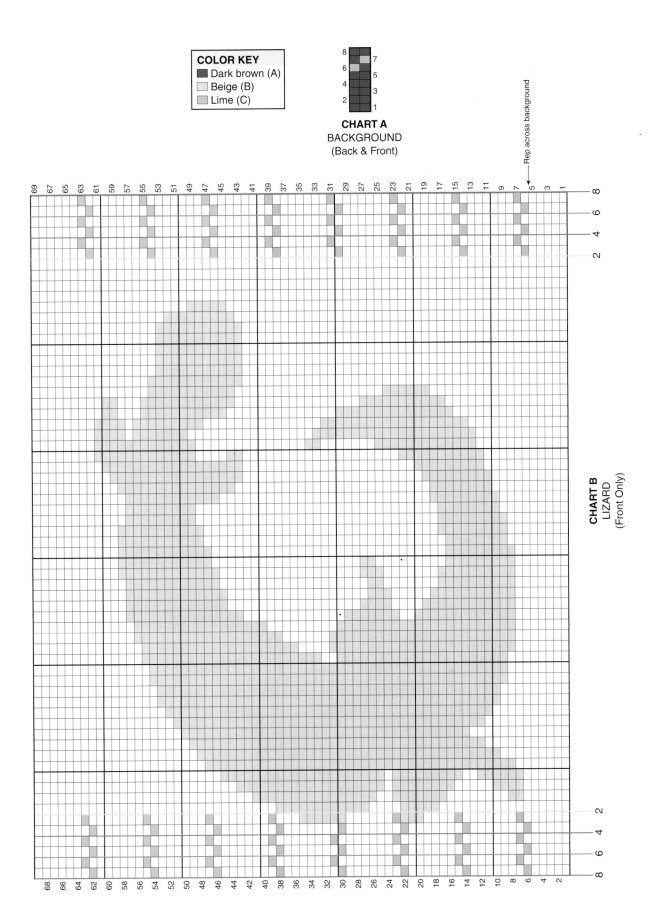

COLOR KEY
- Dark brown (A)
- Beige (B)
- Lime (C)

CHART A
BACKGROUND
(Back & Front)

Rep across background

CHART B
LIZARD
(Front Only)

and k 52 (56, 60, 64) sts evenly around neck edge.

Pm between first and last st.

Next 8 rnds: *K2 A, p2 C. Rep from * around.

Change to larger needles and B.

Knit 1 round, purl 1 round.

Bind off very loosely.

Finishing

Refer to photo for embroidery placement.

Using chain st, embroider lizard's toes with C, tongue and back stripe with B.

Sew on buttons for eyes.

Measure down 6 (6¼, 6½, 6¾) inches from shoulder seam on front and back and mark for underarm.

Sew top of sleeve to body between markers.

Sew sleeve and side seams. ✦

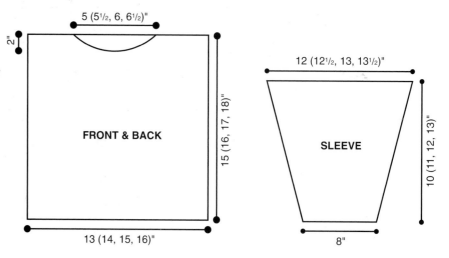

Rascal Raccoon Pullover

Design by Celeste Pinheiro

A cunning raccoon frolics on the front of this pullover. The colorwork background is reminiscent of country hills and streams.

Skill Level

Advanced****

Size

Boy's 2 (4, 6, 8) Instructions are given for smallest size, with larger sizes in parentheses. When only 1 number is given, it applies to all sizes.

Finished Measurements

Chest: 26 (28, 30, 32) inches

Length: 15 (16, 17, 18) inches

Materials

* Plymouth Encore Worsted 75 percent acrylic/25 percent wool worsted weight yarn (200 yds/100g per skein): 1 skein each denim #436 (A), dark brown #1444 (B), beige #240 (C), taupe #1405 (D), fir #670 (E), lime #1552 (F)
* Size 6 (4.25mm) straight and double-pointed needles
* Size 8 (5mm) needles or size needed to obtain gauge
* 2 (⅜-inch) light-colored buttons
* 1 (½-inch) dark-colored button

Gauge

16 sts and 24 rows = 4 inches/10cm in St st using larger needles

To save time, take time to check gauge.

Pattern Stitches

A. Corrugated Rib

Row 1 (RS): *K2 B, p2 C, rep from * across row.

Row 2: *K2 C, p2 B, rep from * across row.

Rep Rows 1–2 for pat.

B. Seed Stitch

Row 1 (RS): *K1, p1, rep from * across row.

Row 2: *P1, k1, rep from * across row.

Rep Rows 1–2 for pat.

C. Sleeve Stripe

Work in St st and stripe sequence of 4 rows F, then 4 rows E.

Back

With smaller needles and A, cast on 52 (56, 60, 64) sts.

Knit 2 rows.

Work in Corrugated Rib pat for 8 rows, ending with a WS row.

Next row (RS): Knit with C.

Work even in Seed st for 5 rows. Change to larger needles.

Referring to Chart A, work even until back measures 14½ (15½, 16½, 17½) inches, ending with a WS row.

Back neck shaping

Next row (RS): K 17 (18, 19, 20) sts, join 2nd ball of yarn and bind off next 18 (20, 22, 24) sts, k to end of row.

Working on both sides of neck with separate balls of yarn, [dec 1 st each side of neck] once. (16, 17, 18, 19 sts remain for each shoulder)

Work even until back measures 15 (16, 17, 18) inches. Bind off.

Front

Work as for back, keeping background in pat from Chart A and

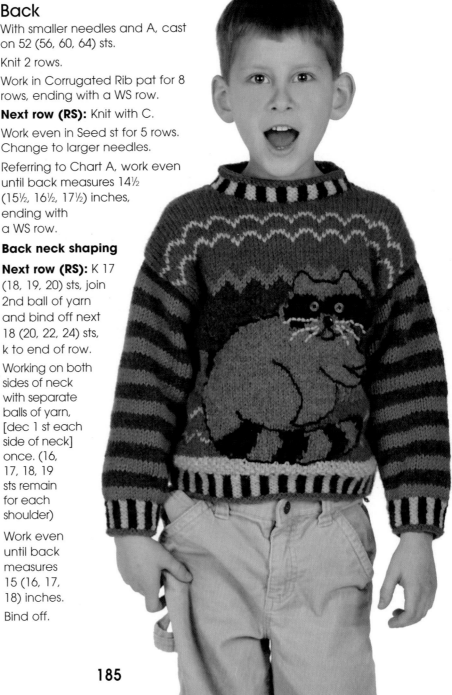

superimposing Chart B over it. When front measures 13 (14, 15, 16) inches, begin neck shaping.

Front neck shaping

Next row (RS): Work in established pat across 22 (24, 26, 27) sts, join 2nd ball of yarn and bind off next 8 (8, 8, 10) sts for front neck, work to end of row.

Working on both sides of neck with separate balls of yarn, bind off at each neck edge [3 sts] once, then [2 sts] once.

[Dec 1 st at each neck edge every row] 1 (2, 3, 3) times. (16, 17, 18, 19 sts remain for each shoulder)
Bind off.

Sleeve

With smaller needles and A, cast on 32 sts.

Work Corrugated Rib as for back. Change to larger needles and Stripe pat.

Beg with 12th row, [inc 1 st each end every 6th row] 8 (9, 10, 11) times. (48, 50, 52, 54 sts)

Work even until sleeve measures 10 (11, 12, 13) inches.
Bind off.

Sew shoulder seams.

Neck Band

With smaller dpn and A, pick up and k 52 (56, 60, 64) sts evenly around neck edge.

Pm between first and last st.

Next 8 rnds: *K2 B, p2 C. Rep from * around.

Change to larger needles and A.

Knit 1 round, purl 1 round.

Bind off very loosely.

Finishing

With B, outline raccoon in backstitch as in photo.

Sew on buttons for eyes and nose.

Backstitch whiskers with C.

Measure down 6 (6¼, 6½, 6¾) inches from shoulder seam on front and back and mark for underarm.

Sew top of sleeve to body between markers.

Sew sleeve and side seams. ✦

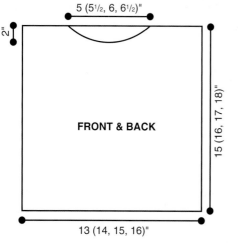

5 (5½, 6, 6½)"

2"

FRONT & BACK

15 (16, 17, 18)"

13 (14, 15, 16)"

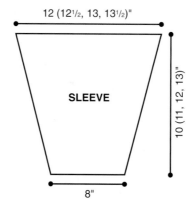

12 (12½, 13, 13½)"

SLEEVE

10 (11, 12, 13)"

8"

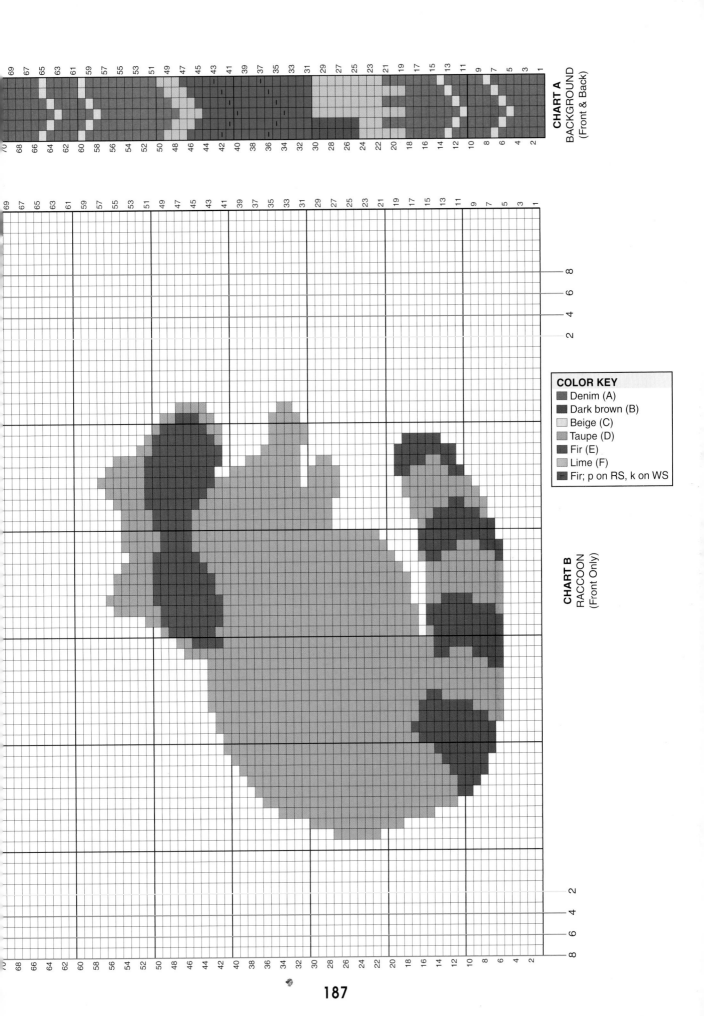

CHART A
BACKGROUND
(Front & Back)

CHART B
RACCOON
(Front Only)

COLOR KEY
- Denim (A)
- Dark brown (B)
- Beige (C)
- Taupe (D)
- Fir (E)
- Lime (F)
- Fir; p on RS, k on WS

187

Fold first 6 rows of pants to inside to form casing. Pin in place.

Remove provisional cast on and loosely sew casing to inside, leaving an opening for inserting elastic.

Cut elastic to measure 1 inch more than waist. Thread elastic through casing and sew ends securely.

Close remaining portion of opening.

Booties

Cuff

With size 6 needles, cast on 23 (28, 28) sts.

Knit 3 rows. Change to size 8 needles.

Work 13 rows in St st, ending with a RS row.

Shape ankle

Row 1: P3, [p2tog, p3] 4 (5, 5) times. (19, 23, 23 sts)

Eyelet row: K2, *yo, k2tog, rep from * to last st, k1.

Row 3: P2tog, p to last 2 sts, p2tog. (17, 21, 21 sts.)

Divide for instep

Row 1: K12 (14, 14), turn. Mark this row.

Row 2: P7, turn, sl remaining sts to holder.

Work even in St st on 7 sts only until instep measures 1 (1½, 2) inches above marker, ending with a purl row. Cut yarn, sl sts to holder.

With RS facing, join yarn at back edge.

K 5 (7, 7) sts from holder, pick up and k 7 (7, 9) sts evenly along right edge of instep, k across 7 sts of instep, pick up and k 7 (7, 9) sts evenly along left side of instep, then k remaining 5 (7, 7) sts on holder. (31, 35, 39 sts)

Knit 5 rows.

Shape sole

Row 1: K2, ssk, k8 (10,12), k2tog, k3, ssk, k8 (10, 12), k2tog, k2. (27, 31, 35 sts)

Row 2: Knit.

Row 3: K2, ssk, k6 (8, 10), k2tog, k3, ssk, k6 (8, 10), k2tog, k2. (23, 27, 31 sts)

Row 4: Knit.

Row 5: K2, ssk, k4 (6, 8), k2tog, k3, ssk, k4 (6, 8), k2tog, k2. (19, 23, 27 sts)

Bind off purlwise.

Finishing

Sew back and foot seams.

Cut a 36-inch length of yarn and fold in half.

Make a twisted cord by inserting a pencil on 1 end and twisting until yarn folds back on itself. Tie ends.

Thread cord through eyelet row and tie in bow at front.

Hat

With size 6 dpn, cast on 48 (60, 72) sts.

Join without twisting, pm between first and last st.

Work in garter st for 6 rounds.

Change to size 7 dpn and knit 8 rnds.

Begin pat

Rnd 1: *P8, C4, rep from * to end of round.

Rnd 2 and all even-numbered rnds: Knit.

Rnd 3: *P8, k4, rep from * to end of round.

Rnd 5: Rep Rnd 1.

Rnd 7: Rep Rnd 3.

Rnd 8: Knit, dec 0 (4, 0) sts evenly. (48, 56, 72 sts)

Shape crown

Rnd 1: *K6, k2tog, rep from * around. (42, 49, 63) sts.

Rnd 2 and all even-numbered rnds: Knit.

Rnd 3: *K5, k2tog, rep from * around. (36, 42, 54 sts)

Rnd 5: *K4, k2tog, rep from * around. (30, 35, 45 sts)

Rnd 7: *K3, k2tog, rep from * around. (24, 28, 36 sts)

Rnd 9: *K2, k2tog, rep from * around. (18, 21, 27 sts)

Rnd 11: *K1, k2tog, rep from * around. (12, 14, 18 sts)

Rnd 13: *K2tog, rep from * around. (6, 7, 9 sts)

Finishing

Cut yarn, leaving a 12-inch tail.

Draw yarn through remaining sts twice, draw up tightly and secure. ✦

Goose in the Flowers Hat

Continued from page 68

Gather edge sts and draw into a ball, stuffing with a bit of yarn before closing completely.

Finishing

Referring to photo and chart, embroider small flowers around area where goose is standing. Embroider one flower in goose's beak.

Sew back seam.

Sew bobble to top of hat. ✦

COLOR KEY
- ⊠ MC
- ☐ Yellow
- ▨ Orange
- ᕹ Magenta lazy daisy stitch
- ╱ Green straight stitch

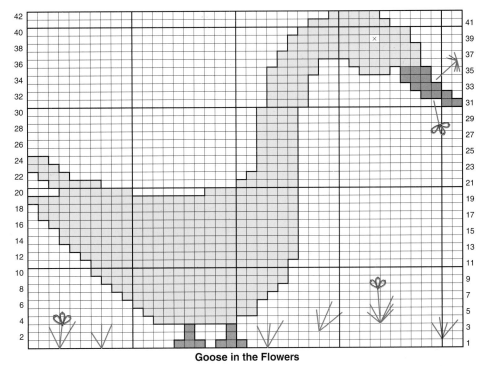

Goose in the Flowers

Grape Confetti & Scarf Set

Continued from page 141

Scarf

With straight needles, very loosely cast on 13 (13, 15, 15) sts.

Row 1 (RS): K1, *p1, k1, rep from * across row.

Row 2: P1, *k1, p1, rep from * across row.

Rep Rows 1 and 2 until scarf measures 38½ (42, 45½, 49) inches.

Bind off very loosely in rib.

Fringe

Cut strands of yarn, each 6 inches long.

Holding 2 strands tog for each fringe, use crochet hook to attach 1 group of fringe in every other st across cast-on edge of scarf.

Trim fringe evenly.

Rep along bound-off edge. ✦

Jazzy Jewels Set

Continued from page 140

Mittens

(Make both alike)

With B and smaller needles, cast on 27 (29) sts.

Work in 1/1 Rib for 2 (2¼) inches, ending with a WS row.

Change to MC and larger needles.

Next row (RS): K2tog, [k1, k2tog] 8 (9) times. (18, 19 sts)

Work Rows 2–4 of Body pat.

Beg thumb gusset

Row 1: P9, pm, inc 1 st in next st, pm, p8 (9).

Row 2: Knit.

Row 3: K9, inc 1 st in each of next 2 sts, k8 (9).

Row 4: Purl.

Row 5: K9, [inc 1 st in next st, k1] twice, k8 (9).

Row 6: Purl.

Row 7: P9, inc 1 st in next st, p3, inc 1 st in next st, p1, p8 (9). (8 sts between markers for gusset)

Row 8: Knit.

Thumb

Next row: K9, drop yarn and place these sts onto holder, remove

marker, join 2nd ball of yarn, k 8 sts for thumb, remove 2nd maker, sl remaining 8 (9) sts to holder.

Working on thumb sts only and keeping in pat st, work 5 more rows.

Dec row: K2tog across row. (4 sts)

Cut yarn leaving a 12-inch length.

With tapestry needle, draw end through sts on needle and fasten snugly.

Sew thumb seam.

Hand

Sl sts from first st holder to RH needle; sl sts from 2nd st holder to LH needle.

With RS facing and using previous dropped strand of yarn at base of thumb, k to end of row. (17, 18 sts)

Work even in Body pat for 11 (13) rows.

Shape top

Next row: K2tog across. (9 sts)

Row 2: P2 tog across, ending with p1. (5 sts)

Cut yarn leaving an 18-inch end.

With tapestry needle, draw end through sts on needle and fasten snugly.

Sew side seam. ✦

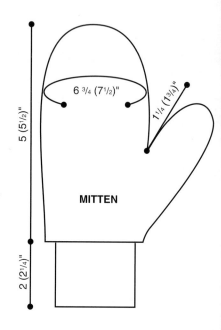

MITTEN

6 ¾ (7½)"

1¼ (1¾)"

5 (5½)"

2 (2¼)"

Star Player Pullover

Continued from page 173

Work even until sleeve measures 9½ (11½, 12½, 13½) inches.

Bind off all sts.

Join front & back

Bind off front and back shoulder sts tog, using 3-needle bind off as follows: Hold needles containing shoulder sts parallel with RS tog. With 3rd needle, k first st on front and back needles tog, * k next st on both needles tog, bind off 1, rep from * until all sts are worked.

Rep for 2nd shoulder.

Neck Band

With RS facing using smaller circular needle and MC, pick up and k 21 (21, 23, 23) sts across back neck, 15 (15, 20, 20) sts along left neck edge, 13 sts across front, 15 (15, 20, 20) sts along right neck edge. (64, 64, 76, 76 sts)

Join, pm between first and last st.

Work in k1, p1 rib for ¾ inch. Cut MC and join C.

Knit 1 rnd, work in k1, p1 rib for 1 rnd.

Bind off loosely in rib.

Finishing

Measure down 5½ (5½, 6, 6) inches on either side of each shoulder seam and mark.

Sew sleeves into armholes between markers.

Sew sleeve and side seams. ✦

Little Master Denim Set
Continued from page 171

Sew crotch and leg seams.

Sew buttons to back waistband.

Hat

Skill Level
Easy **

Size
Child's 2–4 (6–8) Instructions are given for smaller size, with larger size in parentheses.

Finished Measurements
Circumference: 16 (19) inches

Materials
- Plymouth Wildflower D.K. 51 percent cotton/49 percent acrylic DK weight yarn (137 yds/50g per ball): 1 ball denim #10 (MC), small amounts red #46 (A), off-white #40 (B)
- **Size 2–4 only:** Size 4 (3.5mm) 16-inch circular and double-pointed needles or size needed to obtain gauge
- **Size 6–8 only:** Size 5 (3.75mm) 16-inch circular and double-pointed needles or size needed to obtain gauge

Gauge
24 sts and 32 rows = 4 inches/10cm in St st with smaller needles

20 sts and 28 rows = 4 inches/10cm in St st with larger needles

To save time, take time to check gauge.

Special Abbreviation
M1 (Make 1): Make a backward loop and place on RH needle.

Pattern Notes
Both sizes are worked with same number of sts. Needle size determines finished hat size.

Change to dpn when number of sts becomes too small to fit on circular needle.

Stars or hearts are worked on brim in duplicate st after hat is complete.

Brim
With MC and circular needle, cast on 90 sts. Join without twisting, pm between first and last st.

Odd rnds 1–11: Knit.

Rnd 2: *P4, M1, rep from * around. (110 sts).

Rnd 4: Purl.

Rnd 6: *P5, M1, rep from * around. (132 sts)

Rnds 8, 10 and 12: Purl.

Bind off knitwise.

Sides
With MC and circular needle, pick up and k 88 sts along cast-on edge of brim.

Join, pm between first and last st.

Next row: *M1, k44, rep from *. (90) sts.

Knit 27 rnds.

Shape top

Rnd 1: *K43, k2tog, rep from *. (88 sts)

Rnd 2: *K9, k2tog, rep from * around. (80 sts)

Odd rnds 3–15: Knit.

Rnd 4: *K8, k2tog, rep from * around. (72 sts)

Rnd 6: *K7, k2tog, rep from * around. (64 sts)

Rnd 8: *K6, k2tog, rep from * around. (56 sts)

Rnd 10: *K5, k2tog, rep from * around. (48 sts)

Rnd 12: *K4, k2tog, rep from * around. (40 sts)

Rnd 14: *K3, k2tog, rep from * around. (32 sts)

Rnd 16: *K2, k2tog, rep from * around. (24 sts)

Rnd 17: *K1, k2tog, rep from * around. (16 sts)

Rnd 18: *K2tog, rep from * around. (8 sts)

Cut yarn leaving an 8-inch tail.

Draw yarn through remaining sts twice and pull tightly.

Darn in end on WS. ✦

Special Thanks

We would like to thank Plymouth Yarn Co. for providing all the yarn used in this book. We really appreciate the help provided by Uyvonne Bingham and the Plymouth staff throughout the publishing process. We've enjoyed working with them. We also thank the talented knitting designers whose work is featured in this collection.

Standard Abbreviations

beg	begin(ning)
CC	contrast color
ch	chain
cn	cable needle
dec	decrease
dpn	double-pointed needle
g	gram(s)
inc	increase
k	knit
LH	left hand
MC	main color
oz	ounce(s)
p	purl
pat	pattern
pm	place marker
psso	pass slipped stitch over knit (or purl) stitch
rep	repeat
RH	right hand
rnd	round
RS	right side

sl	slip
ssk	slip, slip, knit (a left-slanting decrease): slip 2 stitches individually as if to knit to right-hand needle, reinsert tip of left needle and knit 2 stitches together through back loops
st(s)	stitch(es)
St st	Stockinette stitch
tbl	through back loops
tog	together
WS	wrong side
wyib	with yarn in back
wyif	with yarn in front
yo	yarn over
"	inch(es)
*	repeat instructions from asterisk as directed
[ ]	repeat instructions within brackets number of times stated